W9-CBL-379

THE POWER OF VISUAL STORYTELLING INFOGRAPHICS

JASON LANKOW / JOSH RITCHIE / ROSS CROOKS

Founders of Column Five

WILEY

John Wiley & Sons, Inc.

Copyright © 2012 by Column Five Media. All rights reserved.

Published by John Wiley & Sons, Inc., Hoboken, New Jersey.
Published simultaneously in Canada.

No part of this publication may be reproduced, stored in a retrieval system, or transmitted in any form or by any means, electronic, mechanical, photocopying, recording, scanning, or otherwise, except as permitted under Section 107 or 108 of the 1976 United States Copyright Act, without either the prior written permission of the Publisher, or authorization through payment of the appropriate per-copy fee to the Copyright Clearance Center, Inc., 222 Rosewood Drive, Danvers, MA 01923, (978) 750-8400, fax (978) 646-8600, or on the web at www.copyright.com. Requests to the Publisher for permission should be addressed to the Permissions Department, John Wiley & Sons, Inc., 111 River Street, Hoboken, NJ 07030, (201) 748-6011, fax (201) 748-6008, or online at http://www.wiley.com/go/permissions.

Limit of Liability/Disclaimer of Warranty:
While the publisher and author have used their best efforts in preparing this book, they make no representations or warranties with respect to the accuracy or completeness of the contents of this book and specifically disclaim any implied warranties of merchantability or fitness for a particular purpose. No warranty may be created or extended by sales representatives or written sales materials. The advice and strategies contained herein may not be suitable for your situation. You should consult with a professional where appropriate. Neither the publisher nor author shall be liable for any loss of profit or any other commercial damages, including but not limited to special, incidental, consequential, or other damages.

For general information on our other products and services or for technical support, please contact our Customer Care Department within the United States at (800) 762-2974, outside the United States at (317) 572-3993 or fax (317) 572-4002.

Wiley publishes in a variety of print and electronic formats and by print-on-demand. Some material included with standard print versions of this book may not be included in e-books or in print-on-demand. If this book refers to media such as a CD or DVD that is not included in the version you purchased, you may download this material at http://booksupport.wiley.com.

For more information about Wiley products, visit www.wiley.com.

ISBN 978-1-118-31404-3 (paper); ISBN 978-1-118-42006-5 (ebk); ISBN 978-1-118-42159-8 (ebk); ISBN 978-1-118-43164-1 (ebk)

Printed in the United States of America

10 9 8 7 6 5 4 3 2

INFOGRAPHICS

THE POWER OF VISUAL STORYTELLING

CONTENTS

CHAPTER

06

BRAND-CENTRIC INFOGRAPHICS 160

CHAPTER

07

DATA VISUALIZATION INTERFACES 182

CHAPTER

10

THE FUTURE OF INFOGRAPHICS 220

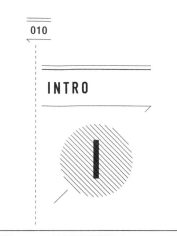

INTRO

fig. I.1-I.4

INTRODUCTION

The world around us is changing. The Information Age has fundamentally changed the way we think and communicate. We are now a culture that thrives on learning and sharing—much of this is facilitated by the increasing ubiquity of social media. This influx of information needs to be consumed and processed, which requires new methods of communication. Infographics, in many different forms, are at the forefront of this new way of thinking. The visualization of information is enabling us to gain insight and understanding quickly and efficiently, utilizing the incredible processing power of the human visual system. Accessing and harnessing this power is not only valuable, but necessary, as we navigate the vast amounts of data presented to us daily.

This is an especially prevalent need in the business world. Consumers are increasingly cynical with regard to advertising and marketing efforts, an attitude which borders on callous. In order to communicate their messages, brands must appeal to consumers in a new way. Hard-sell advertisements are no longer effective. Brands now need to provide a unique value to their audiences, beyond the propositions of their products and services. This value comes in the form of information presentation. In order to build and engage an audience, an increasing number of companies are finding success in taking cues from publishers—presenting purely editorial content with the aim of informing and entertaining readers. How do infographics fit into this picture? With a massive amount of content being created and distributed daily on the web, it has become much more challenging to catch and keep the attention of viewers. Infographics provide a format that utilizes engaging visuals that not only appeal to an audience hungry for information, but also aid in the comprehension and retention of that material.

"The aim of the poet is to inform or delight, or to combine together, in what he says, both pleasure and applicability to life.

In instructing, be brief in what you say in order that your readers may grasp it quickly and retain it faithfully.

Superfluous words simply spill out when the mind is already full."

Horace
(Epistolas Ad Pisones De Ars Poetica)

Though this was written over 2,000 years ago with regard to the role of the poet, every business can benefit from this timeless wisdom as it pertains to any communication. Whether you are informing, delighting, or both, succinct messaging that provides real, interesting knowledge to consumers is not only the new face of marketing, but of any brand communications.

A BRIEF HISTORY OF INFOGRAPHICS

The design of information is nothing new. From the earliest cave paintings to modern-day data visualization, humans have always utilized graphic depictions as a representation of information. Their efficacy has been proven as far back as the Victorian Era, as evidenced by the infographic in Figure I.1, created by Florence Nightingale to show the causes of mortality of the British Army during the Crimean War. This was presented to Parliament, who had previously been unresponsive to concerns of health and hygiene of the troops, and brought about a new way of thinking about the spread of disease (Kopf, p. 390-392).

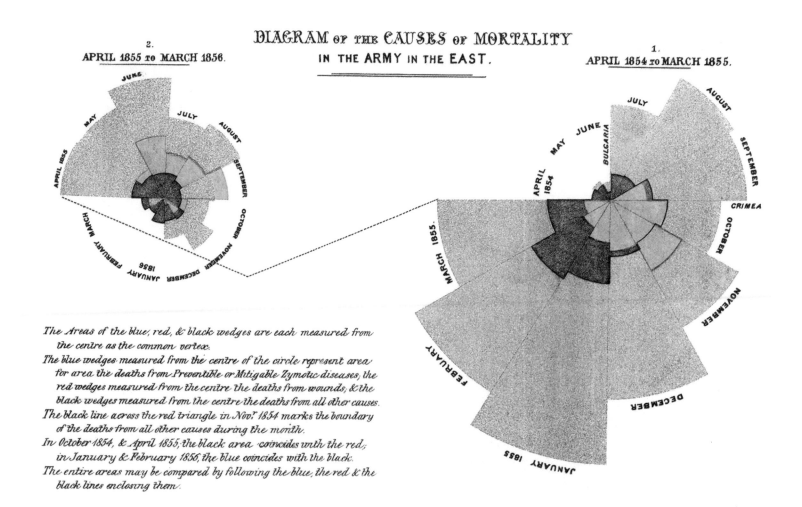

DIAGRAM of the CAUSES of MORTALITY
IN THE ARMY IN THE EAST.

2.
APRIL 1855 to MARCH 1856.

1.
APRIL 1854 to MARCH 1855.

The Areas of the blue, red, & black wedges are each measured from
the centre as the common vertex.

The blue wedges measured from the centre of the circle represent area
for area the deaths from Preventible or Mitigable Zymotic diseases; the
red wedges measured from the centre the deaths from wounds; & the
black wedges measured from the centre the deaths from all other causes.

The black line across the red triangle in Nov. 1854 marks the boundary
of the deaths from all other causes during the month.

In October 1854, & April 1855, the black area coincides with the red;
in January & February 1856, the blue coincides with the black.

The entire areas may be compared by following the blue, the red & the
black lines enclosing them.

Figure I.1
Diagram of the Causes of Mortality in the Army in the East.
Florence Nightengale.

They were popularized for editorial use in the late 1930s and early 1940s, with *Fortune* magazine being one of the most well-recognized early purveyors. These illustrations in Figure I.2 are the embodiment of true craftsmanship, characterized not only by an iconic style, but painstaking attention to detail.

Since then, they have found more broad applications in everything from academic and scientific research to modern marketing. We will discuss more on the history of these uses in Chapter 1 (Importance and Efficacy) and highlight the current applications throughout the book.

Figure I.2
Fortune *magazine infographics.*

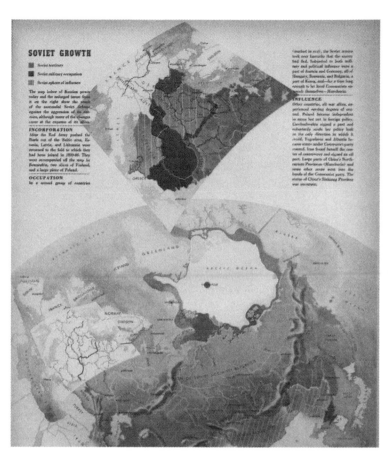

pragmatic reconciliation of theory and changing circumstance. It stamps the course of events with inevitability and calls it historic destiny that capitalists are monopolists, that monopolists are fascists, and that all of them are pitted against the Soviet Union. But this rigidity of theory in no wise prohibits the greatest flexibility of application: words of friendship and words of distrust, pacts with the friendly and pacts with the unfriendly, blunt telling of truth and blunt telling of lies, appeasement and resistance, intervention and isolation, publicity and secrecy, war and peace. Soviet policy reveals itself to no single events, but only in a progression of them. No one can take snapshots of its intentions, but only a motion picture of its motivations. The purpose of this article is to project the motion picture.

One group of Soviet motivations was, in the early days at least, highly subconscious. Lenin and Trotsky roundly repudiated the legacy of Czarist Russia even to the extent of horrifying the outside world by publishing documents of the secret archives. They believed in fish-bowl, not top-hat diplomacy, and they denounced both special privilege and territorial maneuver. But

the legacy remained: Soviet Russia inherited the geography of Czarist Russia along with many of the mental habits that, interacting with geography, had given Russia its shape and its history. The Russia of Lenin and Trotsky was still a Russia with an almost pathological urge for security. Its landlocked, enemy-rimmed insecurity had involved it continually in scrambles at home and abroad. As early as the reign of Ivan the Terrible in the sixteenth century, Russians had found it necessary to purge an entire feudal class at home the better to gird for war abroad. They had long been conscious of a cordon sanitaire, set up by Western nations against them. They had even heard of a plan for a new anti-Russian coalition and for invasion of Russia from the north.

Indeed it was not until the cordon sanitaire had fallen apart —Germany was dismembered, Poland weak—that Russia began to grow in strength under Peter the Great. Yet even then security seemed to demand a reaching out toward the Dardanelles, toward the Baltic, toward the Kingdom of Sweden, toward Poland, toward the Pacific Ocean. Russia breathed, her territory now expanding, now contracting, according to the strength and

THE PURPOSE OF THIS BOOK

The utility and application of infographics are expansive and diverse. In this book, we will focus primarily on their implementation in improving business communication, from their new-found use in marketing to their more traditional application in reporting and gaining business insight. Along the way, we will also discuss some of the related purposes for their use in other fields, which will shed light on the approach and critical framework for analyzing their quality and efficacy that we will establish toward the end of the book. Our primary purpose is to provide an in-depth understanding of the value of their use, and inform as to the proper approach and implementation of the medium. We hope you will leave informed and inspired by the tools of infographic thinking, ready to visually transform your company's communication.

WHAT THIS BOOK IS NOT

This book is not intended as a central resource for the design of infographics. We will, however, highlight some of the tools that can be used to create visualizations, and provide resources for designers to learn more about this practice. In addition, the framework and considerations provided regarding the concept, research, and messaging will prove very helpful for designers. We do hold in high regard the design skills necessary to create beautiful infographics, and believe that the principles and instruction taught in design schools are central to the creation of effective visualizations, whatever the medium.

The examples of formats and applications provided in this book are not intended to be a comprehensive list of all possible uses for infographics. Rather, we chose to recognize some of the key areas where infographics can provide great value to businesses, and discuss the proper approach to each at length, based on our experience working with hundreds of brands over the years, both big and small. There are certainly areas left unrecognized in this book that can bring both clarity and engagement to a brand's messaging—this is all part of the fun. Whether in business, art, or science, people are finding new ways to utilize this incredible medium of infographics for myriad purposes. This is exactly what makes infographics so inspiring—the excitement and beauty of discovering new ways to inform and delight—visually.

A NOTE ON TERMINOLOGY

To be clear about the topics that this book covers, we must define the terms that we will be using frequently. Some are nuanced and might seem redundant. There are a variety of disciplines that deal with information and data, visualization, and design—and the people in all of them have different thoughts and opinions about the way these terms should be used. As such, these are not technical or official definitions; they are simply those that serve us best for the applications we will be discussing in this book.

Information
Knowledge in the form of words, numbers, or concepts that can be communicated.

Data
Quantifiable information. Though data can take various forms, in this book we typically consider data to be numerical. It is debated whether the word "data" should be treated as singluar or plural. From its Latin origins, it is plural; the singular form of the word is "datum." In modern language, however, it is most commonly used as a singular mass noun.

Data Set
A categorized collection of data that has been filtercd at some level, the insights of which people can recognize more simply through visualization.

Design
The concept, functionality, and graphic output intended to solve a specific problem.

Illustration
A hand-drawn or vector-based depiction of an object. In infographics, we can use illustration to display the anatomy of an object or to add aesthetic appeal.

Visualization

We will use this term to mean "information visualization." A photograph or painting is technically a visualization; however, in order to give the term meaning for this context, it will refer to the process of making visual whatever is communicating specific knowledge. This may include the visualization of data, or simply the use of visual cues to illustrate, differentiate, or show a hierarchy of information.

Members of the scientific and academic communities often use the term visualization to refer to graphics that are automatically generated using software. Such programs can process different information, in a similar format, with a different visual result. We include this visualization method in our definition, but also the manual processing, plotting, and design of information and data that are unique to an application. While the traditional definition is very suitable for scientific and academic purposes, this book covers a variety of media and applications, so we must use a broader definition.

Data Visualization

A visual representation of data or the practice of visualizing data. Common forms include pie charts, bar graphs, line charts, and so forth. However, relationships in data can be quite complex. For that reason, there is an opportunity to find unique ways to visualize these values to accurately portray such relationships. These visualizations enable us to detect trends, patterns, and outliers that we can use to derive insight.

Information Design

The practice of representing information in a visual format. We'll also use this term to refer to the field of study and practice as a whole. A visual representation of information could include visualizing data, processes, hierarchy, anatomy, chronology, and other facts. While a chart is technically an information graphic, most information graphics are multifaceted and contain explanations or insightful descriptions.

Infographic

An abbreviation of "information graphic." This term has gained popularity recently based on the increased use of graphics in online marketing over the past few years. Some use this term to connote the unique format that has been widely adopted for this application, which is characterized by illustration, large typography, and long, vertical orientation displaying an assortment of facts. We refer to such graphics as editorial infographics, which can also be presented in different formats.

We will use the terms information graphic and infographic interchangeably, and we feel the need to maintain a very broad definition for both of these terms. Simply put, an infographic uses visual cues to communicate information. They do not need to contain a certain amount of data, possess a certain complexity, or present a certain level of analysis. There is no threshold at which something "becomes" an infographic. It can be as simple as a road sign of a man with a shovel that lets you know there is construction ahead, or as complex as a visual analysis of the global economy.

Editorial Infographic

An infographic for use in print, an online publication, or a blog. While newspapers have used these for decades, they've recently found a new form and life on the Internet. Content marketing—the practice of using informational, editorial content to bring attention and thought leadership to a company blog to engage both current and prospective customers—has driven much of this growth. An example of such a visual content marketing campaign is the series of graphics created for Marketo, shown in Figure I.3.

Qualitative Graphic Elements

Anything nonnumerical, this can include both information and illustration.

Quantitative Information

Information that involves a measurement of any kind, typically taking a numerical form (Figure I.4).

Narrative

An approach to information design that seeks to guide the viewers through a selected set of information that tells a story. This is best used for infographics that communicate value judgments and are designed to leave the viewers with a specific message to take away.

Figure I.3
Example of editorial infographic campaign.
Column Five for Marketo.
(Continued on page 22)

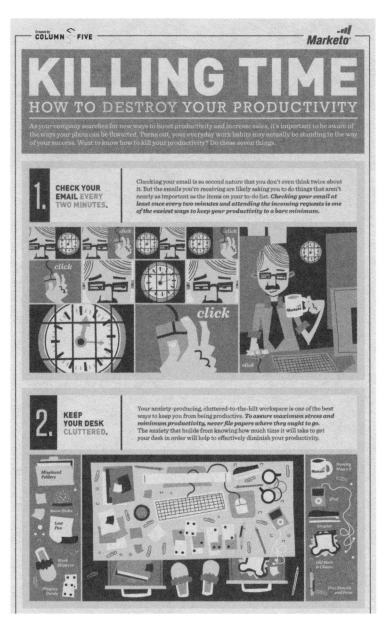

Figure I.3
Continued.

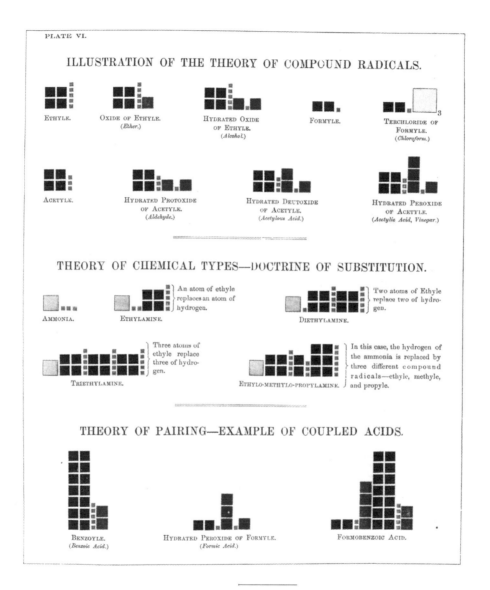

Figure I.4
Example of quantitative information display.

HOW TO USE THIS BOOK

There are countless applications for information design and visualization in the business world today. However, the needs of each company are unique, so it is necessary to create custom solutions to solve communication problems. We have structured this book to enable you to consume and learn the information that is relevant to your needs and goals, while giving you the freedom to leave behind sections that do not apply. You can think of it as a resource to reference regularly, as you identify needs and seek opportunities for new applications. Just as one designs a visualization based on the information it displays, so should you craft a visual strategy to fit your company's needs and opportunities. This book serves as a guide to these various strategies and applications.

We've outlined the book's structure in this section to give you an idea of what to expect in each chapter. You can use this to determine the relevance of a particular chapter to your company. When in doubt, please explore a chapter further. This is a great way to identify new opportunities for visualizing information, and can help evolve and transform your overall communication and marketing strategy.

Some sections of this book will be essential reading in order to understand the underlying concepts that will be discussed in further detail within each application.

ESSENTIAL READING CHAPTERS

CHAPTER 1

IMPORTANCE AND EFFICACY:
WHY OUR BRAINS LOVE INFOGRAPHICS

CHAPTER 2

INFOGRAPHIC FORMATS:
CHOOSING THE RIGHT VEHICLE FOR YOUR MESSAGE

CHAPTER 3

THE VISUAL STORYTELLING SPECTRUM:
AN OBJECTIVE APPROACH

CHAPTER 8

WHAT MAKES A GOOD INFOGRAPHIC?

CHAPTER 9

INFORMATION DESIGN BEST PRACTICES

CHAPTER 10

THE FUTURE OF INFOGRAPHICS

However, you can read (or not read) other chapters based on your interest and/or need. The applications chapters will contain some examples that you will find relevant, and some that you will not. We do encourage you to explore even those that might not apply to your current needs, as these chapters can also provide fresh ideas for using infographics in new strategies. And of course, you never know when your needs are going to change.

▲

PICK-AND-CHOOSE CHAPTERS

CHAPTER 4

EDITORIAL INFOGRAPHICS

CHAPTER 5

CONTENT DISTRIBUTION: SHARING YOUR STORY

CHAPTER 6

BRAND-CENTRIC INFOGRAPHICS

CHAPTER 7

DATA VISUALIZATION INTERFACES

The following are brief explanations of what you can expect from each chapter.

CHAPTER 1

IMPORTANCE AND EFFICACY:
WHY OUR BRAINS LOVE INFOGRAPHICS

This chapter will present the science behind the efficacy of visual communication and will explain how best to use it. While the value of visualization can seem somewhat intuitive in certain settings, it is important that we understand exactly what makes it so effective in order to execute properly. We look at the various objectives one might have in creating an infographic, and establish correspondent priorities of the various values infographics provide.

CHAPTER 2

INFOGRAPHIC FORMATS:
CHOOSING THE RIGHT VEHICLE FOR YOUR MESSAGE

This chapter will explore the various forms that information design and data visualization take, including static, interactive, and motion graphics. We'll describe each format in detail, and cite some applications where it may be used.

CHAPTER 3, 4, 6, AND 7

APPLICATIONS

These chapters will address the various uses of infographics in the business world. Chapter 3 outlines The Visual Storytelling Spectrum, a framework by which we can consider the following three applications:

- Chapter 4: Editorial Infographics
- Chapter 6: Brand-Centric Infographics
- Chapter 7: Data Visualization Interfaces

We will look at each application as an opportunity to move away from the status quo by showing you how to create engaging and intelligent visual content. In areas where visual content is fairly common, such as presentations or dashboards, we will consider some of the opportunities to improve and innovate with your content to ensure that your visualizations provide clarity and excite your audience.

CHAPTER 5

CONTENT DISTRIBUTION: SHARING YOUR STORY

In this chapter, we will discuss the best approach to spreading your content far and wide. You're not done once you've created great visual content; you need people to see it, too. Here we will discuss the strategies involved in distributing and promoting your content using social media to make sure people see it—and, more important, share it.

CHAPTER 8

WHAT MAKES A GOOD INFOGRAPHIC?

This subjective and controversial topic is high on our FAQ list. Therefore, this chapter will outline a critical framework by which we can judge information design across various applications.

CHAPTER 9

INFORMATION DESIGN BEST PRACTICES

This book is not intended to be an instructional on how to design infographics, but rather how to best apply them to your communication strategies. However, it is necessary that you have a sound understanding of the basic principles of information design if you are going to be involved in the production process with a designer or in the publication process as an editor. As such, Chapter 9 will give you a cursory knowledge of the dos and don'ts of infographics, so that you can identify their misuse and guide the process of making them interesting, informative, and effective.

CHAPTER 10

THE FUTURE OF INFOGRAPHICS

It is essential in all areas of business to stay on top of the latest trends and technologies. The world of information design is no different, especially as it relates to your particular organization and industry. This final chapter will look at some of the emerging applications of infographics in the not-so-distant future.

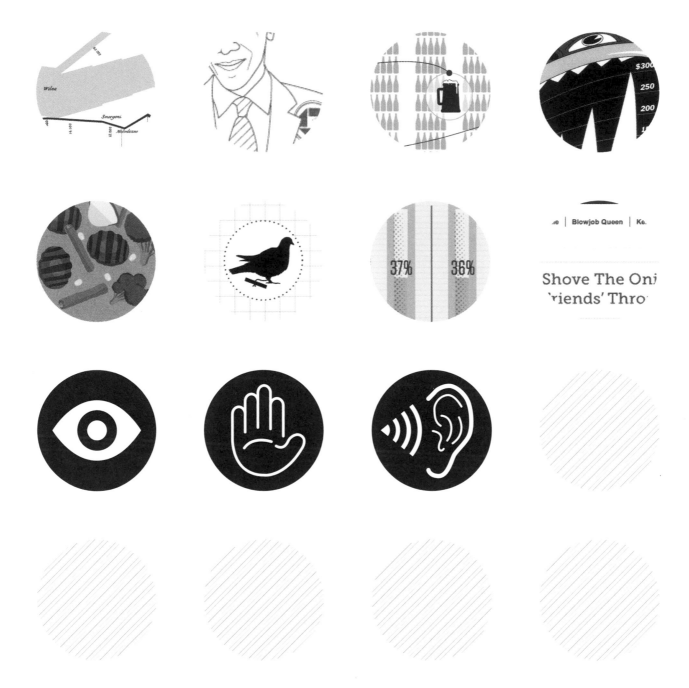

CHAPTER

★ ESSENTIAL READING CHAPTERS

01

fig. 1.1-1.17

01 – 02 – 03 – 08 – 09 – 10

IMPORTANCE AND EFFICACY:

WHY OUR BRAINS LOVE INFOGRAPHICS

In *De Architectura*, Roman architect and engineer Vitruvius states that there exist three standards to which all structures should adhere: soundness, utility, and beauty. In their paper, *On the Role of Design in Information Visualization*, authors Andrew Vande Moere and Helen Purchase point out that these standards can and should also be applied to information design and the various applications that serve this purpose. They state that a good visualization should be sound; that is, the design's form should be suitable for the information it depicts. It should be useful, enabling the viewer to derive meaning from it. And of course, as with all design, it should have aesthetic appeal that attracts the viewer's attention and provides a pleasing visual experience.

This framework provides a solid basis that anyone can use to judge the value of visualization. However, we will use a slightly different categorization for the purpose of discussing the positive effects of infographics. We will refer to beauty as *appeal*, and divide utility into the areas of *comprehension* and *retention*—as these are the three basic provisions of all effective verbal or visual communication methods:

1. *Appeal*
   Communication should engage a voluntary audience.
2. *Comprehension*
   Communication should effectively provide knowledge that enables a clear understanding of the information.
3. *Retention*
   Communication should impart memorable knowledge.

We will address the need to have a sound design on a more practical level in Chapter 9 (Information Design Best Practices) when we discuss principles for the practice of information design.

Images and graphics should always look appealing and encourage viewers to engage in the content. It is important that we examine why this is the case and identify the primary elements that lead to this appeal. This is certainly the first and potentially most challenging step in conveying a message: getting the recipient to commit to hearing what you have to say.

People have long accepted the notion that a picture can replace a thousand words, and similarly, that a simple graph can replace a table full of numbers. Basic visualization allows us to immediately comprehend a message by detecting notable patterns, trends, and outliers in the data. This chapter will look at how visualization achieves this feat so easily while other forms of communication fall short.

Further, we'll determine how we can make those visualizations more memorable. The democratization of media, especially online, has given us a great variety of options that we can use to consume our news, videos, and funny pictures—and generally educate ourselves on myriad topics. However, the downside to this exponential increase in stimuli is that we tend to lose much of this knowledge shortly after we gain it. While no one should lament forgetting a mediocre LOLcat, it pays to be memorable—especially in the business world. Fortunately, connections have been made recently between the illustrative elements of graphics and the retention rates of the information displayed—and these connections can help us all figure out how to have people remember our material.

This chapter will also discuss the fact that information design lends itself to achieving these objectives, and will seek to understand exactly how and why it does this, based on the way our brains process information. We will not be getting into too much heavy science; rather, our main goal is to understand which elements of design help us reach our specific communication goals, and to leave behind those that do not. For this we will lean heavily on several key works that have covered the science of visualization exhaustively, most notably Colin Ware's thoughtfully written *Information Visualization: Perception for Design*.

Finally, we will identify several of the divergent schools of thought. We've concluded that the differences in these approaches are largely rooted in the failure to recognize that varied objectives necessitate varied approaches to the practice. That is, a design whose primary objective is to give the viewer information for analysis cannot be considered, designed, or judged in the same way as one whose primary goal is to be appealing and entertaining while informing. We will discuss these varied approaches to each unique objective and elaborate on the practice in the applications chapters (3, 4, 6, and 7). We will then discuss how we can use these different methods to serve our three basic communication provisions: appeal, comprehension, and retention.

VARIED PERSPECTIVES ON INFORMATION DESIGN: A BRIEF HISTORY

Many a heated debate over the proper approach to information design is raging online nowadays, which seems to raise the question: Why all the conflict in the friendly field of pretty picture creation? The debate surrounds just that: The role of aesthetics and decoration in the design of infographics. To understand the underlying tension, a bit of background is necessary.

Science and publishing have used information design and visualization as a communication tool for centuries. However, study and development in the field has mostly been dominated by academics and scientists, who are concerned primarily with understanding the most effective way to process and present information to aid viewers' analyses. These efforts are driven by loads of research, with highly theoretical consideration; when practical, the focus is on using software to process and visualize data sets. For years, only a select few—an educated, knowledgeable, and skilled group of individuals—have discussed and practiced visualization in this sense. Then the Internet caught on. Around 2007, interest in infographics (mostly editorial in nature) began to grow on the web, as people shared old infographics like Napoleon's march on Moscow (Figure 1.1) and newer creations such as those published by *GOOD Magazine* (Figure 1.2). Suddenly, a whole new group of "experts" was praising, sharing, and critiquing (mostly critiquing) any infographic they could find.

Since then, an impressive number of new infographics have been created as various industries and areas identified different applications for their use. One of the most common was to use editorial infographics for commercial marketing purposes. This new breed of visual took a bit of a different path, both in format and content. The long, skinny graphic, designed to fit within a blog's width, became ubiquitous and almost instantly synonymous with the term *infographic*. These pieces used illustration and decoration much more than their traditional counterparts. And as with most marketing efforts, their goal was to use their content and design to attract attention, interest, and adoration for the company that produced them—making each brand a "thought leader" in its industry. This was quite a divergence from the traditionally stated purposes of the field, which was purely to use visual representation to aid in the processing and comprehension of data.

As you can imagine, the new field of infographic designers often lacked knowledge of best practices for information design. In other words, people were winging it. As with any field experiencing this kind of growth, overall quality of designs vary drastically—which has attracted criticism (read: utter disdain) from the academic and scientific visualization community. The Internet had usurped infographics.

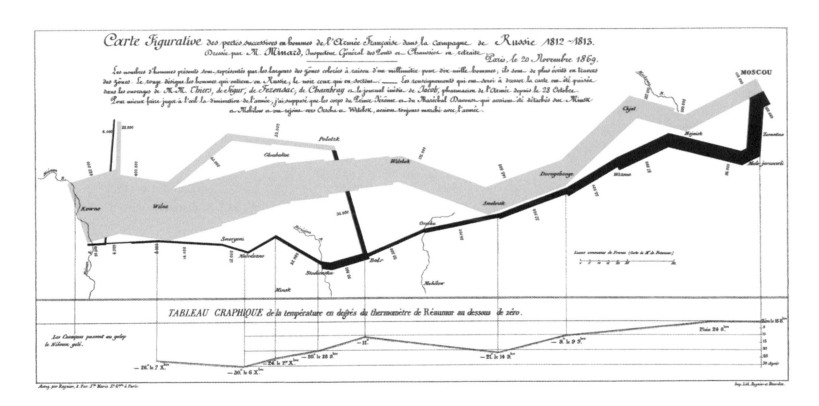

Figure 1.1
Flow map of Napoleon's Russian Campaign of 1812.
Charles Minard.

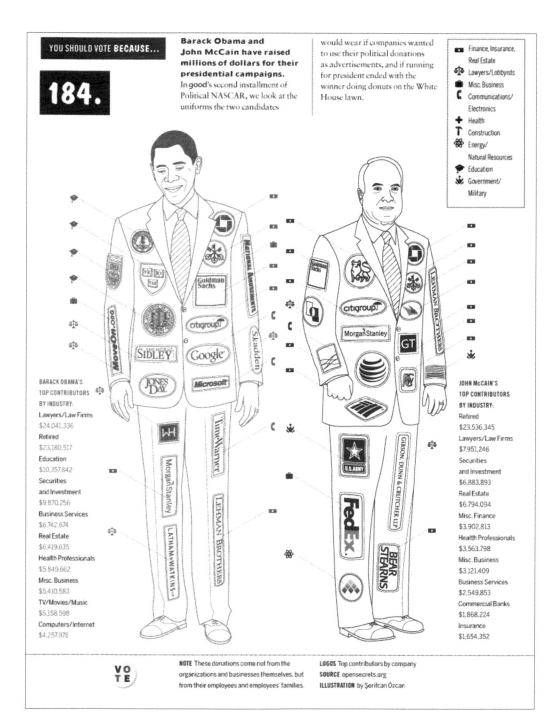

Figure 1.2
You Should Vote Because.
Open, NY for GOOD.

EXPLORATIVE NARRATIVE

CHARACTERISTICS

EXPLORATIVE	NARRATIVE
MINIMALIST	ILLUSTRATIVE
ONLY INCLUDES ELEMENTS THAT REPRESENT DATA	DESIGN-FOCUSED
SEEKS TO COMMUNICATE INFORMATION	SEEKS TO APPEAL TO VIEWER WITH ENGAGING VISUALS
IN THE MOST CLEAR, CONCISE MANNER	INFORMS AND ENTERTAINS

APPLICATIONS

EXPLORATIVE	NARRATIVE
ACADEMIC RESEARCH	PUBLICATIONS
SCIENCE	BLOGS
BUSINESS INTELLIGENCE	CONTENT MARKETING
DATA ANALYSIS	SALES AND MARKETING MATERIALS

Figure 1.3

Approaches to infographic design.

The debate over what should be considered an infographic continues to this day, as people seek to find concrete definitions in an area that's constantly becoming more nebulous. Among the most known and quoted voices in this area is Yale University statistics professor Edward Tufte, who has written some of the most acclaimed and comprehensive works on the topic of information design. Tufte has contributed much to its popular terminology by coining terms such as *chartjunk* (unnecessary graphic elements that do not communicate information) and developing the data-ink ratio—a measurement of the amount of information communicated in a graphic as it relates to the total number of visual elements in it. Tufte's thoughts on the topic represent a conservative lean on the spectrum of approaches to infographic design (Figure 1.3), which is typical of those who have an academic or scientific background. He argues that any graphic elements of a design that do not communicate specific information are superfluous and should be omitted. He believes that chartjunk such as unnecessary lines, labels, or decorative elements only distract the viewer and distort the data, thus detracting from the graphic's integrity and decreasing its value (Figure 1.4). Although Tufte does concede that decorative elements can help editorialize a topic in some instances, his teachings typically discourage their use.

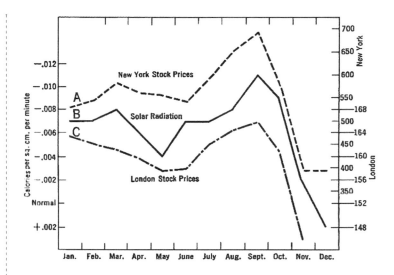

Figure 1.4
Example of explorative graphic approach using minimalist design.

The work and writing of British graphic designer Nigel Holmes characterizes the opposite end of the spectrum, which supports the heavy use of illustration and decoration to embellish information design (Figure 1.5). Holmes is best known for his illustration of editorial "explanation graphics" in *Time* from 1978 to 1994. The perspective that Holmes' work supports the notion that using illustration and visual metaphor to support and reinforce the topic makes the graphic appealing to viewers. Recent studies show that these decorative elements can also aid in the retention of the information presented, which we will examine later in the chapter.

So which is the correct approach? Both are. What people often overlook in these debates is the most central issue to any design: the objective. While Tufte and Holmes might want to represent the exact same data set, they likely would be doing it for very different reasons. Tufte would aim to show the information in the most neutral way possible, to encourage his audience to analyze it without bias. Conversely, Holmes's job is to editorialize the message in order to appeal to the viewer while communicating the value judgment he wants readers to take away. Tufte's communication is *explorative*; that is, it encourages the viewer to explore and extract his or her own insights. Holmes's, on the other hand, is *narrative*, and prescribes the intended conclusion to the viewer. The difference is inherent in their areas of work, as the objectives of science and research are much different than those of the publishing world. There's no need to establish a universal approach to govern all objectives; rather, different individuals and industries should develop best practices unique to each application's specific goal.

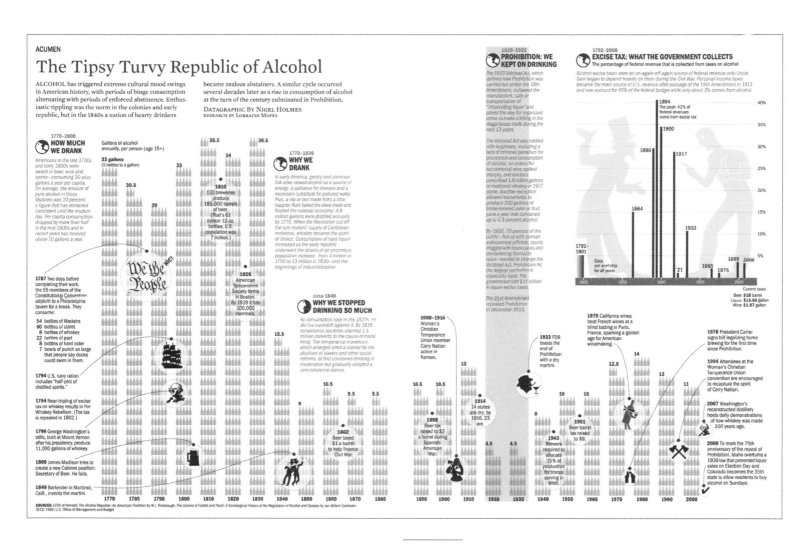

Figure 1.5

The Tipsy Turvy Republic of Alcohol.

Nigel Holmes.

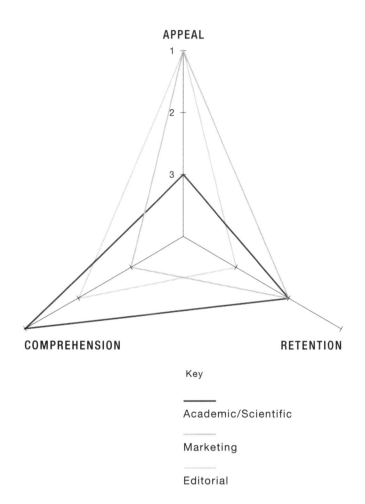

APPEAL

1

2

3

COMPREHENSION

RETENTION

Key

——— Academic/Scientific

——— Marketing

——— Editorial

Figure 1.6
Infographic priorities by application.

OBJECTIVES OF VISUALIZATION

Of course, we must first look at what each infographic is trying to achieve before we can establish the best practices for its application. By definition, all information graphics are aimed at communicating information. What varies is the purpose for doing so—and understanding this purpose is what determines a graphic's priorities. These priorities account for a necessary difference in approach to each design.

For example, if an infographic is intended to communicate information in the most clear and unbiased manner possible, then the first priority for the designer is *comprehension*, then *retention*, followed by *appeal* (Figure 1.6). This is common in academic, scientific, and business intelligence applications, as these areas typically lack any agenda aside from conveying and having viewers comprehend knowledge. Appeal is less necessary in this setting, as the viewer most typically needs the information and seeks it out as a result. Appeal is only useful when it keeps the viewers' attention to enable further comprehension. Such a graphic typically would be used as a resource for information—which is why retention is also a secondary priority. If the viewer needs the information and it is a readily accessible resource, then he or she can revisit it as needed to retrieve it again. There's no need for it to take up any more valuable brain space than necessary.

However, a graphic created with a commercial interest in mind will have much different priorities. Brands primarily seek to get viewers' attention and eventually (hopefully) convert those users into paying customers. As evidenced by Super Bowl commercials, companies will go to almost any length to get this attention. The order of priorities of a commercial marketing graphic would be *appeal*, *retention*, and then *comprehension*. Brands are looking to catch viewers' attention and make a lasting impression—which usually means that viewers' comprehension of content is frequently the brands' last priority. The exception to this would be infographics that are more focused on the description of a product or service, such as a visual press release, since designers in these cases would want the viewer to clearly understand the material as it relates to the company's value proposition. However, being appealing enough to prospective customers to get them to listen is always goal number one.

Publishers that create editorial infographics have a slightly different mix: *appeal*, *comprehension*, and *retention*. Since the appeal of a magazine's content is what will make it fly off the newsstand, it shares this top priority—improving sales—with companies in other industries. A publisher's survival is based solely upon its ability to spark readers' interest. The quality of content or graphics produced on a consistent basis helps drive this interest by making a strong impression on readers—and this is where *comprehension* comes into play. A publication's quality is based on the content it produces, which is intended to help readers understand a given topic. However, whether or not the reader can *recall* that topic with the same level of understanding one week later is of little importance to a publisher's bottom line. The common denominator between commercial and editorial interests is that they both desire to compel the consumer to take a specific action.

APPEAL

In 2010, Google CEO Eric Schmidt famously stated that we now create more information in two days than we created from the dawn of man up until 2003. This staggering statistic obviously necessitates clarification of what constitutes information and its creation. Regardless, the message is clear and uncontested: humanity is creating and consuming far more information than it ever has before. As a result, it is increasingly difficult to get people's attention, since they're constantly bombarded with various stimuli throughout the day—material that ranges from breaking news to funny photos to Facebook updates. Marketers, salespeople, brand evangelists, and publishers must all figure out how to grab a slice of this attention—a task that is becoming more challenging by the day. How do you get people's attention, and keep it long enough to share your message with them? Due to the sheer volume of "stuff" out there, it's a formidable task to make yours stand out.

How do you appeal to an audience in a world of information overload in which people constantly face new inputs, options, and decisions? Ask the world's biggest company, Apple. With a cash reserve larger than the total valuation of all but fifty companies worldwide (as of early 2012), this organization surely must have some insight into what people like. In the battle for MP3 player dominance, the iPod came in early and overshadowed the competition. What was, and still is, the key differentiator between this and other products? The simple answer is design. While features such as OS compatibility, memory, and screen size certainly factor into the decision, the most outstanding difference between the iPod and its competitors is its impressive design. As Steve Jobs preached, good design not only garners additional appeal for an item, it can also actually incite an emotional reaction. Few can deny the good feeling of pulling a new Apple product out of the box.

So how does this translate to best practices for information design? Our consumer culture is becoming increasingly design focused in areas that extend beyond graphics and consumer electronics, and that play a role in many other industries. Home products company IKEA, for example, has made clever furniture design mainstream. British mega-brand Virgin brought sexiness to the airline industry, with an interior design that looks more like a chic lounge than a mode of mass transit. Regardless of whether they can articulate it—or if they even know it—consumers connect with these brands because of designs that continues to attract new fans and followers. The ever-growing media landscape makes it increasingly important to use great design to differentiate your brand from the crowd.

Even if your goal is to present information for a purely analytical objective—that is, without any desired action from the reader—it is still beneficial to have aesthetic appeal.

DESIGN IS TO DATA AS CHEESE SAUCE IS TO BROCCOLI.

(That analogy is on the SAT, if you don't remember.) In other words, people need an added incentive to eat their vegetables—especially when those vegetables are as cold and dry as research studies and analytics reports. Presenting information by way of engaging visuals immediately attracts readers and entices them to dig deeper into the content.

Possessing this appeal to your audience is not a "nice to have" for businesses; it is a "must have." You can't sell magazines if no one picks them up, and you can't sell products if you can't get potential customers' attention.

The modern marketer can learn a lot from Horace's quote in the introduction, and the notion that delighting people with your content is a must. It has become a necessity in order to build trust with your audience and capture their attention often. We will discuss how to do this further in Chapter 3 (The Visual Storytelling Spectrum) and Chapter 4 (Editorial Infographics), in the sections pertaining to Editorial Infographics. For now, it is important for us to focus on the first step: How to get their attention in the first place.

Just what appeals to us when we become interested in consuming information? We are drawn to formats that we see as efficient, engaging, and entertaining (Figure 1.7). It's highly unlikely that someone would prefer to read a lengthy article than view a multimedia display presenting the same information. A diversity of media keeps our brains engaged in the material, and the visualization can enable us to digest it more efficiently and facilitate understanding.

Figure 1.7
Source: Reprinted with permission of THE ONION.
Copyright 2012, by ONION, INC.
www.theonion.com.

Further, a recent study from the University of Saskatchewan suggests that viewers prefer a greater use of illustration in visual representations. When presented with both a simple chart and one that contained an illustration by the aforementioned Nigel Holmes (Figure 1.8), participants consistently opted for the Holmes version in a number of different areas (Figure 1.9). While this conclusion—that a more dynamic and stimulating visual is preferable to a plain one—seems somewhat obvious, it's important to consider in design approach. It's not enough to make your content visual; you must also make it visually interesting. You can do this by using representative iconography, illustrative metaphor, or relevant decorative framing mechanisms—all powerful tools for communicating your message. However, you always want to remember your objective. The appropriateness of decorative and illustrative elements will vary based on an infographic's application and use. For example, an editorial graphic in the Sunday newspaper on the topic of corporate profits could find great use in the illustration of a rotund executive sitting atop a throne of gold bullion. Shareholders, on the other hand, might not share the same appreciation for such a work of art if it adorned the pages of an annual report containing similar data.

If used incorrectly, decorative elements have the potential to distract the viewer from the actual information, which detracts from the graphic's total value. Mastering this execution and finding the balance between appeal and clarity can be a nuanced process. We will discuss the proper use of illustration and decorative elements further in Chapter 9 (Information Design Best Practices), where we'll cover the principles and best practices of information design.

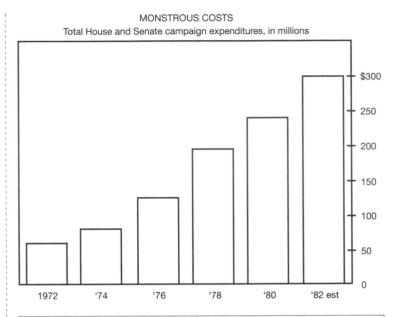

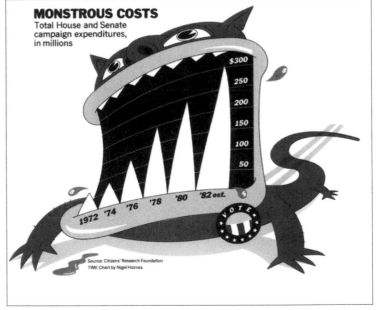

Figure 1.8
Illustrative Nigel Holmes graphic with simplified equivalent.

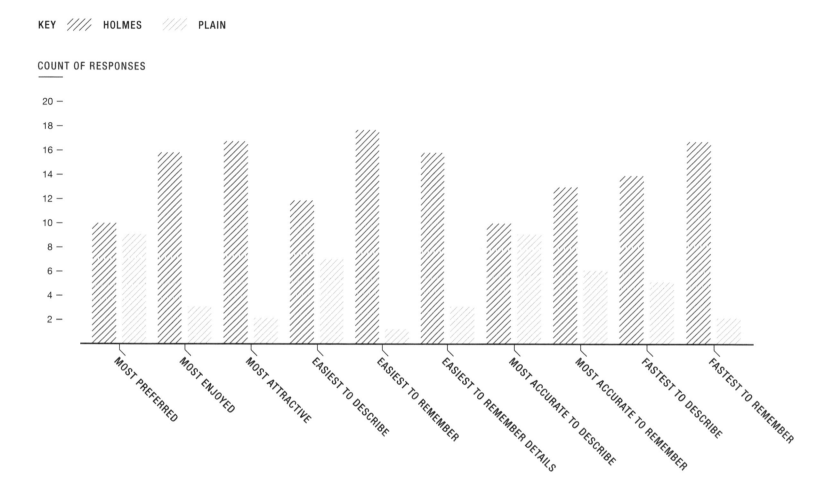

Figure 1.9
University of Saskatchewan study results.

COMPREHENSION

You often hear someone claim to be a "visual learner," which simply means that they need to see something in order to understand it. Researchers have studied and modeled learning styles in a number of different ways over the past several decades, and the origins of this specific visual style of thinking can be traced to Neil Fleming's VAK model. One of the most commonly known and quoted models of thinking, it states that when comprehending information, people learn best with one of three types of stimuli:

Visual learners best comprehend information that is presented in pictures, diagrams, charts, and the like; auditory learners do best when hearing this information spoken; and tactile learners need to touch and learn by doing. While this theory is commonly accepted, it has been highly scrutinized in the scientific community, which posits that there is little to no evidence that any one preferred method of learning is actually more beneficial for comprehending and retaining information.

Regardless of this ongoing debate, it is important to consider the media structure and channels through which people obtain information. It is less important to identify how people *prefer* to learn, and instead figure out how they are *actually* learning—and these experiences are occurring increasingly online today, a channel based primarily on visual display. The use of audio-only content on the web is relatively minimal outside of music sites—and until virtual reality is able to provide interactive, tactile experiences, the majority of information on the Internet will be communicated visually.

Given that people are more likely to consume information visually, the value of using visuals in our communication—instead of just words—is truly significant. As Colin Ware states in *Information Visualization: Perception for Design*,

"The human visual system is a pattern seeker of enormous power and subtlety. The eye and the visual cortex of the brain form a massive parallel processor that provides the highest-bandwidth channel into human cognitive centers. At higher levels of processing, perception and cognition are closely interrelated, which is why the words *understanding* and *seeing* are synonymous (p. xxi)."

Ware goes on to state that we are able to acquire more information through our visual system than we do through all our other senses combined (p. 2). This is largely because visualizations contain certain characteristics called preattentive attributes, which our eyes perceive very quickly (within 250 milliseconds) and our brains process with impressive accuracy—without any active attention on our part. Force-feeding for the mind—how convenient! To use a common illustration of this concept, refer to Figure 1.10. Try to count the number of 7s in the number set. How long did that take?

Now, try the same exercise with Figure 1.11. A color change makes recognition almost instant, since color is one of several preattentive attributes, displayed in Figure 1.12. All visualizations contain such attributes, and using them properly to convey information is the key to visual communication. Our brains are able to recognize and process many of these visual cues simultaneously through a course of action called preattentive processing. All this action precedes any cognitive attempts to focus on any specific area; rather, it is purely involuntary and will simply proceed wherever our eyes are pointed.

These natural functions that result from the connection between the eyes and brain can be quite handy when we want to communicate to people who don't have a lot of time—or a long attention span. We know that we can use these visuals to attract people by appealing to them aesthetically, but we can also decrease the amount of time it takes them to comprehend the message by using these same tools.

That said, you can't tell a story through color alone, or craft compelling messaging using only shapes and symbols. So how do words factor into information design? Within the context of a society that speaks the same language, words—as compared to symbols—have a distinct advantage in terms of familiarity. No set of symbols has universal ubiquity; rather, most are isolated to specific social or cultural settings. This necessitates a cost-versus-benefit analysis of using visualization instead of verbal communication. Symbols can take longer to interpret than language when conveying a concept to someone who is unfamiliar with the symbols. In this case, communication should favor text descriptions. To someone who knows the symbols, however, this comprehension process is far easier; in this case, communication should rely more upon visualization methods.

Ware provides a sound breakdown of the general value of each medium by explaining that "images are better for spatial structures, location, and detail, whereas words are better for representing procedural information, logical conditions, and abstract verbal concepts" (p. 304). The practical reality is that we don't need to choose between the two. The strongest visualizations are those that are supported by descriptions as well as narratives, especially in editorial applications. Using words in this way helps to bring both personality and clarity to an infographic.

```
2   1   4   3   9   5   6   7   8   2   3   6   5   9   4   0   1

6   7   9   3   4   9   0   5   6   2   5   8   4   0   5   2   6

9   8   2   6   3   5   9   3   2   9   3   7   2   6   3   4   8

8   1   6   2   3   8   7   9   5   0   2   3   9   2   8   4   3

0   9   1   8   5   4   2   9   4   7   4   6   8   4   0   2   9

3   9   2   7   3   6   6   5   2   9   4   0   4   9   4   8   6

5   2   4   3   6   4   8   1   0   3   9   4   8   4   7   3   2

8   6   2   3   0   8   7   3   6   2   5   4   4   8   3   5   0
```

Figure 1.10
Preattentive Processing Test 1.

```
2  1  4  3  9  5  6  7  8  2  3  6  5  9  4  0  1

6  7  9  3  4  9  0  5  6  2  5  8  4  0  5  2  6

9  8  2  6  3  5  9  3  2  9  3  7  2  6  3  4  8

8  1  6  2  3  8  7  9  5  0  2  3  9  2  8  4  3

0  9  1  8  5  4  2  9  4  7  4  6  8  4  0  2  9

3  9  2  7  3  6  6  5  2  9  4  0  4  9  4  8  6

5  2  4  3  6  4  8  1  0  3  9  4  8  4  7  3  2

8  6  2  3  0  8  7  3  6  2  5  4  4  8  3  5  0
```

Figure 1.11
Preattentive Processing Test 2.

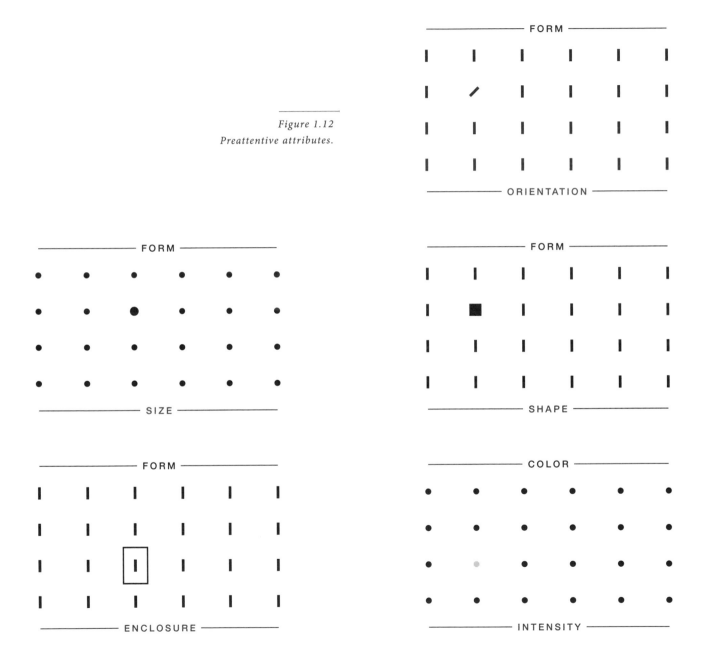

Figure 1.12
Preattentive attributes.

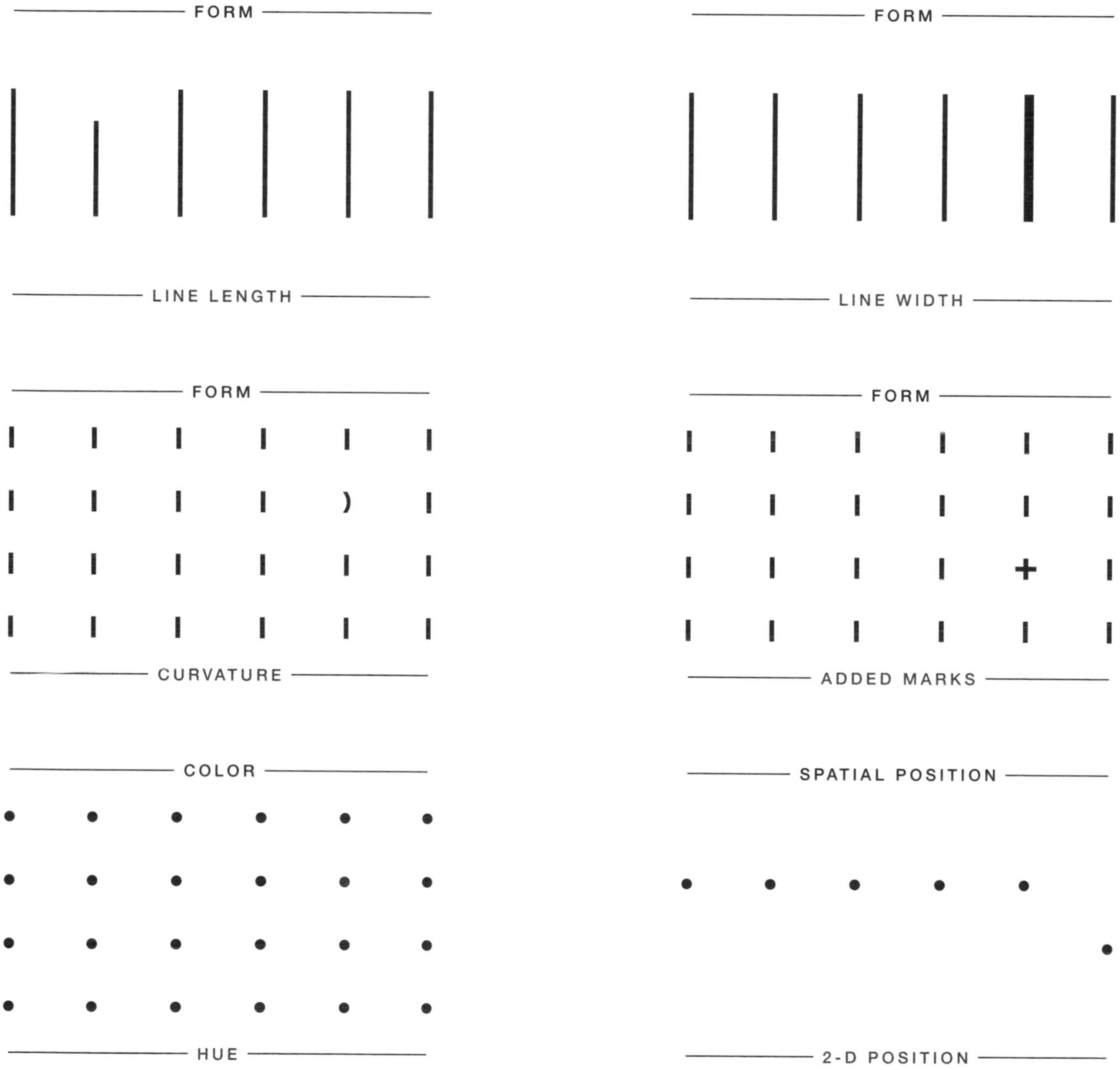

————— FORM —————

————— LINE LENGTH —————

————— FORM —————

————— LINE WIDTH —————

————— FORM —————

————— CURVATURE —————

————— FORM —————

————— ADDED MARKS —————

————— COLOR —————

————— HUE —————

————— SPATIAL POSITION —————

————— 2-D POSITION —————

RETENTION

The third main benefit of using infographics in communication is their ability to help people retain information, as the graphics are able to extend the reach of our memory systems. Visualizations do this by instantly and constantly drawing upon nonvisual information that's stored in our long-term memory (Ware, p. 352). The human brain can recall familiar symbols, scenes, and patterns, allowing us to make rapid connections to already stored information and to quickly comprehend what we're seeing. This prompts the question: Which visualization methods best serve recall for various different types of memory?

There are three main types of memory that relate to viewing images. The *iconic memory* is the snapshot of a scene that you retain for a brief instant after looking at something. It is stored for less than a second, unless it is analyzed and connected to something that is already stored in your brain (Sperling via Ware, p. 352). *Long-term memory* stores information from our experiences that we will retain for long periods of time, and from which we draw upon in order to process new information. Long-term memory is further divided into three areas: episodic memory, semantic memory, and procedural memory. *Episodic memory* is the primary device for recalling images and scenes that we've experienced, and the feelings associated with those experiences. *Semantic memory* enables us to recall knowledge that has no specific context or experience associated with it, and could generally be considered the storage of "common knowledge." *Procedural memories* are those that recall processes of doing—such as typing or tying a tie—that we access involuntarily without conscious thought. These memories often build on themselves, which is why you are able to recall that the "M" arm position comes after the "Y" when the Village People are played at a wedding reception.

Visual working memory is what lies in between iconic and long-term memory, and is most essential to processing visual information. When we see an object that requires further attention, we move it from iconic to visual working memory. Visual working memory then calls upon semantic memory (long term, nonvisual) to understand its meaning. All this happens in about 100 milliseconds (Ware, p. 353). With our vision transmitting massive amounts of information into the brain, and the brain accessing its stored knowledge to provide context, we are able to understand much more quickly than with any other combination of sensory perception and processing.

So what visual elements should be used to best ensure that individuals store this understanding for long-term recall? While academics have typically argued against using decorative elements in information design—claiming that they only serve to distract the viewer—this isn't always the case. A very interesting finding from a University of Saskatchewan study conducted by Scott Bateman and his colleagues from the Department of Computer Science uncovered that a more illustrative approach to design actually benefits information recall significantly. All participants were shown a set of alternating graphics, some plain and some in Holmes's illustrative style, such as that depicted in Figure 1.8. The researchers split the participants into two groups: half were part of an immediate recall group, and the other half were in the long-term recall group. After seeing all the graphics, the immediate recall group played a five-minute game to clear their visual and linguistic memory. They were then questioned regarding the information in each graphic. The long-term recall group was scheduled to come back for their recall session two to three weeks following the initial observation.

Each participant had to answer questions about the graphic's subject, the categories displayed within it, and the general trend of the chart. They also had to describe whether there was a value judgment presented in the chart; that is, a perceived opinion that the graphic's creator had presented.

The immediate recall group showed no significant differences between Holmes's graphics and their plain counterparts in terms of how well they'd retained information about the subject, categories, or trends (Figure 1.13). Yet there was a significant difference in their identification of whether a value judgment had been presented. However, the long-term recall group experienced notable differences in their ability to recall information in all areas (Figure 1.14). The subjects, categories, trends, and value messages within Holmes's graphics stuck with users more prominently after two to three weeks.

Bateman et al. offer up three possible explanations for the findings in this experiment:

1. Additional imagery enabled people to encode information more deeply, as there were more visual items to recall and use memory to draw upon.
2. The variety of Holmes's style gave it a unique advantage in being memorable over the style of the plain graphics, which all had a similar look.
3. The user preference (as described earlier in the Appeal section) provided a hidden factor: The participants' emotional responses to the graphic, combined with the imagery used, helped to solidify the image in their memories.

KEY ///// HOLMES ///// PLAIN

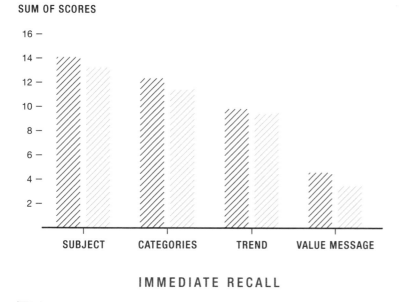

Figure 1.13: Results of immediate recall group.

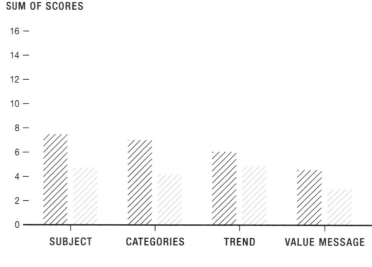

Figure 1.14: Results of long-term recall group.

So what does all of this tell us about using infographics, particularly for commercial objectives? Graphics that contain visual embellishment beyond the information being displayed may be superior not only in terms of appeal, but also in their ability to ensure that viewers understand and retain your message—which is likely value-based. Appealing to someone not only aesthetically but also emotionally prompts a deeper connection with the information, which makes them more likely to remember it.

While design style is something that varies greatly and often cannot be categorized neatly, there are certain devices that we can use to facilitate understanding and retention. We refer to these collectively as illustrative design:

1. *Visual Metaphor*
   We use this often at Column Five and it works incredibly well when implemented effectively. You can do this by containing information within a framing mechanism that is indicative of your subject matter (Figure 1.15).

2. *Symbols and Iconography*
   The success that these achieve depends largely on cultural context. Your audience must universally understand your icons and symbols for them to be effective. When this is the case, they can provide a great communication shortcut by using visual elements in the place of verbal explanation (Figure 1.16).

3. *Decorative Framing*
   Using design elements that appeal to your target audience lets them connect with infographics on an emotional level, thereby deepening their interest in and retention of the information (Figure 1.17).

Illustrative design can also have its negative effects, so it is important to determine when it might potentially detract from rather than support your message. The main pitfall here is the designer's accidental or intentional distortion of the display of data. Illustrations should complement visualization elements, but never at the expense of misleading the viewer. Whether intentional or not, you always want to avoid altering accurate information representation.

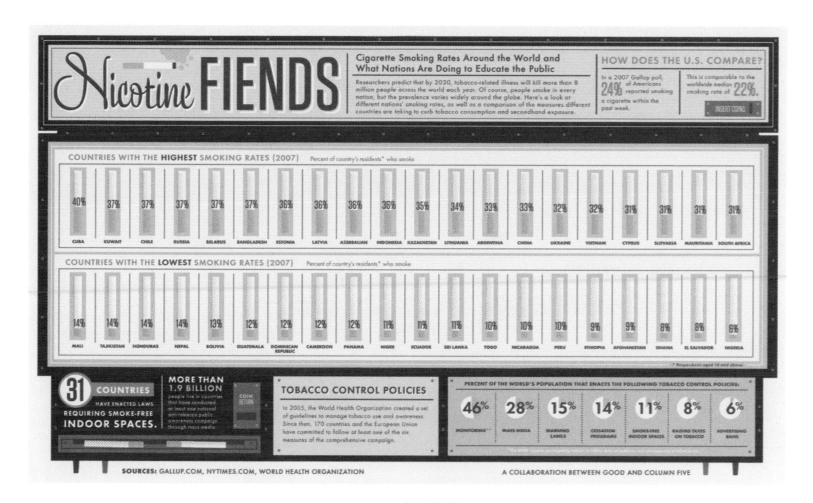

Figure 1.15
Example of visual metaphor.
Column Five for GOOD.

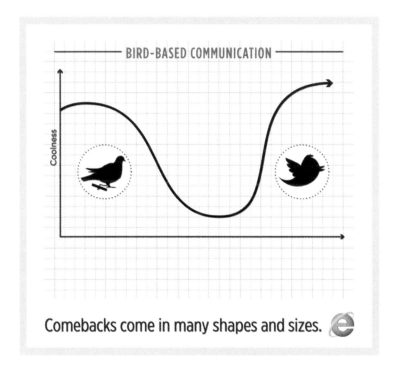

Figure 1.16
Example of use of symbols and iconography. Column Five
for Microsoft.

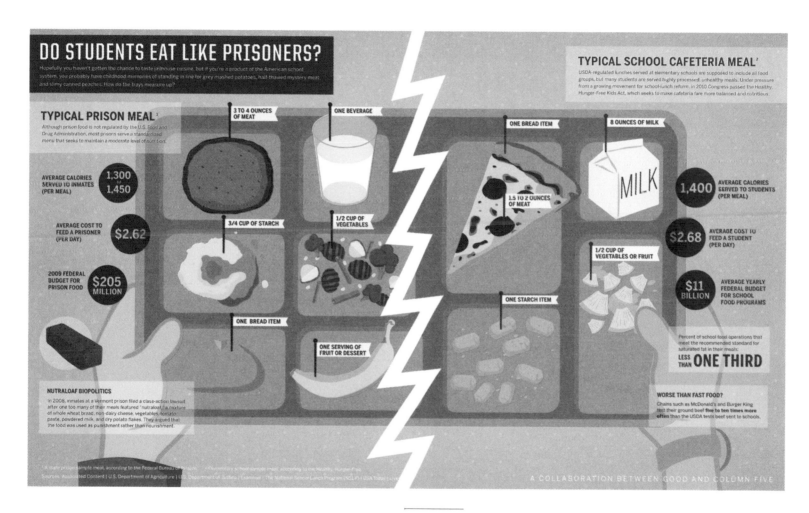

Figure 1.17
Example of decorative framing.
Column Five for GOOD.

CHAPTER

★ ESSENTIAL READING CHAPTERS

fig. 2.1-2.14

(01) – (**02**) – (03) – (08) – (09) – (10)

INFOGRAPHIC FORMATS:

CHOOSING THE RIGHT VEHICLE FOR YOUR MESSAGE

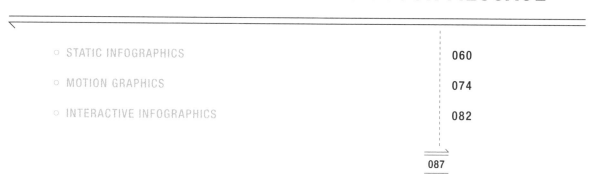

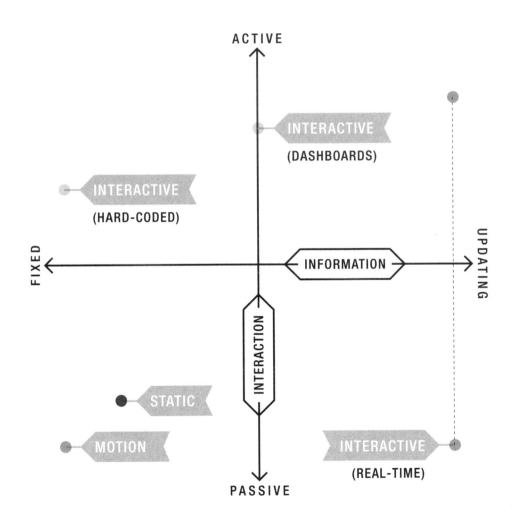

Figure 2.1
Infographic Formats Quadrant.

As you embark on the journey to becoming a more visual company through using infographics, it is important to understand which format will help deliver your message most effectively. The key formats that can house infographic communication are static images, interactive interfaces, and motion content (Figure 2.1). There is no implied hierarchy, as the best format is determined by how effective it is at containing and delivering the information that you want to communicate. It is helpful to understand the attributes of each format, and to consider that many artistic mediums can be used within each of these categories.

1. *Static*

    Typically *fixed information*. User interaction consists of viewing and reading. Display output is a *still* image. Works best as a *narrative* but can be explorative in some cases.

2. *Motion*

    Typically *fixed information*. User interaction consists of viewing, listening if there is voiceover, and reading. Display output is animated, or *moving*. Works best as a *narrative*, almost never *explorative* without being used in combination with interactive content.

3. *Interactive*

    Can be *fixed* or *dynamic information* input. User interaction consists of clicking, searching for specific data, actively shaping the content displayed, and choosing which information is accessed and visualized. Can be *narrative, explorative, or both*.

Static images can be used in a wide range of applications, and while they are the simplest to execute of the three, and perhaps the least expensive, they are often the most versatile. The ability to create them more quickly than interactive and motion content makes them optimal for many applications, such as delivering visual content related to time-sensitive news. We will look at how the context and purpose of static infographic content determines the layout and size of the image itself.

We also touch on the use of infographics in motion content. We mostly focus on the use of infographics in short animation and as augmented reality-style overlays on top of live action footage. Because a motion project requires manual updates to the information, it is difficult to make changes once your content is finalized. We will talk about how this impacts the type of information that you want to communicate through this format. It is extremely important to finalize the information and script at an early stage, rather than trying to make changes after animation is completed.

In the last format section, we take a look at the different types of interactive interfaces based on the information visualized. These can range quite dramatically—from the simplest form as a clickable series of slides, to a living, breathing data visualization that updates before your eyes in real-time. While interactive interfaces can obviously be a central aspect of software, this chapter will focus mostly on describing interfaces for visual representation of information on the web. You can keep in mind, however, that interactive content can also be used for live displays at events, or in a dashboard feature of your web application or software product.

It is vital to consider the type of information you will want to display, and how frequently it will need to be updated. The order of the sections within this chapter is meant to reflect the range from fixed information inputs, which are typically utilized in static and motion content, to dynamically updated information, which usually requires an interactive interface. Collectively, these sections will give you a framework for understanding the characteristics of each format so that you can choose the best approach for effective visual storytelling.

STATIC INFOGRAPHICS

First, we will focus on the static infographic, which is the most prevalent format for utilizing information design. In this section, we will show some brief examples of how they are used so that you can get an understanding of the fundamental characteristics and versatility of this format. People use infographics most commonly in static format as an image for print, web, or both. While the purpose of the content may vary, the overall size and shape of your infographic is mostly determined by the demands of your publishing context, such as a blog roll or magazine spread. Whether it is for a print publication, or a report to shareholders, static infographics are very effective at representing rich data in a single image.

There are three main types of static infographic content that are utilized by businesses:

1. Internal reporting and presentations
2. Editorial content for blogging and social/PR distribution
3. Brand-centric content for blogging and social/PR distribution

One of the main benefits (and reasons for the ubiquity) of static content is the relative ease of creating a static image versus an interactive interface—especially if you want to use the infographic to cover time-sensitive material or breaking news. This efficiency also makes this content relatively affordable compared to motion and interactive content. Another key factor in the rising popularity of static infographics is their ease of shareability, as they can easily be embedded in blogs.

One challenge inherent in using the static infographic for certain reports is that the information can become dated. An infographic that visualizes a regularly updated, fixed set of data (such as a monthly index) will still maintain value as a reference to the data at a specific moment in time. However, you will need to manually update the infographic for people looking for the most current information available (which are, arguably, most people out there). This need to present updated information is also an opportunity, even if it can be more time-consuming. For example, you can further your brand by consistently publishing a new infographic each month, based on updated data in a proprietary index of your own creation, to build an audience that begins to anticipate the next release. Column Five has done this with *The Wall Street Journal*'s Home Price Scorecard, which aggregates all home price indices into one simple graphic (Figure 2.2).

Home-Price Scorecard

They take different approaches, but home-value indexes tackle the same question: Are prices up or down?

S&P/Case-Shiller	LPS	FHFA	FNC
-3.6%	-4.4%	-2.8%	-4.7%

CoreLogic	Radar Logic	Clear Capital	Zillow
-3.9%	-5.4%	-2.2%	-5.1%

Note: Latest year-over-year data as of Dec. 22.

THE WALL STREET JOURNAL. COLUMN FIVE

Figure 2.2
Home Price Scorecard.
Column Five for Wall Street Journal.

Sometimes a data visualization created by software powerful enough to process larger data sets will be output to a format such as scalable vector graphics (SVG). The SVG format allows us to visualize data in a vector format that contains all of the underlying data in the editable image file, which can be imported into Adobe Illustrator to edit or to provide additional context or visual cues. This allows us to then utilize the data visualization within a broader infographic that provides further information, such as qualitative descriptions or even editorial illustration and text. The advantage to this approach is that it lets presenters guide viewers through the messages they're conveying, towards specific conclusions. While you could certainly take an explorative approach with certain information and allow the viewer to peruse a large body of information, it is best to put a reasonable limit on the amount of information that you try to cram into one static infographic, and to take a narrative approach. The narrative infographic's goal, after all, is to express meaning, and to enable a viewer to quickly comprehend the story in the information that you present. If you want to make the static infographic's underlying data open for exploration by your viewers you can link them to the dataset.

One of the best uses for the static graphic is to display evergreen content that will stay relevant without a frequent need to have the underlying information updated. While certain data can indeed become dated, there are plenty of opportunities to create static infographics with perpetual value. There are certainly many types of data that will allow for an infographic to have a long shelf-life, such as Census data that is mostly updated only once per decade. However, there is also potential to explain concepts, use diagrams and maps, and even to create content that is entertaining and has the potential to go viral.

Let's look at two typical audiences in business communication to further understand the various shapes that a static infographic might take: first, for internal reporting within your organization, and then for external-facing content for distribution outside of your company. We will look more closely at other applications of static infographics in the coming chapters, so these two examples will serve to help understand the varying purposes and formats of static infographics.

STATIC INFOGRAPHIC EXAMPLE: REPORTS FOR INTERNAL USE

Companies often come to Column Five to get help designing reports containing important information to be shared internally throughout the organization or for other confidential use. Whether it is a global company wanting more clarity in sales reports for internal communication, or a venture capital firm that wants to keep their institutional investors informed about portfolio performance at a glance, there are countless opportunities to visualize information. The raw data is intimidating to some, and can often take far too long to review. Even a well-written 30 page summary of a research initiative and its underlying data can often go unread by the executives who need the information the most, but who only have time for the highlights. Our goal, therefore, is to clarify the high-level story, while pairing the infographic summary with the underlying data so that the intended audience is able to get the granular details—if and when they have time.

Companies often want to be able to empower internal people to ultimately create these reports, so that they can quickly disseminate the information at their fingertips. But they've traditionally used programs that are not particularly revered for their ability to output beautiful charts and graphics. Letting someone in your organization handle design work by "driving without a license," so to speak, can lead to a disjointed visual language throughout your company and misrepresentation of data. For example, let's say that Jeff in Accounting loves creating butterfly-themed PowerPoint decks with orange and purple 3D pie charts for his presentations using Comic Sans, while Ruth in Marketing is using Excel to make blue and yellow bar charts. It gets really exciting when Jeff likes one of Ruth's charts and throws it into his presentation deck. This is a challenge many organizations face when non-designers have no guideposts for communicating important information. We will talk more in Chapter 6 (Brand-Centric Infographics) about how you can use information design in presentations. Some companies prefer to work with outside agencies for these projects so that their employees can stay focused on what they are good at.

Whether you do it yourself, or hire someone else to create infographics for your reports, it is essential to identify the most important information at an early stage, and for all the project's stakeholders to agree up front about the points that are worth highlighting in the infographic. Think hard to determine who can, should, or will give feedback that you will want (or have) to consider, and get them involved at the information outline stage rather than waiting until the design work begins. Furthermore, it is important to think of all scenarios where the information will be presented—is it for print, web, presentations, white papers, or some combination of all of them? This will help determine the actual orientation, size, and shape of the canvas that is used so that you don't have to radically alter the design later to fit a different purpose or audience.

Even if you don't, assume that you already have the brand guidelines sorted for now, and that you are working with the appropriate designer (or doing it yourself with the appropriate software) for your infographic. When you need a print version, it is very important to design the information as a static image (Figure 2.3). If you want a browser-based interactive interface as well (which we'll discuss in depth shortly in the interactive format sections), you must give careful attention to how people will view the different layers of information such an interface would

include in printable reports. For this example, imagine that you want to manually create a static infographic report that uses a fixed set of information—say, your quarterly sales metrics—and assume that the information is a fixed snapshot at a specific point in time.

DISPLAY UPDATES

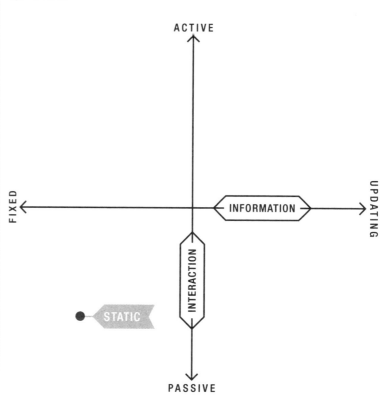

Figure 2.3
Static infographics typically consist of fixed information with passive user interaction.

JOEY DONUT'S YEAR IN REVIEW

2011

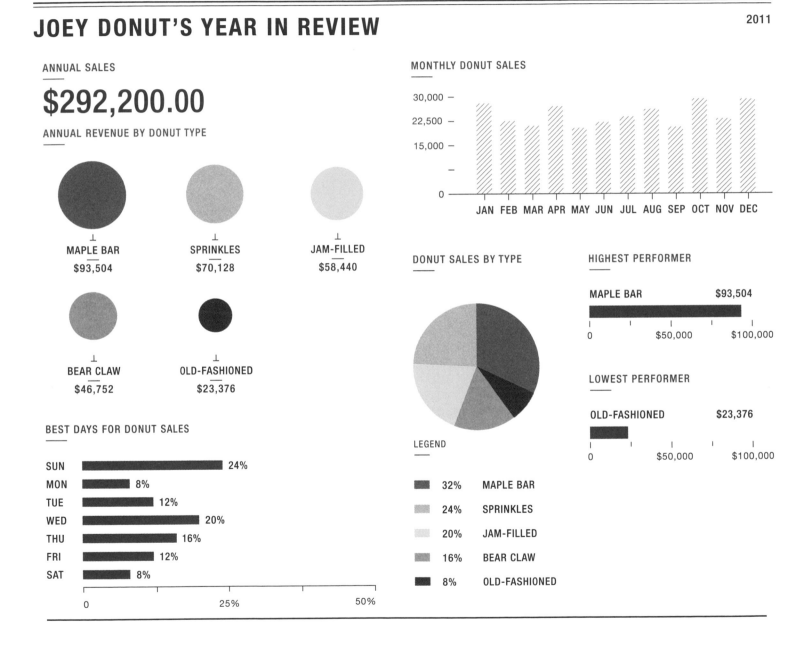

ANNUAL SALES

$292,200.00

ANNUAL REVENUE BY DONUT TYPE

MAPLE BAR
$93,504

SPRINKLES
$70,128

JAM-FILLED
$58,440

BEAR CLAW
$46,752

OLD-FASHIONED
$23,376

MONTHLY DONUT SALES

DONUT SALES BY TYPE

HIGHEST PERFORMER

MAPLE BAR $93,504

0          $50,000 $100,000

LOWEST PERFORMER

OLD-FASHIONED $23,376

0          $50,000 $100,000

LEGEND

32%	MAPLE BAR	
24%	SPRINKLES	
20%	JAM-FILLED	
16%	BEAR CLAW	
8%	OLD-FASHIONED	

BEST DAYS FOR DONUT SALES

SUN	24%
MON	8%
TUE	12%
WED	20%
THU	16%
FRI	12%
SAT	8%

0   25%   50%

Figure 2.4: Example of brand-centric report for internal use.

One advantage to this internal-use-only, brand-centric report is that you are communicating to a smaller audience—likely a group that you know well. Because you don't have to think about how complete strangers will receive the message, you don't have to worry as much about emotional or mass appeal; you just have to think about how to appeal to the investor holding your purse strings or the person who signs your paycheck (no pressure).

The ultimate goal here is to give a clear, easy-to-digest explanation of the information that you need to share throughout your organization or to a trusted group of insiders.

As you saw in this chapter's introduction, the output of a static image at a given point in time does not necessarily mean that the underlying information is fixed or manually input, because we can create an interface that allows us to process an up-to-the-second static snapshot of real-time data. You could run these reports at intervals of every minute, day, or month. An example of this would be an analytics report with annotation of milestones and company events that provide explanations for spikes and dips in traffic or conversions. It wouldn't require much manual labor (depending on your analytics platform) to simply run an updated report each month for your boss or your own reference.

The key takeaway here is that while the underlying data is not permanently fixed, the output—or presentation of it—is a static snapshot of the data at a specific moment in time. The advantage of this approach is that you can tell a story (for internal or external purposes) that shows the data as of a particular date or within your desired date ranges.

The disadvantage is that the viewer might not necessarily be able to get access to refreshed information in real-time, and might not realize that more current information is available. A static infographic won't be enough for large groups that require access to real-time information. If you have such a need, you will either need to build an interface that allows multiple people to process and output updated information into reports, or at least have a system for ensuring that people know how to find updated information.

Because using the static infographic as an internal, brand-centric piece is more likely to be narrative than explorative, you want to ensure that the information flows in a logical order to tell your story (Figure 2.4). This report likely would be best created in landscape orientation so that it also could be used in a presentation deck, although you could certainly create a PDF in portrait layout. This might sound elementary, but it is actually a very important early consideration.

While you can condense some infographic reports into a single page, in cases where you have multiple pages of information design, it is typically ideal to produce it in landscape orientation so that you can print and use it in presentation decks. This makes the content more versatile than a vertically oriented infographic, such as those created for posting on blogs, which require the viewer to scroll. It is also helpful to keep in mind that you don't have to force all of the information in an "infographic-based presentation" into an infographic format, and that some of your qualitative slides can certainly consist of text only.

STATIC INFOGRAPHIC EXAMPLE: CONTENT FOR SOCIAL/PR DISTRIBUTION

Now, to get that image of presenting your quarterly figures to the boss or investors out of your mind, you can focus on creating a message for the friendly masses on the Internet! In addition to content in which you share a slice of your proprietary data with the public, editorial content related to your company's broader industry has become an outstanding vehicle for establishing your expertise and driving brand awareness. Let's consider an example of both in order to understand the context in which the static infographic is commonly applied on the web.

Visual Press Release

First, let's focus on what most people think they want and need most: content about ourselves! Pretend you are a start-up, and you have recently pivoted for the third time and have your Facebook killer drawn up on a napkin. It's time to tell the world your story, right? However, it is extremely difficult to get the tone of such content just right. No one likes the person at the party who simply talks about himself or herself the whole time. The challenge is that people are constantly bombarded by companies talking about themselves, and while we live and breathe our own brands, in most cases Joey Donut could care less about your company. This sounds harsh, but it is The Way of the Internet.

The answer lies in fighting the urge to talk endlessly about yourself and your company, and letting the interesting story in your data shine through. While there are certainly opportunities for telling qualitative stories about your brand in static form, we will focus on an example that is driven by proprietary, quantitative data. We have found the visual press release to be most successful in helping companies share aggregated data about their own businesses. There are so many ways to do externally facing, brand-centric content wrong (Make the logo bigger!), and sometimes you have to experience the growing pains to find the best practices that allow you to tell your story in a way that engages people. We will discuss this further in Chapter 6 (Brand-Centric Infographics).

For example, we worked closely with Hunch (which was acquired by eBay) to show the tastes and preferences of self-identified Mac versus PC users (Figure 2.5). Because the underlying topic was about a story that was bigger than Hunch itself, we were able to tap into a broader audience than we would have been able to reach by simply talking about Hunch and its product. The beauty is that the data were all generated by Hunch users, and we were able to work closely with them to craft a narrative that was meant to entertain a wide audience. As you can see, the image was optimized for sharing the entire piece on the web, and the individual charts within the graphic can be cropped for use by a journalist or blogger as images in a post.

Editorial

The application of static infographics in editorial content (Figure 2.6) has grown exponentially in the last few years. The popularity of the long, scrolling vertical format came about as a by-product of most blogs' restricted width. Further, using a width in the 550- to 600-pixel range has made it very easy for other bloggers and publications to pick up and repost the infographic. This has made it a popular form of the classic infographic medium for purposes of PR, branding, search engine optimization (SEO), link building, and social media marketing. There have been quite a few rants against the ubiquity of this application of infographics, and many journalists have mistakenly applied their wrath about spammy use of infographics to the medium as a whole. The sheer novelty of the infographic in the digital world has worn off as more people have used them; however,

Figure 2.5
Example of static infographic for Social/PR distribution.
Column Five for Hunch.
(Continued on pages 68–70)

CORE DEMOGRAPHICS

PC people are 22% more likely than Mac people to be ages 35-49.

22% more likely than PC people to be ages 18-34.

36% of PC people are liberal.

58% of Mac people are liberal.

PC people are 18% more likely to live in the suburbs and 21% live in a rural area.

52% of Mac people live in a city.

54% of PC people have completed a four-year college degree or higher.

The same can be said for 67% of Mac people.

PERSONALITY

PC people are 26% more likely to prefer fitting in with others.

Mac people are 13% more likely than PC people to say they want to be "perceived as unique and different to make my own mark."

PC people are 23% more likely to say they seldom throw parties.

Mac people are 50% more likely than PC people to say they frequently throw parties.

PC people are 33% more likely than Mac people to say that two random people are more different than alike.

Mac people are 21% more likely than PC people to say that two random people are more alike than different.

PC people are 38% more likely than Mac people to say they have a stronger aptitude for mathematical concepts.

$F(X) = \dfrac{\blacktriangle}{T}$

Mac people are 12% more likely than PC people to say they have a stronger verbal (vs. math) aptitude.

Figure 2.5
Continued.

FASHION, TASTE, & AESTHETICS

PC people are 21% more likely than Mac people to prefer impressionist art.

Mac people prefer modern art and are design enthusiasts.

71% of PC people identify their styles as casual and trending toward jeans.

18% and 14% of Mac people describe their style as designer/chic/upscale and unique/retro, respectively.

69% of PC people would rather ride a Harley than a Vespa.

52% of Mac users would go for the Vespa.

FOOD & DRINK

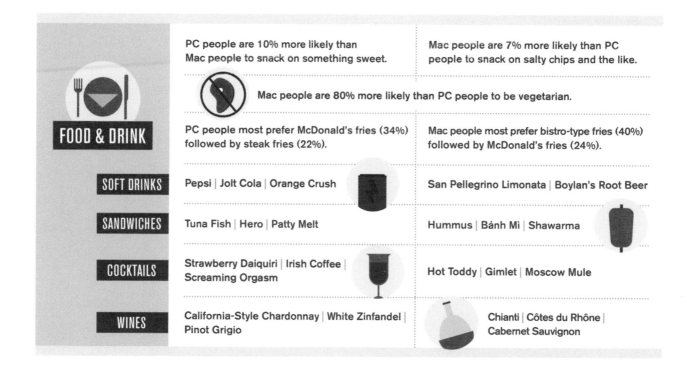

PC people are 10% more likely than Mac people to snack on something sweet.

Mac people are 7% more likely than PC people to snack on salty chips and the like.

Mac people are 80% more likely than PC people to be vegetarian.

PC people most prefer McDonald's fries (34%) followed by steak fries (22%).

Mac people most prefer bistro-type fries (40%) followed by McDonald's fries (24%).

SOFT DRINKS

Pepsi | Jolt Cola | Orange Crush

San Pellegrino Limonata | Boylan's Root Beer

SANDWICHES

Tuna Fish | Hero | Patty Melt

Hummus | Bánh Mì | Shawarma

COCKTAILS

Strawberry Daiquiri | Irish Coffee | Screaming Orgasm

Hot Toddy | Gimlet | Moscow Mule

WINES

California-Style Chardonnay | White Zinfandel | Pinot Grigio

Chianti | Côtes du Rhône | Cabernet Sauvignon

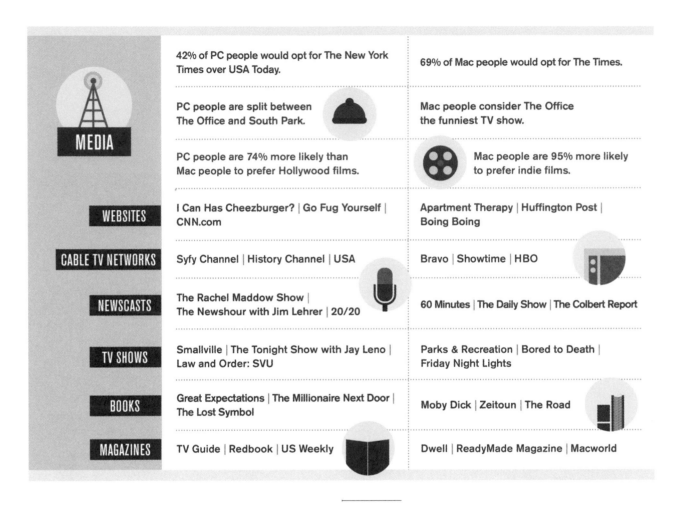

MEDIA

42% of PC people would opt for The New York Times over USA Today.

69% of Mac people would opt for The Times.

PC people are split between The Office and South Park.

Mac people consider The Office the funniest TV show.

PC people are 74% more likely than Mac people to prefer Hollywood films.

Mac people are 95% more likely to prefer indie films.

WEBSITES

I Can Has Cheezburger? | Go Fug Yourself | CNN.com

Apartment Therapy | Huffington Post | Boing Boing

CABLE TV NETWORKS

Syfy Channel | History Channel | USA

Bravo | Showtime | HBO

NEWSCASTS

The Rachel Maddow Show | The Newshour with Jim Lehrer | 20/20

60 Minutes | The Daily Show | The Colbert Report

TV SHOWS

Smallville | The Tonight Show with Jay Leno | Law and Order: SVU

Parks & Recreation | Bored to Death | Friday Night Lights

BOOKS

Great Expectations | The Millionaire Next Door | The Lost Symbol

Moby Dick | Zeitoun | The Road

MAGAZINES

TV Guide | Redbook | US Weekly

Dwell | ReadyMade Magazine | Macworld

Figure 2.5
Continued.

the medium itself is stronger than ever. Infographics should be individually judged based on the value of the information communicated and the quality of the design, rather than by a blanket assessment of all content created in the medium. We will discuss the critical framework for judging the quality of infographics in Chapter 8 (What Makes a Good Infographic?).

However, one common and still valid argument is that the content within an image file is not very accessible in some cases—specifically, via smaller mobile devices or to visually impaired Internet users. The best way to overcome this limitation is to make the underlying information available in a text format, either as ALT text (the message that is rendered if the underlying image is not visible to a visitor to your site) or as supplementary copy in the body of the article or page where you present the infographic. This also benefits your site by providing more information for search engines to crawl, in turn helping your SEO for the page where the content lives. In Chapter 4 (Editorial Infographics), we will take an in-depth look at shaping a content strategy around such editorial infographics.

COMBINING ARTISTIC MEDIUMS

The static infographic is a valuable weapon in your arsenal because you can create it relatively quickly and inexpensively (as compared to interactive and animated infographics), but it is still extremely effective in aligning results with your content marketing goals. An image's shareability allows you to spread certain editorial content swiftly, and most infographic images created for the web can be fairly easily modified for print as well. Remember that an information graphic can use multiple mediums of artistic expression. For example, we have always enjoyed using photography in diagrams (such as the one shown in Figure 2.6), which shows the economics of the hamburger industry) and each component layer. In another instance, we created a flexible template for retail DNA testing company 23andMe (Figure 2.7) that could be dynamically populated by genetic information for each individual customer. This is a nice application of the ability to use dynamic information to output to a flat image as a report, which we will discuss further in the context of interactive infographics in the following pages. Part of the appeal of this approach came from varying the artistic medium used in each piece, such as hand illustration, custom typefaces, and vintage-photography scans. We teamed up with respected artists from around the globe to create custom artwork for the header and as decorative elements surrounding the individual's genetic information as displayed in The Grand Tree, which is similar to a family tree showing which portion of one's genetic makeup was inherited from which parents and grandparents.

A willingness to experiment with tried-and-true media as visual aids in your infographics can help yield novel and more interesting content. By using unique artistic elements within your information graphics, you can generate beautiful content that entices the viewer to pay attention to—and even care about—the rest of the story.

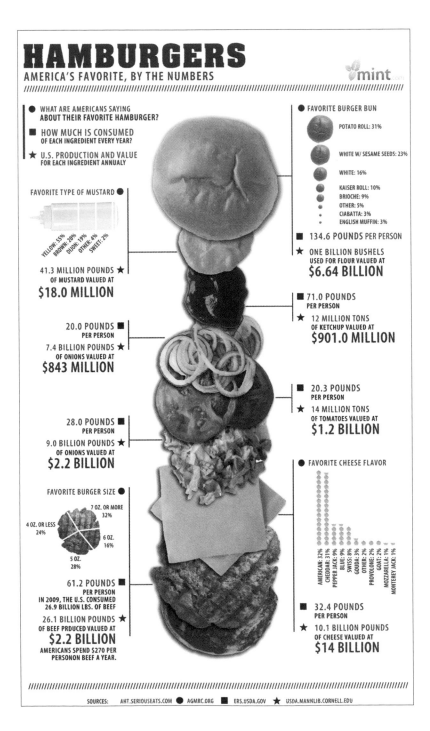

Figure 2.6
An example of photography
use in static infographic
for editorial purposes.
Column Five for Mint.com.

Figure 2.7
Template design with dynamic updates for genetic information.
Column Five for 23andMe. Illustration by Jessica Hische.

DISPLAY UPDATES

● DYNAMIC

○ SEMI-DYNAMIC

● STATIC

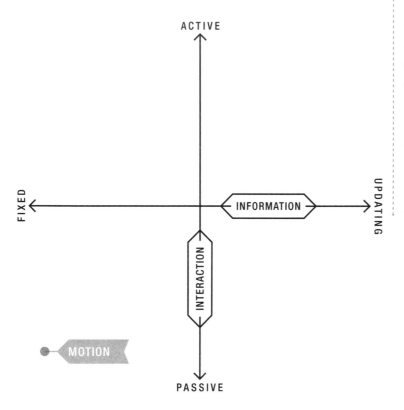

MOTION GRAPHICS

You can also utilize motion graphics to animate your infographic content. There is something special about a motion graphic's ability to engage people in a different way than static or interactive infographics could. Essentially, if there is voiceover, individuals can sit back and have the narrative presented to them in a linear fashion. They don't need to actively choose to engage with the information from moment to moment as they would with viewing a static infographic. The ability to appeal to a viewer emotionally through music while also informing through voiceover and the imagery in motion provides an opportunity to communicate your brand's message in a powerful way. Because it is so time-consuming and expensive to make late stage changes to an animated video, it is typically necessary to utilize fixed information (Figure 2.8), at least when your animation will be delivered in a video player format and syndicated to video platforms like YouTube and Vimeo (Figure 2.9).

Figure 2.8
Motion graphics typically consist of fixed information and passive user interaction.

Another fundamental difference between motion content and static content is time. By definition, static content exists fixed in time, and the visual content within it does not change. Motion content, on the other hand, exists across time. While static content pieces are snapshots—and valuable in their own right—motion pieces have life and movement. Motion graphics traditionally have served a narrative function, with limited and mostly passive user interaction (aside from pressing play/pause, rewinding, fast-forwarding, etc.). As we discuss in the next section, interactive content is traditionally better suited for displaying dynamic information and allowing for exploration, since it allows users to customize their experience and find personally meaningful and relevant information.

Motion graphics are increasingly popular to include in interactive content for the web as HTML5, CSS3, and advanced JavaScript libraries become more widely used, giving us an increased ability to utilize augmented reality style overlays on top of video (Figure 2.10). Some of these cutting edge applications of motion content have tremendous viral potential simply for the sake of their novel methods of production. For most typical businesses, though, use of motion graphics is best when your objective is to communicate a single linear story in order to create visual and emotional appeal that engages viewers on multiple levels (Figure 2.11).

Figure 2.9
Example of motion graphic in Vimeo video player.

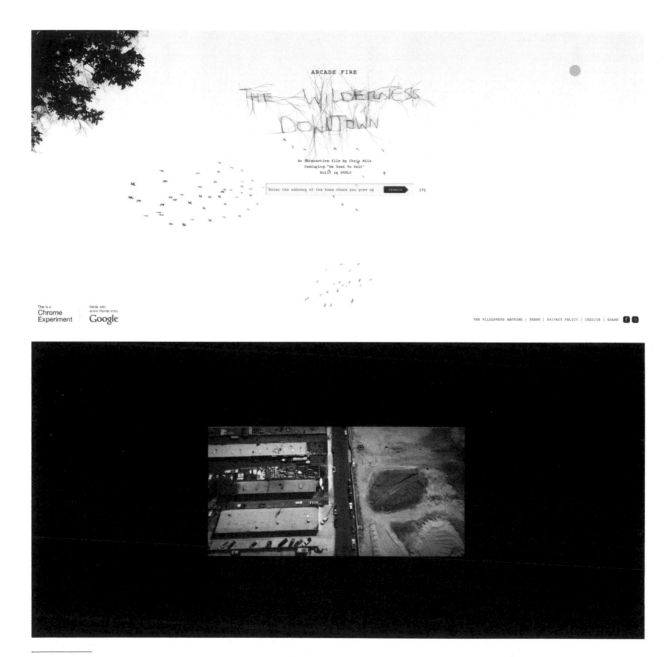

Figure 2.10
An example of location-based information used to customize video for each unique user.
Google + Arcade Fire.

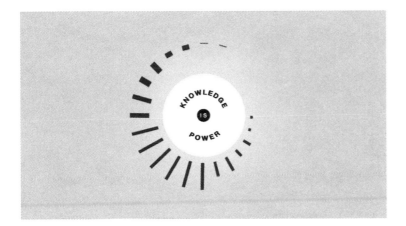

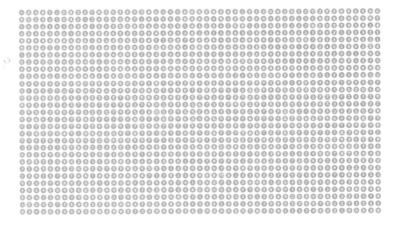

Figure 2.11
Motion graphic stills from *The Value of Visualization.*
Column Five.
(Continued on pages 78-81)

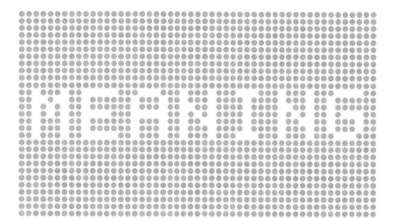

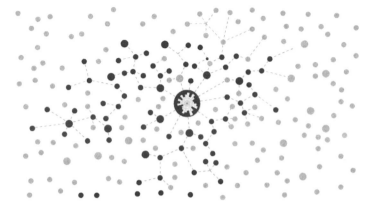

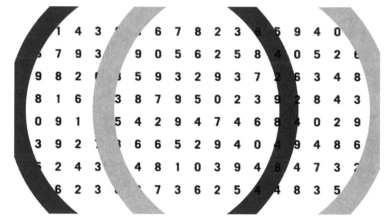

2 1 4 3 9 5 6 7 8 2 3 6 5 9 4 0 1
6 7 9 3 4 9 0 5 6 2 5 8 4 0 5 2 6
9 8 2 6 3 5 9 3 2 9 3 7 2 6 3 4 8
8 1 6 2 3 8 7 9 5 0 2 3 9 2 8 4 3
0 9 1 8 5 4 2 9 4 7 4 6 8 4 0 2 9
3 9 2 7 3 6 6 5 2 9 4 0 4 9 4 8 6
5 2 4 3 6 4 8 1 0 3 9 4 8 4 7 3 2
8 6 2 3 0 8 7 3 6 2 5 4 4 8 3 5 0

2 1 4 3 9 5 6 **7** 8 2 3 6 5 9 4 0 1
6 **7** 9 3 4 9 0 5 6 2 5 8 4 0 5 2 6
9 8 2 6 3 5 9 3 2 9 3 **7** 2 6 3 4 8
8 1 6 2 3 8 **7** 9 5 0 2 3 9 2 8 4 3
0 9 1 8 5 4 2 9 4 **7** 4 6 8 4 0 2 9
3 9 2 **7** 3 6 6 5 2 9 4 0 4 9 4 8 6
5 2 4 3 6 4 8 1 0 3 9 4 8 4 **7** 3 2
8 6 2 3 0 8 **7** 3 6 2 5 4 4 8 3 5 0

INFOGRAPHICS

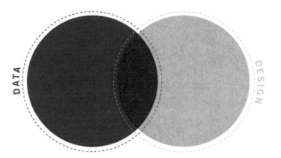

DATA DESIGN

2 1 4 3 9 5 6 7 8 2 3 6 5 9 4 0 1
6 7 9 3 4 9 0 5 6 2 5 8 4 0 5 2 6
9 8 2 6 3 5 9 3 2 9 3 7 2 6 3 4 8
8 1 6 2 3 8 7 9 5 0 2 3 9 2 8 4 3
0 9 1 8 5 4 2 9 4 7 4 6 8 4 0 2 9
3 9 2 7 3 6 6 5 2 9 4 0 4 9 4 8 6
5 2 4 3 6 4 8 1 0 3 9 4 8 4 7 3 2
8 6 2 3 0 8 7 3 6 2 5 4 4 8 3 5 0

2 1 4 3 9 5 6 ⟩ 8 2 3 6 5 9 4 0 1
6 ⟩ 9 3 4 9 0 5 6 2 5 8 4 0 5 2 6
9 8 2 6 3 5 9 3 2 9 3 ⟩ 2 6 3 4 8
8 1 6 2 3 8 ⟩ 9 5 0 2 3 9 2 8 4 3
0 9 1 8 5 4 2 9 4 ⟩ 4 6 8 4 0 2 9
3 9 2 ⟩ 3 6 6 5 2 9 4 0 4 9 4 8 6
5 2 4 3 6 4 8 1 0 3 9 4 8 4 ⟩ 3 2
8 6 2 3 0 8 ⟩ 3 6 2 5 4 4 8 3 5 0

2 1 4 3 9 5 6 7 8 2 3 6 5 9 4 0 1
6 7 9 3 4 9 0 5 6 2 5 8 4 0 5 2 6
9 8 2 6 3 5 9 3 2 9 3 7 2 6 3 4 8
8 1 6 2 3 8 7 9 5 0 2 3 9 2 8 4 3
0 9 1 8 5 4 2 9 4 7 4 6 8 4 0 2 9
3 9 2 7 3 6 6 5 2 9 4 0 4 9 4 8 6
5 2 4 3 6 4 8 1 0 3 9 4 8 4 7 3 2
8 6 2 3 0 8 7 3 6 2 5 4 4 8 3 5 0

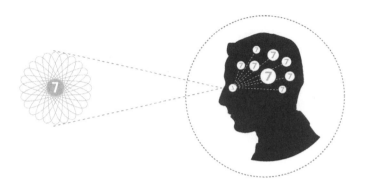

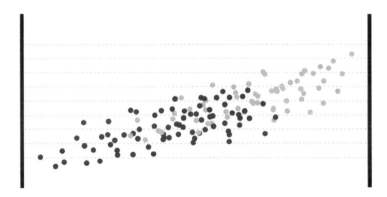

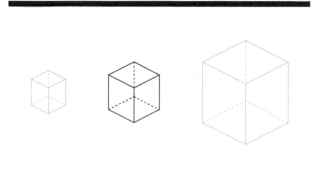

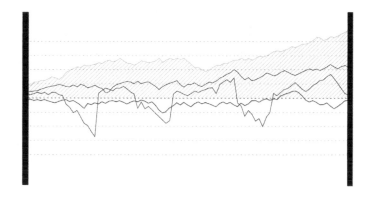

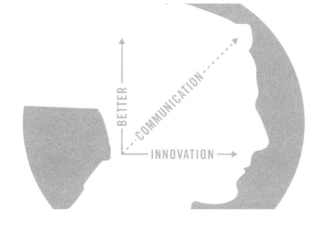

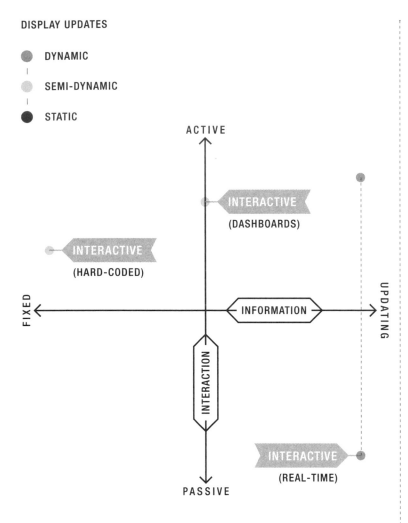

DISPLAY UPDATES

● DYNAMIC

○ SEMI-DYNAMIC

● STATIC

Figure 2.12
Interactives with fixed information which require manual updates
can still encourage active user interaction.

INTERACTIVE INFOGRAPHICS

In this section, we will look at the range of interactive info-graphic interfaces, from the most basic functionality up to the most dynamic. This format is particularly useful if you have vast amounts of data and want to create interactive content that draws the user in to encourage further exploration. The scatterplot displays the varying degrees of user interaction (Figure 2.12). Sometimes you may want the user to browse your information in order to derive meaning that is relevant or interesting to them. Or you may use interactive infographics to guide someone through a specific narrative in a linear fashion, so they grasp the specific story that you want to tell. Keep in mind that this isn't an either/or decision; you can use the narrative/editorial angle to tell people what you see as significant, interesting, or entertaining in order to entice them to view the content, and then encourage them to explore the data further to find information that is relevant to them.

While not everything fits neatly into the categories that follow, we have found them to be helpful for segmenting projects. Additionally, they allow users to determine fairly early in the process which approach is most relevant and useful for the specific information to be visualized. Consider your goals in creating an interactive data visualization in the first place, and let those be your primary guide to choosing whether to keep it simple or to invest a lot of time and resources into something more robust.

INTERACTIVE WITH FIXED INFORMATION (MANUAL UPDATES REQUIRED)

Some narratives are better presented in interactive form, which allows for a nice alternative to the long, vertically oriented infographic. When you have a specific sequence through which to walk people, you can create the equivalent of an interactive infographic slide show, with functionality as simple as clicking to view the next step of the story. If you do limit the interactive functionality to simply allowing people to click through a series of static infographic images, you should use a presentation sharing platform such as SlideShare to distribute your content.

In many other cases, you will be telling a story by presenting data that have multiple layers. One common application of an interactive infographic is a map with multiple variables in the data to be presented. For example, a map of the United States with 20 pieces of information for each state would look horrific on the web if you crammed everything into a static image with callouts drawn from each state. However, you can solve this problem fairly easily by using an interactive map with pop-ups from each state upon the user's hover or click. These pop-ups could also link people to more information about that region.

Whether you develop your project internally or through an agency, it is good to understand the true value of this specific medium within the interactive category, along with the challenges inherent in the format. There are several benefits to using narrative interactive content with fixed information sets as a tool within your content strategy. First, because you only need basic functionality to be programmed, it is potentially the least expensive category within the interactive infographic medium, but it still allows you to showcase your brand in an engaging way. Also, if you want to use interactive infographics as part of your content marketing strategy, this tier of interactivity is typically the best route to go because it can be faster than more complex data visualizations. An interactive U.S. map with state-level data, for example, typically wouldn't be more than two or three times the expense of a static project, depending on whether you utilize Flash (which has a faster timeline) or JavaScript/CSS/HTML (which can potentially take much longer depending on browser support requirements). In this U.S. map example, you'd also be able to show multiple layers of information within a confined space, and to potentially guide the user through the story in a specific order, if you choose to be more narrative than explorative in the piece.

The challenge in using this approach is that you must make all changes manually, since the information is hard-coded into the interactive files. For example, if you just need an update once per year, it might make sense to stick with this option and make manual changes as needed. One upside to the manual approach is that it also allows you to update the design to refresh the style at the same time. It can be more expensive to maintain such a project in the long run than to implement a solution from one of the interactive categories that we describe in the following pages. The frequency of updates needed is typically the primary factor in making the right choice for your interactive application.

INTERACTIVE INTERFACE WITH FIXED INFORMATION SET (DISPLAY UPDATES DYNAMICALLY IF NEW INFORMATION IS MANUALLY UPDATED)

For a bit more up-front work and financial investment, you will be able to update the dynamic interface by simply uploading the new data in the same format as the previous version. For example, online real estate database Zillow has data on real estate transactions at both the ZIP code and county levels. Their proprietary analysis has allowed them to create the Zillow Home Value Index, for which they update data once per month. We worked with the company to create a dynamic interface that allows users to explore the past 10 years of data in order to discover stories at a local, state, and national level. And because you would have to be a masochist to manually hard-code that much data once a month, the approach here was a bit different.

It makes the most sense in this specific example to display the data in a choropleth: a thematic map that employs a color key to visually represent the value ranges on the U.S. map. We chose to focus on modern web browser compatibility because Zillow doesn't have a substantial segment of users on outdated browsers such as Internet Explorer 6. This allowed us to utilize the excellent SVG format, which dynamically creates a vector graphic from the data it contains as XML code. SVG is truly the best solution for developing interactive graphical pieces, especially if you want the work to be functional on most mobile web browsers. It allows you to draw and manipulate complex shapes, and then make them interactive by attaching code that is triggered when someone clicks, drags, or hovers over the shape.

Much of what we implemented utilized the D3 (Data-Driven Documents) JavaScript library, which allows us to dynamically transform the image with smooth transitions as you browse the interactive front-end interface (Figure 2.13). D3 is an advanced JavaScript library for creating visual representations of large data sets that can be displayed graphically in quicker and more responsive and interactive ways. D3 assists in the creation and manipulation of SVG documents, which can help make the user experience more engaging and allow for up-to-date representations of the underlying data. As the data change, whether manually in this instance, or through an automated feed as described in the next section, and/or a user interacts with the page, the way the data is represented in the front-end interface is updated. The flexibility of this technology allows the user to easily navigate through complex data sets, drilling down to the most relevant data points and filtering out anything not immediately relevant.

We chose not to show anything more localized than data at the county level for the national view, because we wanted to strike a balance between displaying the most granular expression of data and information overload. It would be extremely

difficult to take anything meaningful away from a national view of ZIP code–level data, simply because the area covered by any single ZIP code is too small. Still, real estate is a local game, and we had the ZIP code data, so we made it possible for people to search by state, which pulls up individual SVG state maps.

This project's goal was to create a hub for people to explore the rich data, and to see how real estate in the United States has risen and fallen over last 10 years—and then struggled to stabilize. There was also a PR-driven goal to make the data attractive to journalists, so that they would want to use the explorative interface in order to find stories at the local, state, and national levels. Most importantly, we built this tool with the future in mind. When the new Zillow Home Value Index (ZHVI) is released each month, we can instantly incorporate the new data into the historical view on the front-end interface. We provided Zillow with tools that would convert their ZHVI data into a series of JavaScript Object Notation (JSON) files. JSON is a lightweight, text-based format for storing data. Perhaps the best way to visualize how data is stored as JSON is to picture a series of comma-separated files that can be nested one inside the other. This nesting can be as many layers deep as is required to accurately represent the data.

The main challenge in representing the information was in limiting the amount of data that needed to be loaded in the browser in order for the maps to function (particularly important as more people use devices connected through mobile data plans). To reduce the data size and loading time, a national map is loaded when the user first visits the page—and we don't load a second map when the user opts to view the data for a specific state or region. Instead, we use the same national map and zoom to the selected region. This keeps the user from having to download more data and their browser from needing to redraw the map. We simply shift the perspective from which they see the data. And since the map is SVG, increasing the zoom does not

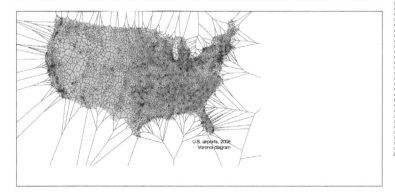

Figure 2.13
Examples from D3 Javascript library.
www.d3js.org.

compromise the image quality because it is a vector image drawn in the browser, which doesn't get pixelated.

DYNAMIC INTERACTIVE (AUTOMATIC UPDATES TO BOTH DISPLAY AND UNDERLYING INFORMATION)

When you want to visualize information on demand across custom time periods, it is helpful to automate the process of feeding the most current data to the dynamic interface. Some common examples of this type of visualization would be in the dashboards of your analytics program or customer relationship management software. Another great example is the content within the user interface for Mint.com, a free, web-based personal finance management service. While it may not be practical for your organization to build something quite so magnificent, it's a useful point of reference for the visualization of a dynamic data feed. Users' banking transactions are automatically updated within their Mint account, and they're able to explore and drill down into specific trends and budget categories (Figure 2.14). These reporting interfaces are useful because you can refresh the data source within the front-end interface itself, so you do not have to wait for someone else to update the underlying data. If you are building the interface for the web, you can use the technological approach we just referenced from the Zillow case study and take advantage of advanced JavaScript libraries and the SVG format as well.

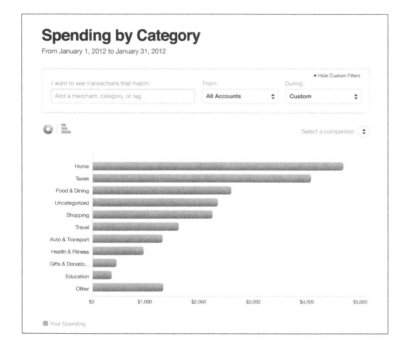

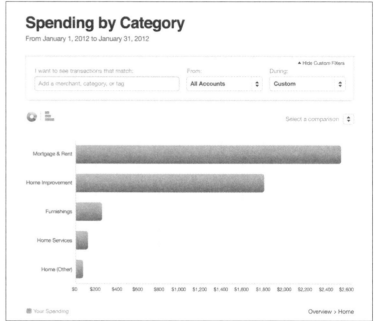

Figure 2.14
Dynamically generated reports for analyzing spending.
Mint.com.

It can be extremely frustrating to find a way to unite information that comes in from so many sources. You almost need an aggregator to manage all of your data aggregators. Since many existing "solutions" are not capable of centralizing everything you need, it becomes necessary to build something proprietary—which can be extremely expensive. For now, however, you should realize that it's also possible to create your front-end dynamic interface to display real-time data without the need for manual input to refresh the most current data. Although most content in this category of interactivity is typically explorative, you can also structure it to tell a narrative.

Outside of a showcase project for branding purposes and cool factor, there are many potential internal applications, such as monitoring network activity. As Hilary Mason, Chief Data Scientist for URL-shortening service bitly, said: "The most important applications of real-time data apply to situations where having analysis immediately will change the outcome. More practically, when you can ask a question and get the answer before you've forgotten why you asked the question in the first place, it makes you massively more productive."

FLEXIBILITY FOR THE FUTURE

Historically, the easiest approach to representing complex data in an interactive interface on the web has typically been to use Adobe Flash. However, it has been necessary to rethink this, given the surge in use of Apple products (specifically iPhones and iPads) that do not support Flash. This became even more vital in November 2011, when Adobe discontinued its development of Flash for mobile browsers as it became clear that HTML5 would power browser-based interactivity and applications on mobile devices in the near future.

Whether you are utilizing fixed information sets or dynamic data feeds, creating interactivity allows you and your audience to engage with the information in a deeper way and to unearth new insights. The beauty is that you are not limited to choosing solely explorative or narrative content when you go interactive. You can entice people with a narrative by drawing out the most interesting information in the underlying data and telling its story, and simply creating another tab that allows people to explore the data for themselves in order to find their own stories, as well as the information that is most meaningful to them.

APPLYING THE RIGHT FORMAT TO YOUR BUSINESS

These overarching infographic formats—static, motion, and interactive— are at the core of a multitude of real business applications that we will cover in the following chapters. In some cases you could potentially use any number of these formats, and you will make your choice based on which one fits within your budget for a particular project. Still, with this basic understanding of the fundamentals of each format—along with some benefits and shortcomings of each—you can begin to think critically about which approach can best empower a real business application that takes priority in your communication or marketing goals.

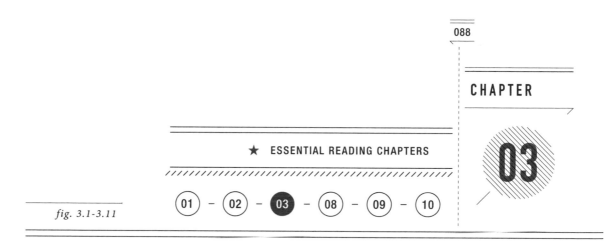

CHAPTER

03

★ **ESSENTIAL READING CHAPTERS**

fig. 3.1-3.11

(01) – (02) – (**03**) – (08) – (09) – (10)

THE VISUAL STORYTELLING SPECTRUM:

AN OBJECTIVE APPROACH

Every brand is different. Therefore, the way your brand should communicate—both internally and externally—will be unique. It will be based on your communication objectives, or your goals. These goals are determined by two very distinct inputs.

- Who is your audience?
- What are you communicating to them?

UNDERSTANDING THE VISUAL STORYTELLING SPECTRUM

We can assume a format-agnostic approach for now, and focus on illustrating the concept above (Figure 3.1). To better understand this concept, let's think of the *Who* as being the label for the *x*-axis, and the *What* as being represented along the *y*-axis.

1. *Audience (x-axis)*—two ends of the axis represented by *targeted* and *broad* audiences.
2. *Content (y-axis)*—two ends of the axis represented by *brand-centric* and *editorial* content.

Figure 3.1: The Visual Storytelling Spectrum

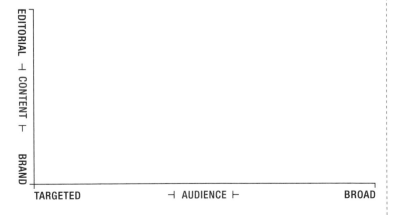

The quality of an application of infographics is largely measured by how it is leveraged to reach its specific objectives. Simply, popularity—or broad reach—should not be misinterpreted as a litmus test for quality, as reaching a large audience is not always the goal. For instance, if you are creating an internal (brand-centric) report for shareholders, it likely will not be interesting to an audience larger than who it was intended for: the shareholders. However, if someone is trying to create a really fun editorial piece, that *they* think will have broad appeal, but in the end it falls on deaf ears, then that my friend is a failure.

You should also think of each application along the visual storytelling spectrum as occupying a territory or range, rather than as a single point. And for each brand, these ranges will have different levels of overlap. For instance, an extremely brand-centric graphic for Facebook will probably have more broad appeal than the same for Joey Donut's donuts.

The more editorial the content is, the more broad its audience tends to be. Conversely, the more brand-centric the content, the more targeted its audience usually is. This is the case for most brands, and as we have mentioned, the individual ranges and the degrees of their overlap vary by company. Essentially, targeted audiences can range in size from very small to very large. While imperfect, this spectrum is a useful visual guide for helping people select each application and understand how it can be useful.

TARGETED AUDIENCE

A targeted audience tends to differentiate between a broader audience's members. For instance, all Internet users constitute a broad audience, whereas all male Internet users in the United States between the ages 18–25 is still a large subset, but it is more targeted. Any brand attempting to reach only this audience can tailor their messaging accordingly, and say, not worry so much about the female non-Internet users aged 65+. A more targeted audience will find more specific information more interesting or more useful, on average, than a broader audience. Thus, how and what you should communicate to them will be different. Typically, you would use brand-centric content to communicate with a targeted audience, especially if the common thread among this targeted audience is based on a shared relationship with your brand.

BROAD AUDIENCE

A broad audience does not differentiate between audience members. Instead, they treat all members as equal, regardless if they are existing customers, or if they've never heard of your brand before. Since this group is larger than a targeted audience, there is more information that this audience will find interesting or useful. Accordingly, your methods of communicating among them will be different than how you would communicate with a targeted audience. Typically you would use editorial content to communicate to a broad audience, as a relationship with the brand won't likely be a common thread among members.

BRAND-CENTRIC CONTENT

Brand-centric content is defined as explanations of your business and/or a communication of its values. Common examples of this include:

1. *"About Us" Pages*
2. *Visual Press Releases*
3. *Product Instructions*
4. *Presentations*
5. *Annual Reports*

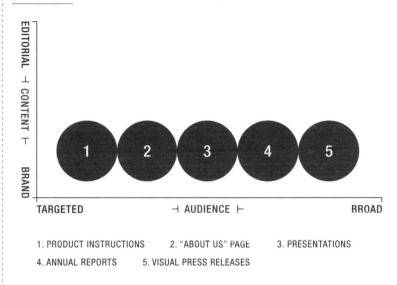

Figure 3.2: a plotting of brand-centric applications.

1. PRODUCT INSTRUCTIONS   2. "ABOUT US" PAGE   3. PRESENTATIONS
4. ANNUAL REPORTS   5. VISUAL PRESS RELEASES

As mentioned above, there tends to be some overlap among the applications within the spectrum. There are some—especially at the far end of brand-centric content—that tend to be more laser-targeted (Figure 3.2). These are typically product instructions, or "About Us" pages—applications with very utilitarian purposes that can often be made more visual. Understandably, this information is typically designed and shared to inform interested readers or even existing customers. Sometimes, because of the design of an application, or because of the size of the company, these targeted applications will reach an audience larger than originally intended.

However, there are some brand-centric applications that have substantially broader appeal than others. The Visual Storytelling Spectrum starts to get interesting with presentations and annual reports, because the content itself can be newsworthy. When the content consists of information that many people find popular for business or personal reasons, journalists will also have an incentive for distributing it. For instance, if the head of a large social networking site were to announce the decision to join the private-sector space tourism industry, there would be a broad audience that would find this information interesting. Journalists who caught wind of such news could base a story around it.

Visual press releases typically have the most mass appeal out of all applications of brand-centric infographic content. By its very nature, a press release is a company's attempt to generate a buzz about something newsworthy that happened to their brand. However, press releases frequently tend to be rather dull, either because the company milestone is boring to anyone outside the company, the company itself is boring, or just because most readers would find the content too niche. Sometimes, however, this type of content can become popular.

The most common instances in which a visual press release can generate mass appeal is when brands choose to visualize findings within their proprietary data. As we've previously mentioned, Mint tracks and anonymously aggregates its users' data. And within this data, they often find newsworthy stories. In these types of situations, a visual press release can generate a lot of attention.

EDITORIAL CONTENT

Editorial content would represent the top half of the y-axis, and it can be defined as the material that's used to tell a story, typically via a company blog treated as a brand's publication. It is very similar to the type of content publications produce. Editorial content does not include messaging about the brand, but it can include messaging about the industry within which the brand operates (Figure 3.3). Within this range, there is one type of content (editorial) but two objectives: thought leadership and virality. Thought leadership content is created with the intention of being recognized as an expert in one's industry, and tends to

be less editorial, and consequently more targeted. Viral content is created with the intention of reaching as broad an audience as possible, and tends to have the most appeal, and consequently is less targeted.

Figure 3.3: A plotting of editorial infographic applications.

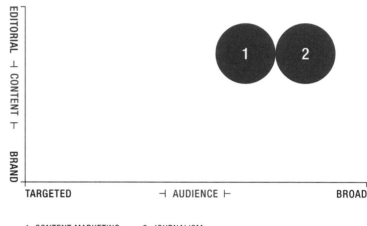

1. CONTENT MARKETING   2. JOURNALISM

When it comes to editorial content, it is difficult for your brand to serve two masters. Because it is intended to appeal to a more targeted audience, content for thought leadership can rarely have viral potential. Frankly, if your goal is to reach as broad of an audience as possible, create content that is capable of doing so. Think of the people that you meet at a party that only want to talk about themselves or their jobs. How many times have you found yourself in this situation, then pretended that you needed a refill on your beer as an excuse to talk to someone else? You don't want people to think of your blog, or your content in this same manner.

Again, this thought leadership content can vary tremendously in terms of audience appeal, based on the size of the brand, its industry, and the nature of the content.

One good example of an editorial infographic that uses proprietary data would be an infographic we created for the recommendation engine, Hunch. The data for this infographic (Figure 3.4) was aggregated from its customers, and they used this data to tell a story about how liberals and conservatives tend to prefer different foods. The content itself had nothing to do with Hunch, or their industry; rather it was simply an interesting story that they were able to generate from their own data.

Many brands produce thought leadership content in order to engage their readers and provide them with something of value. This type of content (as you might guess from its name) typically involves someone at the company speaking on its behalf, sharing their expertise through commentary, or offering analysis of high-level topics relating to the company's industry. In the case of the Hunch graphic, it garnered a much broader audience than we had initially imagined.

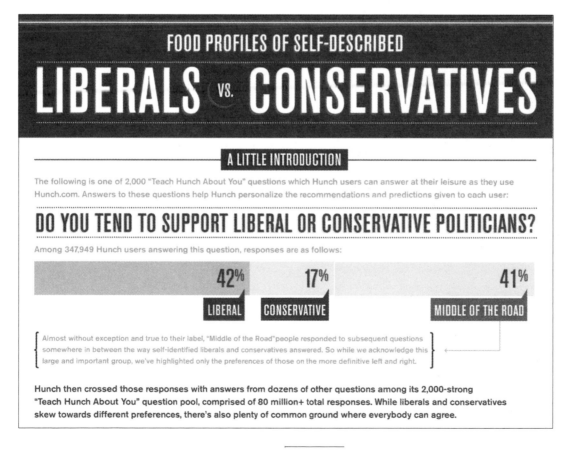

Figure 3.4
The Food Profiles of Self-Described Liberals vs. Conservatives.
Column Five for Hunch.com.

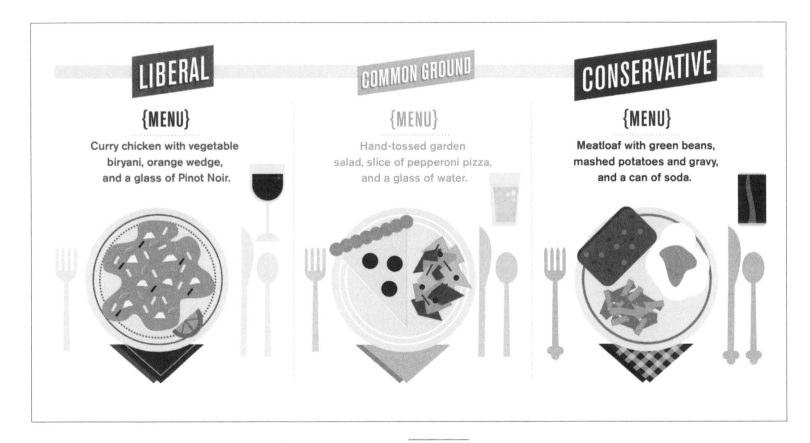

Figure 3.4
(Continued on pages 96-97)

À LA CARTE

FRENCH FRIES

Liberals are 64% more likely than conservatives to prefer bistro-type fries, making these fries their favorite.

An almost equal percentage of liberals and conservatives (9% and 8%, respectively) pass on fries altogether.

Conservatives consider McDonald's fries #1 (they're 38% more likely than liberals to prefer them). They're also 22% more likely to prefer thicker steak fries.

SEAFOOD

Most liberals say they either love seafood and couldn't live without it (38%) or that they enjoy it from time to time (40%).

4% of both political persuasions are fine with seafood, as long as it's deep-fried and covered in a mayonnaise-based sauce.

Conservatives are 10% more likely to say that they enjoy seafood from time to time.

VEGETABLES

Liberals are 3% more likely to prefer their vegetables fresh.

Both liberals and conservatives prefer fresh vegetables over cooked vegetables.

Conservatives are 3% more likely to prefer their vegetables cooked.

FRESH FRUITS

Liberals are 28% more likely to eat fresh fruit daily.

Most liberals and conservatives eat fresh fruit at least once per week.

Conservatives are 35% more likely to eat fresh fruit less often than weekly.

BREAKFAST

Liberals are 17% more likely to eat toast or a bagel in the morning.

Liberals and conservatives (21% and 22%, respectively) enjoy cold breakfast cereal.

Conservatives prefer something else for breakfast. They're also 20% more likely not to eat breakfast at all.

PEANUT BUTTER AND JELLY SANDWICHES

Liberals are 7% more likely to prefer strawberry jelly on their peanut butter and jelly sandwich.

But both liberals and conservatives prefer strawberry jelly. (They also both prefer their sandwiches cut diagonally, though conservatives are 9% more likely to cut them vertically.)

Conservatives are 19% more likely to choose grape jelly.

TACOS

Liberals are 13% more likely to prefer crunchy tacos.

Both liberals and conservatives (57% and 62%, respectively) prefer a soft tortilla over a crunchy corn taco shell.

Conservatives are 9% more likely to prefer soft tacos.

PIZZA CRUST

Liberals prefer thin crust pizza. They're 21% more likely to order it.

Liberals and conservatives are equally likely (35%) to enjoy normal crust.

Conservatives are 33% more likely to prefer deep dish pizza or a thicker crust.

A GOOD HOME-COOKED MEAL

Liberals are more than 100% more likely to cook a coconut curry with lamb and rice at home.

Both liberals and conservatives prefer grilling burgers when they cook at home.

Conservatives are 49% more likely to cook burgers on the grill and 10% more likely to cook comfort food, like tuna casserole or meatloaf.

PASTA SHAPES

Liberals are more likely to prefer hard-to-pronounce pastas, like gnocchi, fusilli, and radiatore.

Everybody loves lasagne.

Conservatives stick to classic pastas, like linguine, rotini, and spaghetti.

DRINK PREFERENCES

 DRINK WITH DINNER AT HOME

Liberals are 57% more likely
to drink wine with dinner at home.

When dining at home, the top drink
choice for both liberals and
conservatives is water.

Conservatives are 57% more likely
to drink milk and 17% more likely
to drink a soft drink or juice.

  BEER

60% of liberals (28% more often
than conservatives) enjoy beer.

Liberals and conservatives who
drink beer prefer a brew that's
pale and refreshing.

Conservatives are 27% more
likely to not like the taste.
Most on Hunch don't like beer.

 SOFT DRINKS

Liberals are 29% more likely to not drink
soda, but when they do they're as likely
(27%) to drink diet as they are regular.

Both political persuasions enjoy
the big brands of Coke and Pepsi
when it comes to soda.

Conservatives are not only more likely
to drink soda. They're also 26% more likely
to drink regular instead of diet.

 TAP WATER

Liberals are 6% more likely
to drink tap water.

The majority of both groups do drink
tap water, and 21% of both liberals and
conservative drink only filtered tap water.

Conservatives are 57% more likely
to not drink tap water.

Figure 3.4
Continued.

ATTITUDES

 ### WHAT'S YOUR IDEA OF EXOTIC ETHNIC FOOD?

Liberals are 31% more likely to consider Pan-Asian/French fusion cuisine to be exotic ethnic food.

Both groups consider Pan-Asian/French fusion cuisine the more exotic ethnic food.

Conservatives are 94% more likely to consider occasional Chinese takeout to be exotic ethnic food.

  ### FAST FOOD

Liberals are 92% more likely to eat fast food rarely or never.

Most liberals and conservatives eat fast food a few times per month.

Conservatives are 64% more likely to eat fast food a few times per week.

 ### VEGETARIANISM

Liberals are 29% more likely to describe a bacon cheeseburger as "disgusting". 10% of them are vegetarians.

Overall, both groups tend to think bacon cheeseburgers are delicious.

3% of conservatives are vegetarians, but conservatives as a whole are 14% more likely to describe a bacon cheeseburger as "delicious."

 ### ON BEING A "FOODIE"

Most liberals on Hunch considers themselves "foodies." Liberals are 39% more likely to consider themselves "foodies."

Hey, we all have to eat!

Conservatives overall aren't really sure what a "foodie" is. They're 52% more likely to claim not to know what makes a person a "foodie."

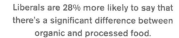  ### ORGANIC VS. PROCESSED FOOD

Liberals are 28% more likely to say that there's a significant difference between organic and processed food.

The majority of both liberals and conservatives agree that there's a significant nutritional difference between organic and processed food.

Conservatives are 50% more likely to say that there's not a significant difference between organic and processed food.

  ### FINE DINING

Liberals are 20% more likely to enjoy fine dining.

Liberals and conservatives overall enjoy fine dining as an occasional splurge.

Conservatives are 39% more likely to say fine dining is too fancy for their tastes.

Stats are based on more than 80 million aggregated & anonymized responses to "Teach Hunch About You" questions answered between March 2009 and May 2011 by about 700,000 users of Hunch.com. Yes, Poindexter, we know that correlation does not necessarily imply causation. Legalese: There are brands listed above that belong to their respective owners, not to Hunch. Find more cool data stuff at hunch.com/info/reports. Tips from your mom: Eat your turnips, vote in the next election, and if you haven't tried Hunch yet, go do that now.
© 2011 Hunch Inc.

Figures 3.5, 3.6, and 3.7 provide other examples of editorial content developed with the intention of establishing thought leadership.

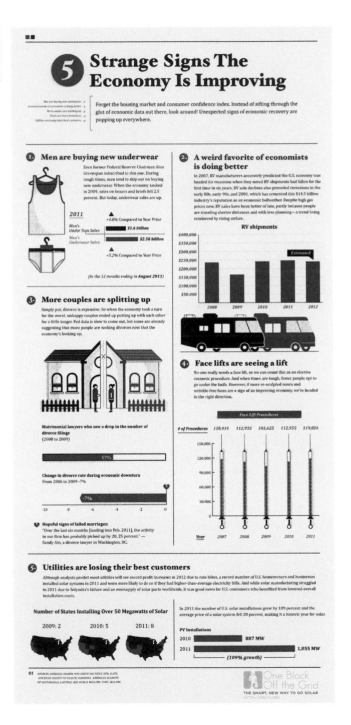

Figure 3.5

5 Strange Signs That the Economy is Improving.
Column Five for One Block Off the Grid.

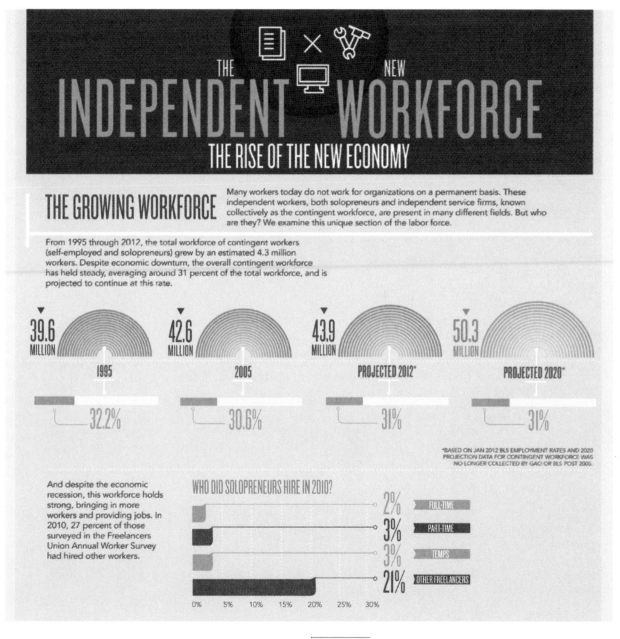

Figure 3.6
The New Independent Workforce. Column Five for Mavenlink.
(Continued on pages 100-101)

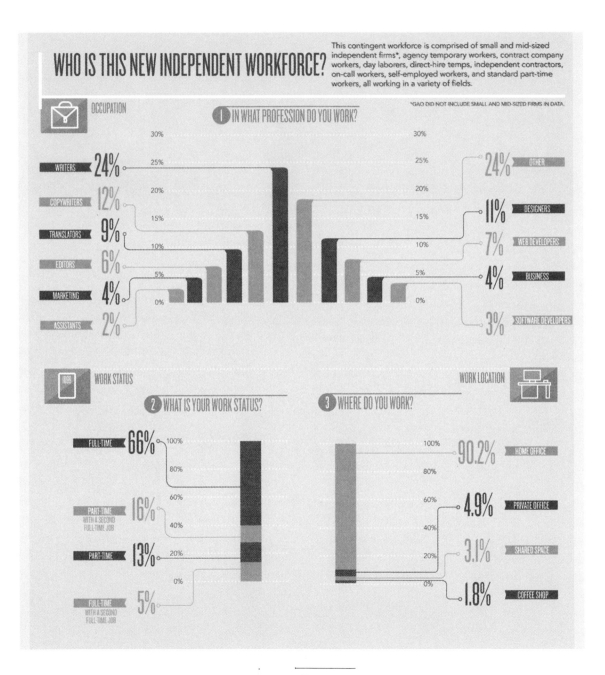

Figure 3.6
Continued.

WHY FREELANCE?

It is a misconception that most solopreneurs enter the independent workforce solely due to layoffs. Below we examine some of the reasons why this type of employment has become so alluring.

WHY DID YOU CHOOSE TO WORK INDEPENDENTLY?

FLEXIBILITY OF SCHEDULE — **25.9%**

TO BE MY OWN BOSS — **15.7%**

SUPPLEMENTAL INCOME — **9.1%**

21.4% FOLLOW MY PASSIONS

14.1% FREELANCE WAS NOT ORIGINALLY PLANNED, FELL INTO IT

13.8% LAY-OFF OR DOWNSIZING

Even through the economic recession, the contingent workforce has held strong, sustaining lower unemployment rates than the national average.

NATIONAL AVERAGE   SELF-EMPLOYED

8.8

5.8

JAN 2012

THE BUSINESS OF CONTINGENCE

The contingent workforce continues to thrive as more and more businesses utilize this segment.

INTEREST FROM THE BUSINESS SECTOR

Savvy businesses are taking advantage of this new shift and turning to independent workers.

90% percent of firms have used freelance or contracted talent.

This trend is only expected to continue.

61% A 2010 Economist Intelligence Unit report found 61 percent of senior executives expect a growing proportion of functions to be outsourced to this labor force.

Tech giant Oracle predicts use of this contingent workforce will increase

40%

over the next 10 years.

$425 BILLION PER YEAR

And spending on this workforce is only growing, expanding to incorporate small independent firms as well as solopreneurs. American businesses spend more than $425 billion per year on contingent labor, according to a 2009 Staffing Industry Analysts Contingent Workforce Estimate.

The strong contingent workforce is evidence of a shift in current employment models. Businesses are pulling resources from the labor force when and where needed, creating a new, more fluid dynamic in the overall workforce.

SOURCES: CNBC.COM I BLS.GOV I 2006 GOA REPORT I 2011 FREELANCE INDUSTRY REPORT I 2011 COUNTING THE INDEPENDENT WORKFORCE I 2010 ECONOMIST INTELLIGENCE UNIT REPORT I ORACLE I STAFFING INDUSTRY ANALYSTS I

jjj mavenlink

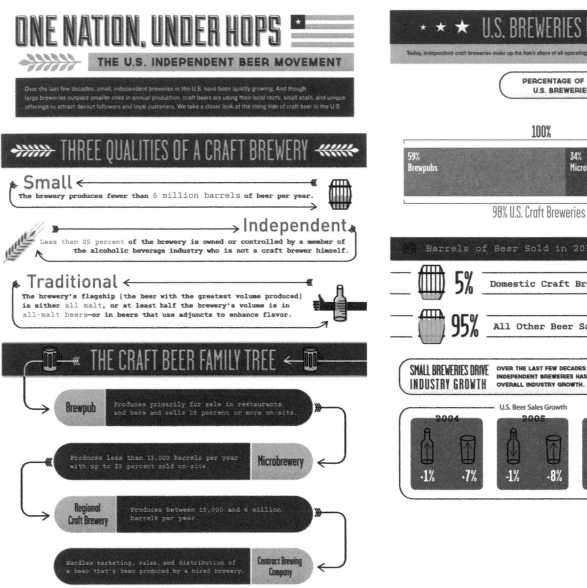

ONE NATION, UNDER HOPS

THE U.S. INDEPENDENT BEER MOVEMENT

Over the last few decades, small, independent breweries in the U.S. have been quietly growing. And though large breweries outpace smaller ones in annual production, craft beers are using their local roots, small scale, and unique offerings to attract devout followers and loyal customers. We take a closer look at the rising tide of craft beer in the U.S.

THREE QUALITIES OF A CRAFT BREWERY

Small
The brewery produces fewer than 6 million barrels of beer per year.

Independent
Less than 25 percent of the brewery is owned or controlled by a member of the alcoholic beverage industry who is not a craft brewer himself.

Traditional
The brewery's flagship (the beer with the greatest volume produced) is either all malt, or at least half the brewery's volume is in all-malt beers—or in beers that use adjuncts to enhance flavor.

THE CRAFT BEER FAMILY TREE

Brewpub — Produces primarily for sale in restaurants and bars and sells 25 percent or more on-site.

Microbrewery — Produces less than 15,000 barrels per year with up to 25 percent sold on-site.

Regional Craft Brewery — Produces between 15,000 and 6 million barrels per year.

Contract Brewing Company — Handles marketing, sales, and distribution of a beer that's been produced by a hired brewery.

★ ★ ★ U.S. BREWERIES BREAKDOWN ★ ★ ★

Today, independent craft breweries make up the lion's share of all operating breweries but only produce a small amount of all U.S. beer sold.

PERCENTAGE OF OPERATING U.S. BREWERIES IN 2010

100%

59% Brewpubs

34% Microbreweries

5% Regional Craft Breweries

98% U.S. Craft Breweries

1% Large Non-Craft Breweries
1% Other Breweries

Barrels of Beer Sold in 2010 (203,576,450 Total)

5% — Domestic Craft Breweries

95% — All Other Beer Sales

SMALL BREWERIES DRIVE INDUSTRY GROWTH
OVER THE LAST FEW DECADES, THE GROWTH OF INDEPENDENT BREWERIES HAS BEEN ECLIPSING OVERALL INDUSTRY GROWTH. HERE'S A GLIMPSE.

ALL BEER | CRAFT BEER

U.S. Beer Sales Growth

2004	2005	2006	2007
-1% / +7%	-1% / +8%	+2% / +11%	-1% / +11%

Figure 3.7
One Nation Under Hops.
Column Five for Intuit.

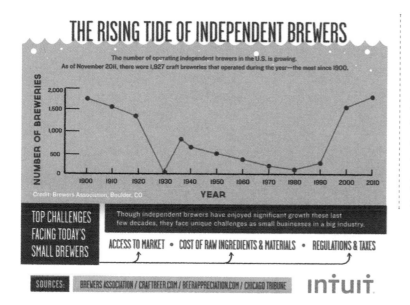

THE RISING TIDE OF INDEPENDENT BREWERS

The number of operating independent brewers in the U.S. is growing.
As of November 2011, there were 1,927 craft breweries that operated during the year—the most since 1900.

NUMBER OF BREWERIES

YEAR

Credit: Brewers Association, Boulder, CO

TOP CHALLENGES FACING TODAY'S SMALL BREWERS

Though independent brewers have enjoyed significant growth these last few decades, they face unique challenges as small businesses in a big industry.

ACCESS TO MARKET • COST OF RAW INGREDIENTS & MATERIALS • REGULATIONS & TAXES

SOURCES: BREWERS ASSOCIATION / CRAFTBEER.COM / BEERAPPRECIATION.COM / CHICAGO TRIBUNE

intuit

We produced a piece titled "If Social Media Were a High School" for Flowtown that is a good example of viral content in Figure 3.8 on the following page. We developed the idea in an effort to create an infographic with as much broad appeal as possible. Some of the key metrics for this piece included nearly 4,000 tweets and over 7,000 Facebook shares. Thankfully, the client in this case entrusted us with their objectives, and allowed us to create content with these in mind. The result was a wildly popular infographic that generated a good amount of attention for our client.

SOCIAL MEDIA HIGH SCHOOL YEARBOOK 2011

CLASS
of
2011

What if social media were a highschool?

FROM THE JOCKS TO THE GEEKS, EVEN THE VAST WORLD OF SOCIAL MEDIA COMES WITH ITS OWN STEREOTYPES AND TEENAGE ANGST.

GOSSIP GIRL

TWITTER

Clubs: President of Gossip Girl, Celebrity Awareness Club, Homepage Queen

Quote: "Everyone is entitled to my opinion." -@madonna

THE PREP

GOOGLE

Clubs: Future Investors of America, Yacht Club, International Billionaires Club

Quote: "Money makes the world go round" -Liza Minnelli

THE JOCK

FACEBOOK

Clubs: Varsity Football, Varsity Angel Funding, Homepage King

Quote: "Veni, Vidi, Vici." -Some Italian Dude

THE NERD

WIKIPEDIA

Clubs: Science Club, Math Club, History Club, Computer Club, Star Trek Club, IQ Above 180 Club

Quote: "Better know nothing than half-know many things." -Friedrich Nietzsche

BAND GEEK

LAST.FM

Clubs: Band Pep Club, Battle of the Garage Bands Founder

Quote: "If it's illegal to rock and roll, throw my ass in jail!" -Kurt Cobain

A/V NERD

YOUTUBE

Clubs: A/V Club, President of the 10 Minute Movie Club, Talking Cats Video Club

Quote: Please follow link for video quote: www.youtube.com/quote

Figure 3.8
What if Social Media Were a High School?
Column Five for Flowtown. (Continued on page 106)

FLICKR

Clubs: Art Club, Photography Club, Creative Commons Club, Hipster Club

Quote: "Look, I'm not an intellectual - I just take pictures."
-Helmut Newton

REDDIT

Clubs: Editor of School Newspaper, Rock the Vote Club

Quote: "I can't prove it, but I can say it."
-Stephen Colbert

MYSPACE

Clubs: Former Member of: Band Club, Photography Club, Pep Club

Quote: "The only thing worse than being talked about is not being talked about."
-Oscar Wilde

WIKILEAKS

Clubs: Lenin Love Club, Freedom of Information Club, Youth Anarchists League

Quote: "I feel your scorn and I accept it."
-Jon Stewart

YELP

Clubs: President of the Debate Club, Culinary Club, Future Better Business Bureau Club

Quote: "There has never been a statue erected to honor a critic."
-Zig Ziglar

ORKUT

Clubs: ESL Club, Foreigners in a Foreign Land Club

Quote: そこに行くあなたは関係なく、覚えておいてください。
-孔子

LIVE JOURNAL

Clubs: Evanescence Fan Club

Quote: "I hurt myself, so I can feel alive."
-Bill Kaulitz

LINKEDIN

Clubs: Class President, President of the 2010 Alumni Club

Quote: "It's not what you know but who you know that makes the difference."
-Anonymous

QUORA

Clubs: Q&A Club, Knowledge Seekers United

Quote: "He who asks a question is a fool for five minutes; he who does not ask remains a fool forever." -Chinese Proverb

TUMBLR

Clubs: Photoshop Club, Shiny Objects Lovers Club

Quote: "I sometimes worry about my short attention span, but not for long." -Herb Caen

FOURSQUARE

Clubs: Mayor's Council, Frequent Diner's Club

Quote: "The shortest distance between two points is often unbearable." -Charles Bukowski

WORDPRESS

Clubs: Creative Writing Club, How To Write and Sell a Novel On The Internet In Ten Days Club

Quote: "If you can't annoy somebody, there's little point in writing." -Kingsley Amis

STUMBLEUPON

Clubs: Content Discovery Team, Jack of all Trades Club, Time-wasters Anonymous

Quote: "I have not told half of what I saw." - James Joyce

DIGG

Clubs: How To Win Friends (Back) And Influence People (Again) Club

Quote: "There are three faithful friends: an old wife, an old dog, and ready money." - Benjamin Franklin

FORMSPRING.ME

Clubs: Askers Anonymous, Teens For The Ethical Treatment of Answers

Quote: "Never hesitate to ask a lesser person." - Confucius

INSTAGR.AM

Clubs: The Ministry of Pretentious Photographers, The Vanity Club, My Life Rules Club

Quote: "There are no rules for good photographs, there are only good photographs." -Ansel Adams

Figure 3.8
Continued.

As you can imagine, there's room for maneuvering within the realm of editorial content, and sometimes the outcome can prove interesting or unexpected. Other examples of editorial content developed with the intention of virality: follow in Figures 3.9-3.10.

Figure 3.9
How to Spot a Yelp! User.
Column Five for Flowtown.

Figure 3.10
The World's Most Demanding Concert Rider.
Column Five for Sonos.
(Continued on page 110)

DRESSING ROOMS

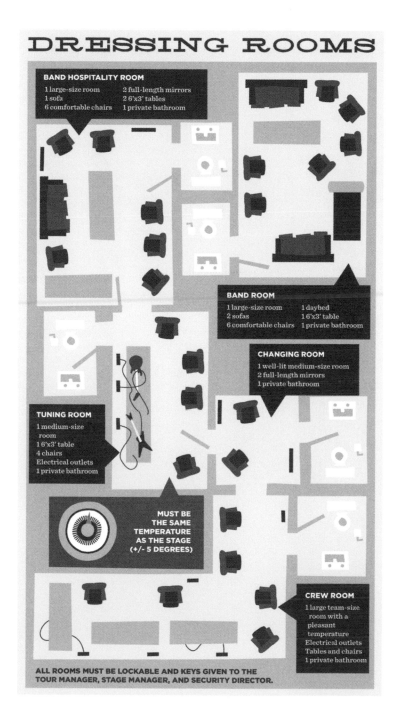

BAND HOSPITALITY ROOM
1 large-size room 2 full-length mirrors
1 sofa 2 6'x3' tables
6 comfortable chairs 1 private bathroom

BAND ROOM
1 large-size room 1 daybed
2 sofas 1 6'x3' table
6 comfortable chairs 1 private bathroom

CHANGING ROOM
1 well-lit medium-size room
2 full-length mirrors
1 private bathroom

TUNING ROOM
1 medium-size room
1 6'x3' table
4 chairs
Electrical outlets
1 private bathroom

MUST BE THE SAME TEMPERATURE AS THE STAGE (+/- 5 DEGREES)

CREW ROOM
1 large team-size room with a pleasant temperature
Electrical outlets
Tables and chairs
1 private bathroom

ALL ROOMS MUST BE LOCKABLE AND KEYS GIVEN TO THE TOUR MANAGER, STAGE MANAGER, AND SECURITY DIRECTOR.

Cheese Tray

Assorted fresh, natural cheeses, including:

Brie Cheddar Muenster Mozzarella Pepper Jack

Vegetables

Fresh, cut vegetable platter, including:

Tomatoes Carrots Celery Scallions Broccoli Cauliflower Assorted dips

Fruit

Fresh, cut fruit platter, including:

Apples Oranges Grapes Pears Melons Kiwi Bananas (whole)

Hot Drinks

Hot coffee (brewed, not instant) Hot water (for tea) Natural and herbal tea bags (Celestial Seasonings) 1 lb. Tupelo honey Sugar

Lipton tea bags 12 fresh lemons with knife and cutting board Cream

Munchies

Potato chips and assorted dips M&Ms Nuts

WARNING: ABSOLUTELY NO BROWN ONES

Pretzels 12 Reese's Peanut Butter Cups 12 assorted Dannon yogurt (on ice)

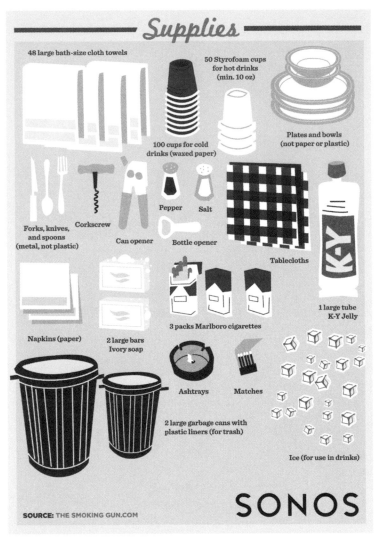

SOURCE: THE SMOKING GUN.COM

Figure 3.10
Continued.

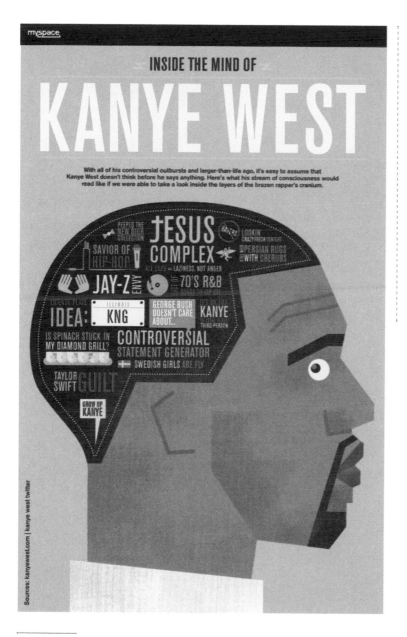

Figure 3.11
Inside the Mind of Kanye West.
Column Five for Myspace.

It's important to note that viral content has its limitations too, in so far as they are not as useful in reaching targeted audience who may in fact be looking for content relating to the brand, or even expert-level content. So as with any decision, you must identify your objectives before you identify your methodology.

In this chapter we illustrated the differences between brand-centric and editorial content and explained how each type has its place, but also its limitations. It is necessary to understand how each content type relates to and should be used to reach various audience sizes and types. At this point you should have a better understanding of the methodology by which you can reach your communication objectives. In the following four chapters we will go into detail about the applications of these content types, as well as how to share your story with the world.

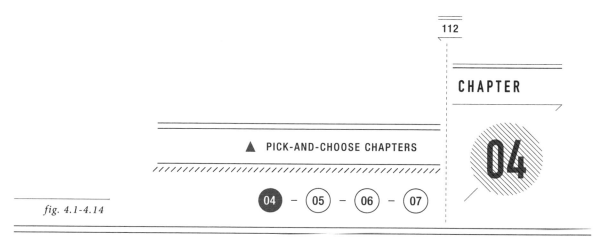

CHAPTER

▲ PICK-AND-CHOOSE CHAPTERS

04 – 05 – 06 – 07

04

fig. 4.1-4.14

EDITORIAL INFOGRAPHICS

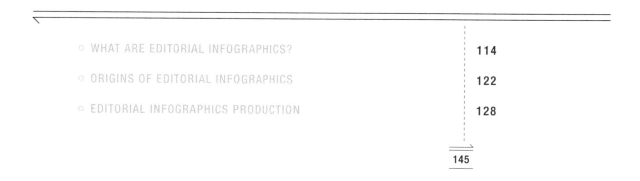

WHAT ARE EDITORIAL INFOGRAPHICS?

An editorial infographic is one that employs a narrative approach. We discussed in the previous section how editorial infographics are designed to have mass appeal, and can position the content producer (in our case, the brand) as a source of information within an industry or on a specific topic. Broadly speaking, editorial infographics have wide distribution potential; people frequently share the best ones online, thereby bringing traffic, links, and brand exposure with them.

While this varies across industry and subject matter, editorial infographic content typically has more mass appeal than brand-centric content. Of course, the more people can relate to the content (e.g., marijuana legislation vs. LARPing), the more mass appeal it will have. According to *Fast Company Co.Design* editor Cliff Kuang, one common mistake that those who produce bad editorial infographics make is to assume that something interesting to them will be interesting to others. As Kuang explains, "People get wrapped up in the process, but they confuse the depth of detail that they had to go through with the amount of detail other people are willing to go through to get the information."

The most important rule to remember is that editorial infographics should *not* reference your company in the content. You can include a company logo at the bottom to let people know the source of the information as it is shared online, but you never want to be hitting people over the head with your brand. Editorial infographics should cover interesting topics that are loosely related to your general industry. For example, a financial services company could display a breakdown of how the Federal Reserve Bank works, or a location-based service could cover a brief history of cartography. The broader and more interesting the topic, the greater the infographic's viral potential—and the more widely distributed it's likely to be.

Many brands succumb to the urge to promote themselves in their editorial content. We couldn't urge more strongly against this. There are other opportunities to talk about your brand elsewhere, which we will address in Chapter 6 (Brand-Centric Infographics). But it can seem sleazy when you take this approach with editorial content. Companies that try to ram brand mentions down people's throats under the auspices of an editorial infographic are easy to identify, because they come off sounding like advertisements. If you want your editorial infographic to succeed, you must avoid this at all costs.

When executed properly, editorial infographics can add value to the readers' lives, either through informing or entertaining an audience. But when done poorly, they read as underhanded attempts to sell something to someone who probably doesn't want whatever it is. So it becomes a question of what type of experience a brand wants to provide to its existing audience (customers) and a possible new audience (potential customers).

Figures 4.1, 4.2, and 4.3 provide a few examples.

Figure 4.1
I'm Big on Twitter.
Column Five for The Emmys.
(Continued on pages 116-117)

MOST POPULAR NOMINEES IN TWITTERSPHERE

(BY TWITTER FOLLOWERS)

ACTORS AND HOSTS

Comedy and reality T.V. genres are hitting it big on Twitter this year, with all of the top ten most popular nominees belonging to one of these two categories.

Jimmy Fallon, who was nominated along with the rest of his team for *Late Night With Jimmy Fallon*, boasts the most amount of fans on Twitter among late night hosts, even beating out redheaded funnyman Conan O'Brien.

Ryan Seacrest
4,851,993

Jimmy Fallon
3,848,883

Chris Colfer
911,238

Bill Maher
650,307

Conan O'Brien
3,451,071

Louis C.K.
506,646

Stephen Colbert
2,482,739

Sofia Vergara
637,329

Elizabeth Banks
472,511

Kristin Chenoweth
360,142

Even though Betty White doesn't have her own official Twitter handle, the former Golden Girl is one of the most talked about celebrities on the microblogging site.

BACK TO REALITY

If Ryan Seacrest's Twitter success proves anything, reality T.V. hosts are quickly seeing their Twitter fan base rise. Here are other notable nominees in the category, along with their followers:

Cat Deeley
138,065

Tom Bergeron
57,110

Jeff Probst
131,585

Figure 4.1 Continued.

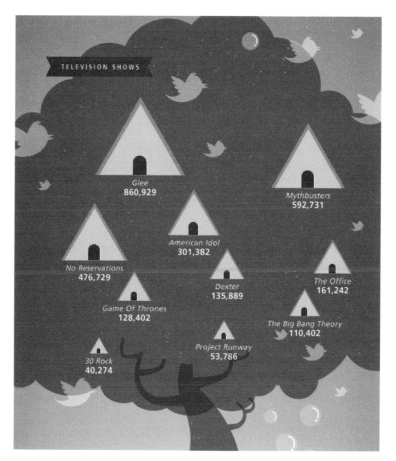

Figure 4.2
How the Foods You Eat Stack Up.
Column Five for Massive Health.

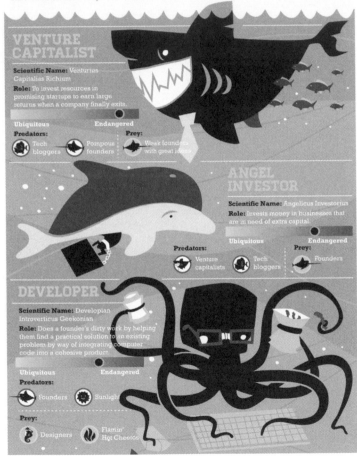

THE STARTUP ECOSYSTEM
PREDATOR VS PREY
WHAT IS YOUR NICHE?

There is a circle of life that makes the Tech Startup Ecosystem self-sustainable. We have put a magnifying glass up to each specimen to determine its role, predators, and prey. Take caution: this ecosystem rests in a delicate balance, for your viewing pleasure only.

VENTURE CAPITALIST

Scientific Name: Venturius Capitalias Richium

Role: To invest resources in promising startups to earn large returns when a company finally exits.

Ubiquitous — Endangered

Predators: Tech bloggers · Pompous founders

Prey: Weak founders with great ideas

ANGEL INVESTOR

Scientific Name: Angelicus Investorius

Role: Invests money in businesses that are in need of extra capital.

Ubiquitous — Endangered

Predators: Venture capitalists · Tech bloggers

Prey: Founders

DEVELOPER

Scientific Name: Developian Introverticus Geekonian

Role: Does a founder's dirty work by helping them find a practical solution to an existing problem by way of integrating computer code into a cohesive product.

Ubiquitous — Endangered

Predators: Founders · Sunlight

Prey: Designers · Flamin' Hot Cheetos

FOUNDER

Scientific Name: Ambitionous Entrepreneurius

Role: Creates marketable solutions to problems that affect a large number of people.

Ubiquitous — Endangered

Predators: Venture capitalists · Pride · Tech bloggers

Prey: Developers · Designers · Sales/business development

DESIGNER

Scientific Name: Creatorious Hipsternium

Role: Makes a product look pretty.

Ubiquitous — Endangered

Predators: Tech bloggers · Corrupt Files

Prey: Funyuns

VP OF MARKETING

Scientific Name: Marketous Egomaniacan

Role: Makes consumers aware of company products that can benefit them.

Ubiquitous — Endangered

Predators: Founders · CEOs

Prey: Consumers

TECH BLOGGER

Scientific Name: Technologicalium Knowitallicus

Role: Provides snarky commentary on products, gossip, and news that often makes or breaks a company.

Ubiquitous — Endangered

Predators: Apple

Prey: Venture capitalists · Founders · CEOs

Figure 4.3
The Startup Ecosystem.
Column Five for Udemy.

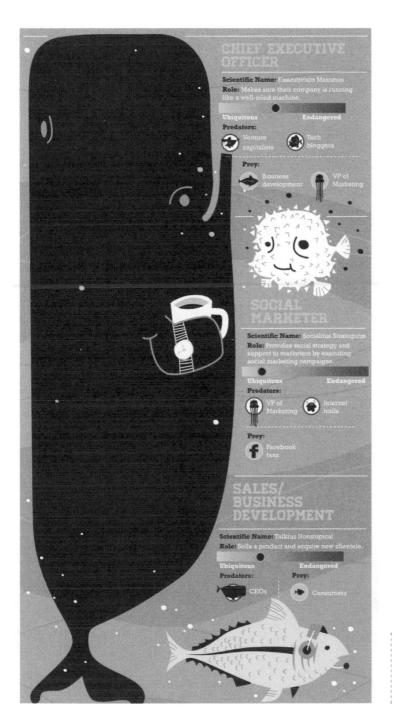

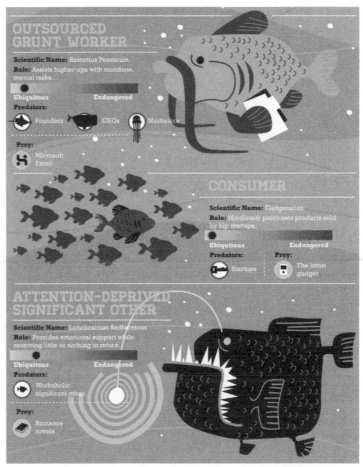

You can see how these graphics take just the right approach, in that they provide useful information and/or entertainment to the reader, and the brand's presence on the graphic (a small logo at the top or bottom) is limited.

ORIGINS OF EDITORIAL INFOGRAPHICS

IN PRINT

By now, most people have seen numerous infographics in both online and print publications. In fact, the use of infographics for editorial purposes is not a new idea, although the trend has recently increased dramatically in various media. While most of this growth has arguably taken place online, the pages of the world's top print publications are becoming filled with more and more infographics. This is evident when you pick up copies of the print versions of magazines such as *GOOD*, *Fast Company*, *Fortune*, and *Wired*, or even older, more conventional newspapers such as *The Wall Street Journal* and *The New York Times*.

While the earliest forms of modern infographics first became prominent in the 19th century, the rise of editorial infographics in their current form can be traced to the latter half of the twentieth century. Pioneers of the editorial infographic—what we can also call "data journalism"—grew in popularity during the 1970s. Nigel Holmes's explanation graphics for *Time* are considered by many to be the first major, mainstream use of a more illustrative approach to infographics. Another designer who helped make this field mainstream was Peter Sullivan (1932–1996), whose work for *The Sunday Times* helped to pave the way in this field from the 1970s until his untimely death.

An additional pioneer in this area was the late Argentinian designer Alejandro Malofiej, who was known mainly for his cartographic abilities. Malofiej was active in the 1970s and 1980s and was considered to be one of the premier infographic designers during this time. In fact, the Malofiej Awards (considered the Academy Awards of visual journalism) are named in his honor. Not coincidentally, the highest award at the Malofiej Awards is the Peter Sullivan Award—essentially the Best Director of editorial infographics.

ONLINE

In the last half decade or so, there has been a dramatic increase in the number of publications that use graphic content to replace more traditional, largely text-based features online as well as in print. This trend spilling over into the online world should come as no surprise, as more people prefer to get their news from the Internet than from newspapers. We should also expect that the leaders for print editorial infographics also will tend to excel in this area on the web.

GOOD is one of the more prominent publications to do this. Considered by many to be a leader in the field, they have made infographics a very prominent feature of both their online and print publications for several years, and publish weekly infographics on their website. Other publications such as *Fast Company*, *Fortune*, and *Wired* have similar approaches to infographics, as well as a generally high regard for design and visuals throughout their content. The best editorial infographics generally tend to come from publications that respect design, have a consistent brand identity, and adhere to the highest journalistic standards.

However, the publication that might best be known for setting the benchmark for editorial infographic content is the multiple-award-winning Graphics Department at *The New York Times*. Widely considered the best in the world at crafting data-driven visual content, this team of more than 30 journalists, designers, and programmers is responsible for some of the most well-executed editorial infographic content you can find anywhere—period. Their work is becoming more interactive and explorative, and you can expect many of the above-mentioned publications, among others, to follow suit in the near to medium future.

Additional examples are shown in Figures 4.4, 4.5, and 4.6.

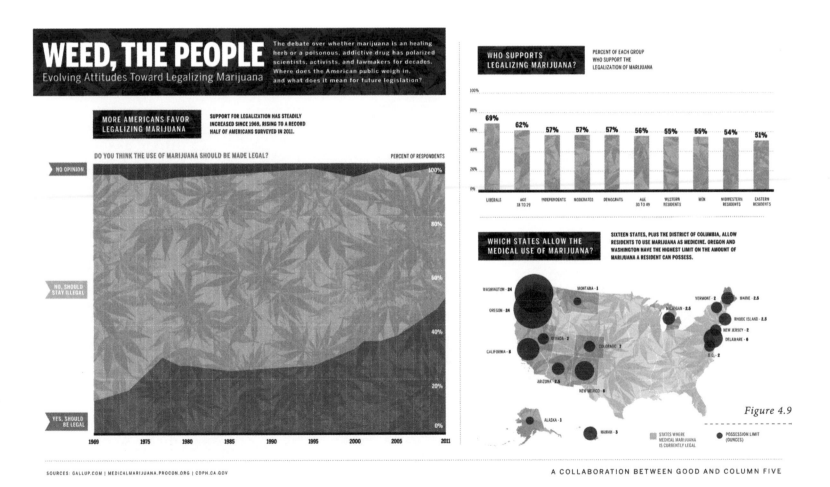

Figure 4.4
Weed, the People.
Column Five for GOOD.

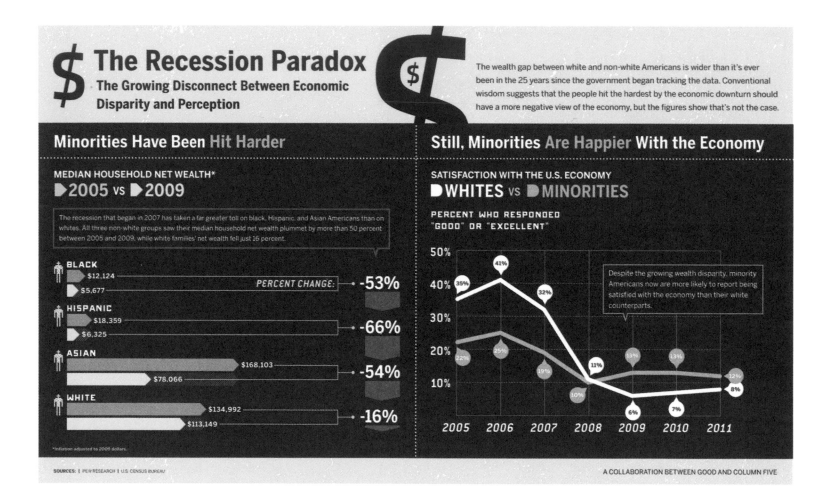

Figure 4.5
The Recession Paradox.
Column Five for GOOD.

Figure 4.6
The Almighty Dollar.
Column Five for Good.

EDITORIAL INFOGRAPHICS FOR CONTENT MARKETING

One of the most interesting things about the recent rise in infographics' popularity is that it has coincided with another trend: the growth of content marketing. The idea behind content marketing should be fairly intuitive; it is content created to reach existing and new audiences. Good content marketers realize that customers are most likely to come from an engaged audience. They aren't going to be people who've never heard of their brand. It is based on the idea that readers or viewers will look favorably upon the brand if they find the content useful.

The underlying goal of this approach is to engage the readers. Further, it assumes that any brand would benefit from having customers consider them to be experts within their industry, or sources on the sometimes complex or debated issues within it. Many marketers view this recognition of engagement with their brand as the most important step in turning a broad audience member into a customer. And even if the audience member doesn't end up buying anything, there is still an intrinsic value in building a fan base of noncustomers—individuals who may someday refer a friend or family member to the brand, or even just share the brand's content online. A good content marketing strategy presents this type of a win-win scenario.

The approach to editorial infographics with broad appeal is what makes an effective content marketing strategy. This is why the commercial sector's wide adoption of editorial infographics should come as no surprise. In the last several years, countless brands—first start-ups, then larger corporations—have learned to leverage editorial infographics as an integral part of their content marketing strategies. They typically do so by publishing these infographics on the company blog—something that brands should always treat as a branded publication, where the brand is featured and ever-present, but not always highlighted in the actual content itself.

As the cost of people's attention constantly grows more expensive, companies have found infographics to be extremely useful for grabbing interest. For one thing, good editorial infographics entice readers to engage with the content. They also get the message across quickly. But perhaps their greatest attribute is the ease with which people can share them via various social channels online. Additionally, infographics are extremely easy to reuse, recycle, repost, or republish—whatever you want to call it—on the web.

Enticing Readers

While this statement is subjective—and risks taking a largely qualitative approach—it's safe to say that to most people, a beautifully designed infographic is more visually enticing than a 250–500 word article, at least at first glance. This has less to do with the differences in efficacy of a text-only based medium vis-à-vis infographic content, and rather more with the amount of content individuals consume each day. In the era of data deluge, we believe that infographics have a better chance of standing out among the mix of various other types of media people come across on a given day.

Getting the Message Across Quickly

People are also using infographics for content marketing more frequently because of the ease and speed with which they permit communication to take place. It's not just that an infographic seems more visually appealing; as we discussed in Chapter 1 (Importance and Efficacy), it can also communicate a message more quickly and effectively than words alone often can. Most people consume a lot of content each day, and make one of two decisions once they read an article or look at a picture; they then move on to the next one, or they share this media with others.

Shareability

Infographics are also definitely more shareable than the average text-based article. A properly configured blog lets readers not only enable one-button sharing via social tools; it can also display the visual content in their social streams. Additionally, infographics are usually hosted in PNG or JPG format and can therefore easily be reblogged. Industry best practices suggest that someone reblogging infographic content should include an attribution link to the original source, and write their own analysis, or brief summary on why the infographic is significant.

Brands and publications should encourage others to reblog their content, as most infographics typically include branding from the original content owners. When your brand's editorial infographics are reblogged, it benefits your other marketing efforts as you attract links, drive traffic, and establish thought leadership, which ultimately can help drive conversions.

EDITORIAL INFOGRAPHIC PRODUCTION

This section will walk you through the typical production of an editorial infographic—from idea to design, and everything in between. Figure 4.7 shows how the process works, in short.

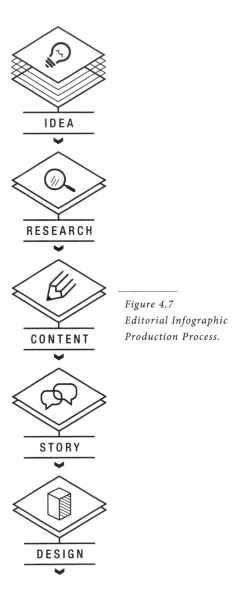

IDEA

RESEARCH

CONTENT

STORY

DESIGN

*Figure 4.7
Editorial Infographic
Production Process.*

WHERE DO IDEAS COME FROM?

The entire process starts with a good idea. Your brand's goals are largely what determine how that infographic is produced. While not mutually exclusive, we like to think of goals as fitting into different buckets, each with their own approach. For example, the tone for an infographic intended to establish a client's position as a thought leader on a given subject or industry would be different than that for a client hoping to create some virality or simply generate web traffic. The goals have everything to do with the audience that the brand is trying to reach, and what they want to do once they have their attention. Do they want to make them laugh? Or do they want to educate them? Admittedly, you can sometimes do both; it's just not always that easy. Less is usually more when it comes to goals, since they tend to be on divergent paths—and it's imperative to keep the vision clear and consistent.

As such, you should choose the information to include in your infographic with your specific goals in mind. We've found that people usually get ideas for infographics from one of several sources. For example, an idea triggered by media consumption—from any number of potential sources, like a radio ad someone heard ten years ago, or an Internet meme they viewed mere minutes prior—can prompt a question for a company to answer using quantitative information. Or a brand can tease out or even discover a story in data, and then editorialize it. Sometimes it's a combination of the two.

At Column Five, most of our ideas come from internal brainstorming sessions that start with the questions "Who is the intended audience?" and "What do we want to say?" acting as primers. Ultimately we try to put ourselves in the shoes of the brand's intended audience and generate ideas that we know they'd find interesting. Spending a lot of time in these sessions (nearly daily) is necessary because an interesting story is not always in the forefront of our brains. And we don't rule out the value of random synapse firings or throwing out offbeat topics. In fact, these seemingly random ideas tend to snowball into actionable ideas, which have ended up being the basis for some of our best infographics.

WHAT MAKES AN IDEA GOOD?

We know that's a loaded question, and one we should frame properly. We judge the quality of "good ideas" for editorial infographics on the objectives we are hoping to reach and the application we're using. We emphasize the value of good ideas, and we spend a lot of time as a company brainstorming ideas for our clients. And while ideas can come from virtually anywhere, what makes an idea "good" is a bit more subjective. The ability to identify the types of content that people would want to consume is more of an art, not a science. That said, we use the following simple checklist to vet our ideas.

1. Is it relevant to your target audience?
2. How does it help you achieve your communication objectives?
3. Is it meaningful?
4. Will other people find this interesting?
5. How is it original?

The answers to these questions shape our approach and help us decide which ideas to pursue. Once we deem an idea worth considering, we move on to an equally important stage: determining whether we can turn this idea into an infographic.

WHAT MAKES A GOOD IDEA ACTIONABLE?

This next step in the process is determining whether an idea is actionable. It's typical for us to work through this question once we do some searching around online to see what research has been done on the topic.

It's not uncommon to have to kill a good idea because we can't figure out how to execute it with integrity. This has mostly to do with being able to find the right sources. And it's especially important in how it relates to data-driven infographics. There are numerous times in which we've developed what we thought was a great idea for a story, only to have to move on because we didn't have access to good, reputable sources. Of course, we take a different approach when the infographic is not meant to be a data-driven piece of content. For example, the Flowtown (Figure 4.8) or Get Satisfaction (Figure 4.9) graphics shown here don't rely on data. Our approach to these infographics was simply to entertain.

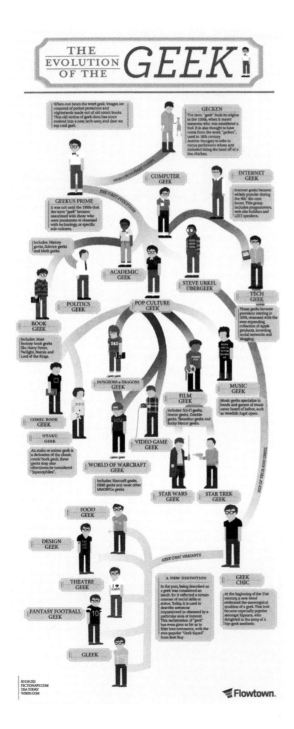

Figure 4.8
The Evolution of the Geek.
Column Five for Flowtown.

Figure 4.9
Super Widget.
Column Five for Get Satisfaction.

AUTO CONNECTION

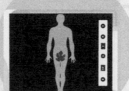

The new SuperWidget© not only allows you to connect to all of your favorite social networks, but it will auto-connect without ever asking for your password or permission. In fact, if you tweet something on your Twitter account, the SuperWidget© will bounce that status update to all of your other social networks and e-mail contacts, and tag it with Google AdWords. The built-in microphone will transcribe your daily conversations and condense them down to appropriate status update-length.

WHEREVER YOU ARE

It is hard to believe how you ever got around without the SuperWidget's Wherever You Are© feature. Not only is your location constantly tracked—in case you get lost—but all of your destinations and pit stops are automatically checked in via Gowalla or Foursquare™.

5G SPEED*

Breathe in the freedom that 5G connectivity offers your tablet experience. This technology will work anywhere—be it city, desert or the stratosphere. Download movies, music and data at lightning-fast speeds!

*5G not yet available in most countries, including the U.S.

GOING GREEN

The greenest tablet on the market, the SuperWidget© runs completely on solar power. The patented micro solar panels on the back of your device will soak up all of the natural energy it needs, so you don't ever have to charge it externally.

Initial charge may take 72 hours. Battery life: 35 minutes.

NEW AIRPLANE MODE

You'll be the TSA's favorite traveling citizen with your SuperWidget's© airplane mode. Simply tap on the airplane icon and the AIT scan mode will permit the TSA agent to scan your possessions and person. This way, you can just skip the line!

This statement has not been reviewed by the FDA, TSA, FBI or PETA. Discontinue use if sores, welts or cancerous tumors develop on skin.

REMOTE

Ever have one of those days when you are simply too tired to stagger across the room to reach your tablet? SuperWidget© now comes with a portable remote, allowing you to access all of the programs and applications on your main device. What if the remote is on the other side of the room too? Don't worry, SuperWidget© comes with a secondary remote for the primary one!

HANDSFREE

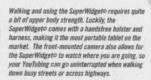

Walking and using the SuperWidget© requires quite a bit of upper body strength. Luckily, the SuperWidget© comes with a handsfree holster and harness, making it the most portable tablet on the market. The front-mounted camera also allows for the SuperWidget© to watch where you are going, so your YouTubing can go uninterrupted when walking down busy streets or across highways.

DOUBLE MOUNT

If you'll be using your SuperWidget© for productive purposes, a double mount is available! How does it work? While one SuperWidget© acts as your primary screen, another doubles as a keyboard. Together, they can even fold flat! No, this is not a laptop.

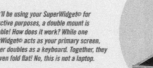

get satisfaction
www.getsatisfaction.com

RESEARCH

In some cases, you will be inspired to create an infographic because you encounter a set of data that is just asking to be designed. In other cases, when the data isn't handy or already in your possession, you will have to search for data that will serve your purposes. Most people have probably had the experience of seeing a well-designed infographic that relies on sources that are dubious at best. Infographics leverage design to help convey an idea or information. But what is the point if the information it displays is incorrect? Many people assume that an infographic is well researched, because it seems like a fool's errand to spend time designing something based on inaccurate information.

Design can be persuasive, but it should never be misleading. That said, there is a lot of responsibility to levy on infographic designers and those shaping the content for design (editors, project managers, creative directors, etc.). These individuals should undertake research with the goals of finding truth and telling a story. A good gauge when conducting research is to ask yourself if the *New York Times* would be satisfied with your employed methodology, as well as the quality of the content that your research yields.

Perhaps the most common infographic research mistake people make is failing to properly contextualize the information. Unfortunately, the increased popularity of infographics has led to an upsurge in bad infographics as well. These are often the ones with the nearly full screen of "sources," typically listed at the bottom left, which are often a smattering of random facts and quotes placed in an order that tells a linear story. However, the readers don't receive proper information about what source relates to what material or how it all relates to each other. In fact, it's becoming quite common to see one of these graphics use data sources that are not only from different years, but also telling different messages, which is problematic.

The ideal scenario is to use research from one source. If, for instance, the graphic is less quantitative yet still involves information that merits design—a how-to guide, a cheat sheet, or tips—we still try and limit the number of sources, for the sake of consistency and coherence. And the source's quality is equally important. Ask yourself whether you'd be able to use a source at an upper-level course at a university; if not, you shouldn't be able to use it in an infographic.

Data and Source Quality

There is no shortage of good data available these days. In fact, we're producing more data every year than ever before. Finding good research is often a matter of seeing an article in a major publication and then going to the original source. Other times, reputable sources compile surveys that answer the question an infographic is asking—or at least address related subject matter. The following is a basic list of our *Rules for Research*:

1. *Make sure the source(s) tell a story.*
   If you're not "telling a story" with your infographics (read: explaining a narrative or allowing a narrative to be explored), then you're doing it wrong. Essentially that story will be derived from the sources that you decide to use. People are going to want to engage an infographic that tells a story that they care to know. In short, there is no shortage of data out there, but not all data is all that interesting, even if it's visualized in a very interesting way.
2. *Make sure your sources are reliable.*
   Not all data producers are created equal. Always use data sets from as unbiased a producer as possible. Good sources include data collected or produced by government agencies, such as the statistics compiled by the U.S. Census Bureau or the Department of Labor. Other top-tier data sources can

include industry white papers, surveys conducted by reputable research organizations, or findings published in academic publications.

It is important to note that surveys conducted by polling agencies or think tanks, while usable, often have a political agenda so always use discretion. Another great source of data is proprietary user data. We have used this for a number of infographics, and if you choose to use this type of data, you should make it easy for people to find out more about the data, such as how it was gathered, how old it is, and how many people were surveyed.

3. *Make sure your sources are relevant.*

The world changes quickly, and the pace of change is accelerating. To ensure you are on the right track for sourcing your infographics, use the most recently published version of the data you've decided to use. Some data producers, such as the Department of Labor, revise their data on an annual or even monthly basis, but this is not always the case for every data producer.

As a rule of thumb, try not to use data that is more than a year old. Two years is acceptable in some cases, if that's the best you can get. Beyond this, use discretion. In all cases, be up front about the age of the data set you are using; you would expect the same from others. Always list the age within the sources or in the graphic's copy. This provides context and clarity, and is a practice no different than writing a college research paper.

If you are using multiple sources, make sure they are complementary. Even if you only use two data sources, they can still create a lot of variance. Using two data sets that clash, such as data collected by think tanks on opposite sides of the political spectrum, makes crafting a narrative difficult. To avoid disseminating inconsistent or biased information, make sure that the sources you use complement each other.

Complementary sources cover the same type of data, collected in the same time frame, using similar questionnaire designs. It is difficult to believe that a coherent message could be created using using data produced by both PETA and the Bookings Institute.

4. *Limit your sources for consistency.*

Finding multiple data sets from multiple sources on one subject can be exciting, but don't get ahead of yourself. It is not possible to create a consistent narrative with 15 different sources. Each additional source you use is another chance of introducing mistakes or biases from the original research into your graphic. The fewer sources you use, the better. A good rule of thumb is to use only one data set, if this is an option. Two or three are acceptable. But the more you add, the more variance you get from different methods, different contexts, and different priorities of the data producers.

COPYWRITING

You want to address copywriting in the same way as research: with integrity. You should employ this part of the process with the intentions of moving the story along and explaining the information's significance.

Quantitative/Data-Driven Infographics

Not all graphics require copywriting. Data-driven editorial infographics (which tend to be more narrative in nature) tell a story and help viewers derive meaning from the visualization (Figure 4.10). In some cases, very explorative graphics can simply consist of a title, graph, and key instructions on how to read the visualization (Figure 4.11) and allow viewers to find meaningful information on their own, not requiring narrative context. And we should start off by establishing that the cardinal rule for this step is to use integrity. In short, write copy that you wouldn't be embarrassed to show your mother.

If your graphic requires some copy, this will invariably come after the research and research organization stage. It's only after you realize what you are trying to say, can you determine how you want to say it. This can be the most pivotal step in the process, one that has the potential to shape the design direction. The infographic producer must make some crucial decisions, such as whether or not to use real numbers or change percentages to tell a story. And while they're also responsible for contextualizing the information, they must primarily be able to prove that the story is worth telling.

Qualitative/Entertaining Infographics

Some of the graphics that we produce don't rely heavily on data (Figures 4.12 and 4.13). We take a more nuanced approach to content development for these. If the goal is to produce an off-beat infographic that entertains and engages audiences, we write copy accordingly. Our approach is typically to try and be as creative as possible—as long as we keep the brand's overarching message in mind while doing so.

BRIEFING

This is the step in which our team collaborates to concept a design, based on the objectives and the content. In doing so, we determine *what* needs to be designed; and consequently *how* it should be designed. While the message is of utmost importance, not all of the information within an infographic will ever be of equal signifiance. Establishing the hierarchy of importance should result in allotting the most space to the most significant information in infographic design. Conversely, the least important information should take the least amount of space on the infographic.

During this stage we determine a plan for design direction as well. This includes identifying ways to visualize the data, or add illustration, or both. For instance, you never want to offend your audience by insensitively applying cartoony illustrations when the subject matter is highly explorative. Conversely, you wouldn't want to bore your audience by applying a dry and uninteresting design to a story that is highly narrative. We'll get into this more in Chapter 9 (Information Design Best Practices). The briefing step serves as a bridge, from crafting the story to visualizing it.

DESIGN

If it weren't for the design stage, we wouldn't have infographics. Our team has a variety of specialists of all types—and in a world rich with data, our approach to each infographic is unique. No content benefits from a "one size fits all" approach; flexibility and creativity are always necessary for good infographic design. A solo designer or team must be able to creatively and accurately convey information with the aim of reaching the brand's objectives. We will address various elements of design best practices throughout the book, especially in Chapter 9 (Information Design Best Practices).

We believe that there should be some conceptual element involved in all infographic design. It can be subtle or obvious, but the reader should be able comprehend the subject matter without having to pore through the text. We also tend to take a primarily "form follows function" approach to design, meaning that the design of an infographic is dictated by the message we are trying to convey and the communication objectives.

Layout + Hierarchy

Since Western languages read from top to bottom, left to right, we keep this in mind when designing. We tend to lay out the information according to its importance, with the most important material presented first, and supporting materials to follow. We do this so that we always convey the most important information first.

Illustration + Design Aesthetic

Since an infographic's design is dictated by the message we are trying to convey, our approach tends to vary from one project to another, and according to application. For instance, we wouldn't advise you to brand an annual shareholder's report with cutesy characters. In the same sense, if you were to create an infographic about how many people watch YouTube on their phones in the office bathroom (Figure 4.14), you shouldn't be a minimalist.

Branding Opportunities

We believe that infographics—especially when used as a content marketing tool—should be an extension of a brand. The goal is for people to know that an infographic belongs to your brand when they see it. And as we've mentioned, you want to do this in a nonaggressive way. Good branding and marketing go hand in hand, so it's always a good idea to use the brand's fonts and colors and to keep illustrations and the overall design aesthetic consistent.

Data Visualization Best Practices

An infographic designer must be aware of the rules and best practices of information design and data visualization. Certain rules apply to the various graph types that are not flexible—under any circumstances. There are also many things for designers to understand and consider between comparisons and data relationships before selecting graphs for visualizing them. We'll go into this in Chapter 9 (Information Design Best Practices) when we talk about the best practices of information design.

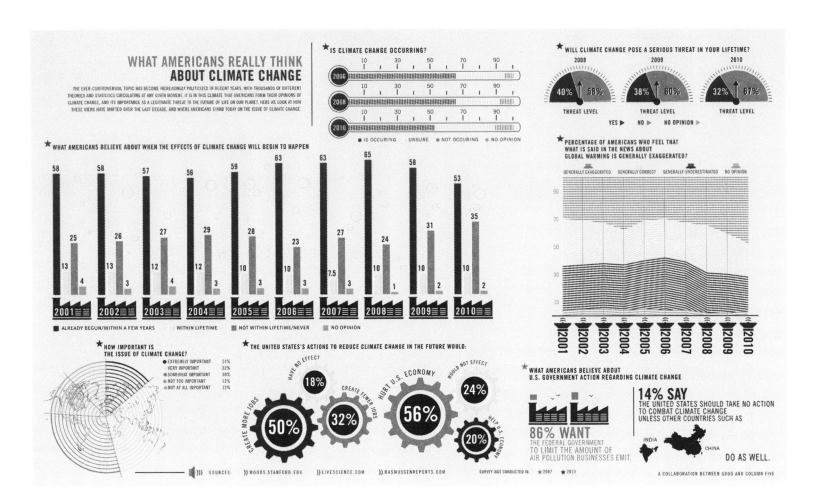

Figure 4.10
Example of a quantitative infographic.Column Five for
GOOD.

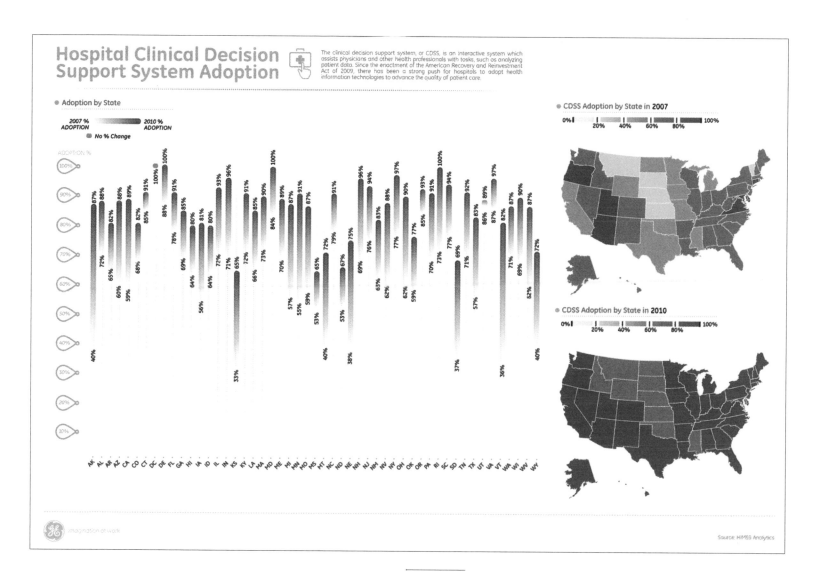

Figure 4.11
Example of a quantitative infographic. Column Five for GE.

The Humanization of Tech
DESIGNING TECHNOLOGY AROUND USERS

Historically, most technology was created to do one thing: increase productivity. No matter how unwieldy or intricate, users had to invest a lot of time to learn how to use these tools. Today, the most commercially successful products on the market are those that are designed around how people naturally do things. Whether through tried-and-true algorithms or empathic design, the user experience is more important than ever. In the modern world, technology learns **you**.

ARTIFICIAL INTELLIGENCE AND THREE PHASES OF MASS PRODUCTION

Artificial intelligence is the science behind creating smart machines and computer programs that understand and simulate human intelligence. Over time, mass production owes much of its evolution to such technologies.

1) MASS PRODUCTION
At the turn of the 20th century, mechanical engineer Frederick Taylor became a notable player in the Industrial Revolution when he developed the idea of **scientific management**—emphasizing technical observations in the workplace to produce standardization and efficiency.

His method went on to inspire Ford's mass assembly line and many other manufacturers and universities.

Frederick Taylor

2) MASS CUSTOMIZATION
Dell, Inc. popularized the idea that simply spurring output isn't enough. Allowing end-users to customize the product according to their own needs under the "built to order" model ultimately makes more sense.

3) MASS PERSONALIZATION
Today, mass production has entered the realm of personalization as products and services are altered to fit users' tastes and preferences. Behaviorally targeted ads are a common example of something that helps achieve this paradigm.

WHAT IS HUMAN-CENTRIC DESIGN?

People can (and have) learned to adapt to traditional technologies.

Think:

Clocks   Musical Instruments   Typewriters

But depending on the complexity of the task, it may take days or even years to learn how to fully acclimate oneself. In some cases, people will never naturally acquire those skills.

Now, as more seek richer user experiences, human-centric design is coming to the forefront. What's the core difference between this design philosophy and others?

The product is built according to how users can, want, and need to use it, instead of forcing people to accommodate to it first.

Think:

Smartphones   Instant Messengers   Social Networks

Figure 4.12
Example of a qualitative infographic.
Column Five for Socialcast by VMware.

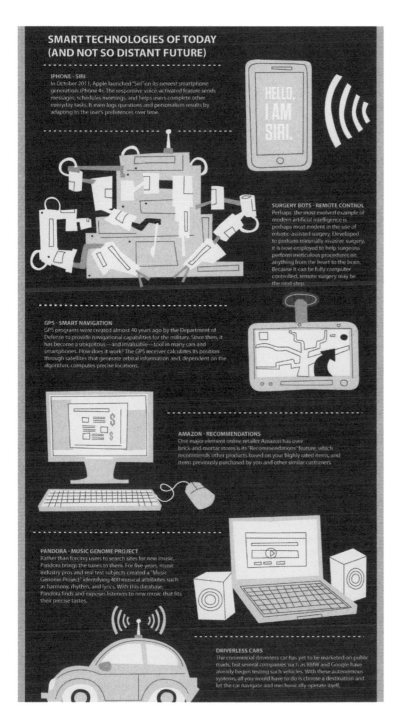

SMART TECHNOLOGIES OF TODAY (AND NOT SO DISTANT FUTURE)

IPHONE - SIRI
In October 2011, Apple launched "Siri" on its newest smartphone generation: iPhone 4s. The responsive voice-activated feature sends messages, schedules meetings, and helps users complete other everyday tasks. It even logs questions and personalizes results by adapting to the user's preferences over time.

HELLO, I AM SIRI.

SURGERY BOTS - REMOTE CONTROL
Perhaps the most evolved example of modern artificial intelligence is perhaps most evident in the use of robotic-assisted surgery. Developed to perform minimally invasive surgery, it is now employed to help surgeons perform meticulous procedures on anything from the heart to the brain. Because it can be fully computer controlled, remote surgery may be the next step.

GPS - SMART NAVIGATION
GPS programs were created almost 40 years ago by the Department of Defense to provide navigational capabilities for the military. Since then, it has become a ubiquitous—and invaluable—tool in many cars and smartphones. How does it work? The GPS receiver calculates its position through satellites that generate orbital information and, dependent on the algorithm, computes precise locations.

AMAZON - RECOMMENDATIONS
One major element online retailer Amazon has over brick-and-mortar stores is its "Recommendations" feature, which recommends other products based on your highly rated items, and items previously purchased by you and other similar customers.

PANDORA - MUSIC GENOME PROJECT
Rather than forcing users to search sites for new music, Pandora brings the tunes to them. For five years, music industry pros and real test subjects created a "Music Genome Project" identifying 400 musical attributes such as harmony, rhythm, and lyrics. With this database, Pandora finds and exposes listeners to new music that fits their precise tastes.

DRIVERLESS CARS
The commercial driverless car has yet to be marketed on public roads, but several companies such as BMW and Google have already begun testing such vehicles. With these autonomous systems, all you would have to do is choose a destination and let the car navigate and mechanically operate itself.

HOW CAN ENTERPRISE CREATE ADAPTIVE INTELLIGENT SYSTEMS?

The smartest system design is one that has a deep understanding of its potential users, along with their wants and needs.

1) USER INTERFACE: MAKE IT INTUITIVE
Apple guru Steve Jobs had it right when he helped develop technology that is not only aesthetically appealing to many, but also easy to navigate and operate.

2) LANGUAGE: KEEP IT SHORT
Brief and concise explanations are key. Steer clear of technological jargon that may confuse users.

3) PURPOSE: FIND A NEED
Why create a product that doesn't target a problem or solve a need? Keep it relevant by asking potential users precisely what they want.

SOCIALCAST

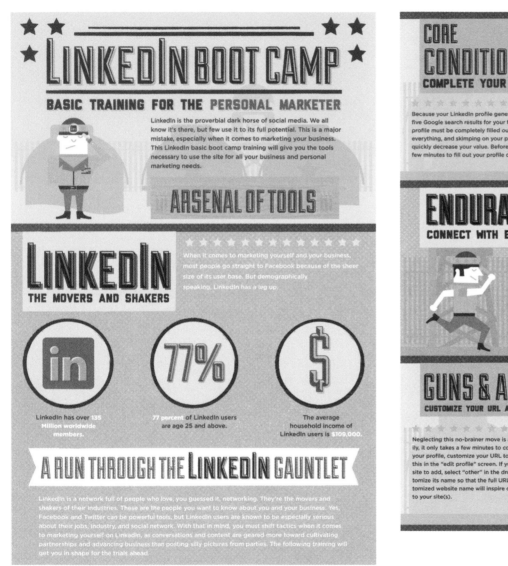

LINKEDIN BOOT CAMP

BASIC TRAINING FOR THE PERSONAL MARKETER

LinkedIn is the proverbial dark horse of social media. We all know it's there, but few use it to its full potential. This is a major mistake, especially when it comes to marketing your business. This LinkedIn basic boot camp training will give you the tools necessary to use the site for all your business and personal marketing needs.

ARSENAL OF TOOLS

LINKEDIN
THE MOVERS AND SHAKERS

When it comes to marketing yourself and your business, most people go straight to Facebook because of the sheer size of its user base. But demographically speaking, LinkedIn has a leg up.

77%

LinkedIn has over 135 Million worldwide members.

77 percent of LinkedIn users are age 25 and above.

The average household income of LinkedIn users is $109,000.

A RUN THROUGH THE LINKEDIN GAUNTLET

LinkedIn is a network full of people who love, you guessed it, networking. They're the movers and shakers of their industries. These are the people you want to know about you and your business. Yes, Facebook and Twitter can be powerful tools, but LinkedIn users are known to be especially serious about their jobs, industry, and social network. With that in mind, you must shift tactics when it comes to marketing yourself on LinkedIn, as conversations and content are geared more toward cultivating partnerships and advancing business than posting silly pictures from parties. The following training will get you in shape for the trials ahead.

CORE CONDITIONING
COMPLETE YOUR PROFILE

Because your LinkedIn profile generally ranks in the top five Google search results for your first and last name, your profile must be completely filled out. First impressions are everything, and skimping on your personal profile will quickly decrease your value. Before moving on, take a few minutes to fill out your profile completely.

ENDURANCE
CONNECT WITH EVERYONE

Some users believe it is only important to stay connected to those you already know and trust, but that only limits your network. Remember, there are 135 million members out there to connect with. Instead of being selective about people you add or accept, start connecting with more contacts and help them connect with each other. The more direct connections you have, the larger your overall network will be, creating more business opportunities in the long run.

GUNS & AMMO
CUSTOMIZE YOUR URL AND WEBSITES

Neglecting this no-brainer move is a rookie mistake. Luckily, it only takes a few minutes to correct. When filling out your profile, customize your URL to reflect your name. Find this in the "edit profile" screen. If you have a blog or website to add, select "other" in the dropdown menu and customize its name so that the full URL doesn't appear. A customized website name will inspire others to click through to your site(s).

Figure 4.13
Example of a qualitative infographic.
Column Five for Mindflash.

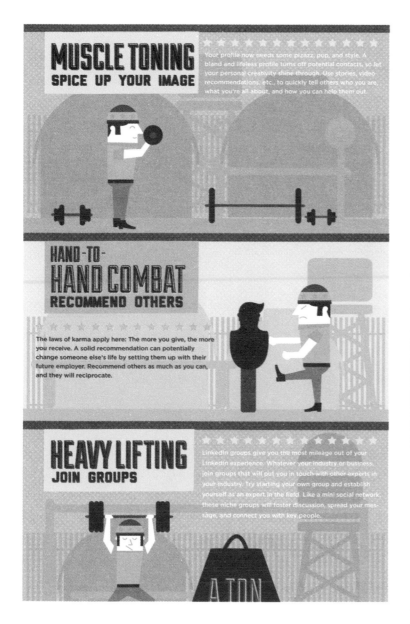

MUSCLE TONING
SPICE UP YOUR IMAGE

Your profile now needs some pizazz, pop, and style. A bland and lifeless profile turns off potential contacts, so let your personal creativity shine through. Use stories, video recommendations, etc., to quickly tell others who you are, what you're all about, and how you can help them out.

HAND-TO-HAND COMBAT
RECOMMEND OTHERS

The laws of karma apply here: The more you give, the more you receive. A solid recommendation can potentially change someone else's life by setting them up with their future employer. Recommend others as much as you can, and they will reciprocate.

HEAVY LIFTING
JOIN GROUPS

LinkedIn groups give you the most mileage out of your LinkedIn experience. Whatever your industry or business, join groups that will put you in touch with other experts in your industry. Try starting your own group and establish yourself as an expert in the field. Like a mini social network, these niche groups will foster discussion, spread your message, and connect you with key people.

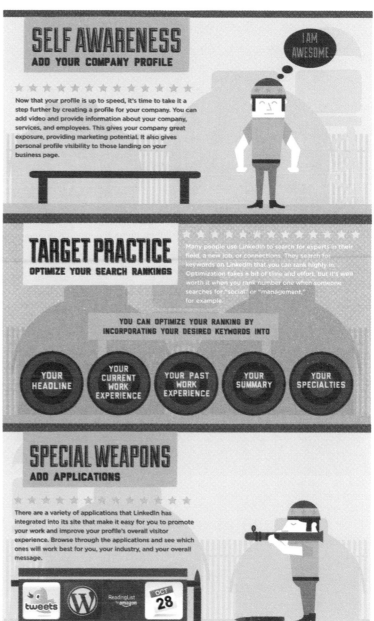

SELF AWARENESS
ADD YOUR COMPANY PROFILE

I AM AWESOME

Now that your profile is up to speed, it's time to take it a step further by creating a profile for your company. You can add video and provide information about your company, services, and employees. This gives your company great exposure, providing marketing potential. It also gives personal profile visibility to those landing on your business page.

TARGET PRACTICE
OPTIMIZE YOUR SEARCH RANKINGS

Many people use LinkedIn to search for experts in their field, a new job, or connections. They search for keywords on LinkedIn that you can rank highly in. Optimization takes a bit of time and effort, but it's well worth it when you rank number one when someone searches for "social" or "management," for example.

YOU CAN OPTIMIZE YOUR RANKING BY INCORPORATING YOUR DESIRED KEYWORDS INTO

- YOUR HEADLINE
- YOUR CURRENT WORK EXPERIENCE
- YOUR PAST WORK EXPERIENCE
- YOUR SUMMARY
- YOUR SPECIALTIES

SPECIAL WEAPONS
ADD APPLICATIONS

There are a variety of applications that LinkedIn has integrated into its site that make it easy for you to promote your work and improve your profile's overall visitor experience. Browse through the applications and see which ones will work best for you, your industry, and your overall message.

tweets | W | ReadingList by amazon | OCT 28

Figure 4.14
Example of infographic that combines qualitative and quantitative elements.
Column Five for Wistia.
(Continued on pages 144-145)

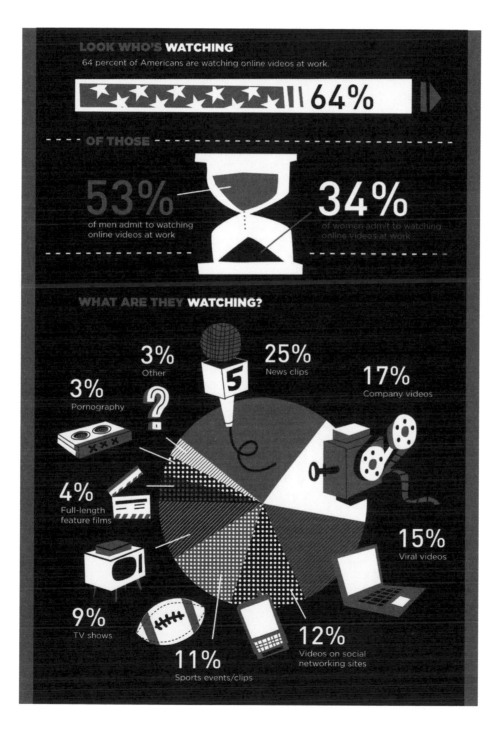

LOOK WHO'S WATCHING

64 percent of Americans are watching online videos at work.

64%

- - - - OF THOSE - - - -

53%
of men admit to watching
online videos at work

34%
of women admit to watching
online videos at work

WHAT ARE THEY WATCHING?

3%
Other

3%
Pornography

25%
News clips

17%
Company videos

4%
Full-length
feature films

15%
Viral videos

9%
TV shows

11%
Sports events/clips

12%
Videos on social
networking sites

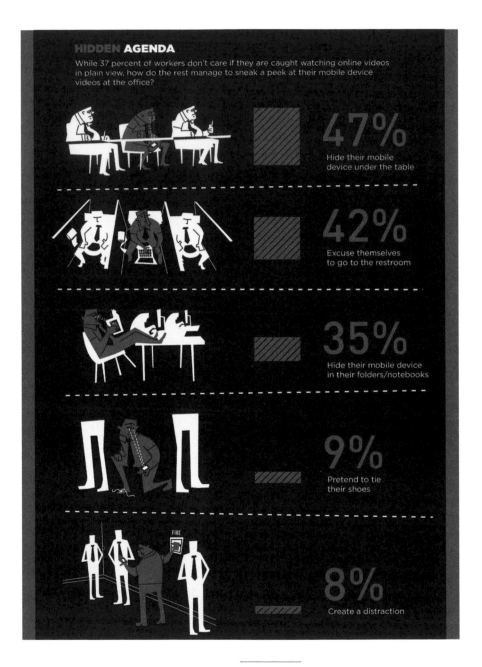

Figure 4.14
Continued.

WHY DO PEOPLE LIKE ONLINE VIDEOS?

36%
Easily shareable
on social networking
sites or email

25%
Engaging and
memorable

14%
More privacy than
TV videos

9%
Context is easier to
understand through
facial expressions

SOURCE: HARRIS INTERACTIVE POLL

Created By
COLUMN FIVE

WISTIA
SHARE VIDEO LIKE A BOSS

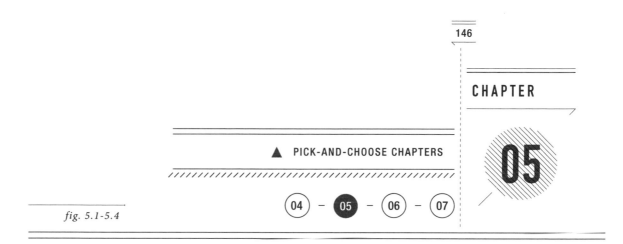

CHAPTER

05

▲ PICK-AND-CHOOSE CHAPTERS

fig. 5.1-5.4

(04) – (**05**) – (06) – (07)

CONTENT DISTRIBUTION: SHARING YOUR STORY

As people consume, curate, and share more original visual content every day, it is more important than ever to utilize infographics as a part of your ongoing content marketing strategy. The medium is becoming more robust as the bar for quality has been raised—which only makes it more challenging to manufacture a message that is a "big hit" in terms of traffic and widespread distribution. Infographics are also being recognized as a vital medium of business communication, as they have value in marketing, communication, and explaining complex processes. As we've discussed in previous chapters, a mounting number of organizations are using infographics to share important information, tell the company story, explain how products work, or to simply make a press release more visual and appealing. And because the medium is so shareable, material spreads faster and further as individuals curate and share content that they love.

There is another interesting characteristic of infographic content that accounts for a difference in the shareability of infographics versus text content. We all learn at a young age not to plagiarize other people's writing. You know that it requires a fair amount of work to reference a written article you like in order to create a quality article that adds unique value to your own readers. And you certainly would never just copy and paste someone else's article in its entirety—even if you cited the original source. However, because an editorial infographic is a single image file, journalists and bloggers can embed the entire story in their own article, then provide additional context or even a critique. Of course, the infographic needs to be properly attributed to the original publisher. They can also include a beautiful infographic in an article as a supplementary resource to make their own content more visual—allowing companies to find value in the process because it spreads their messages further. This ease of embedding to supplement an article is a driving factor in the shareability of infographics. In this chapter, we will give an overview of the promotion process, from publishing your content to making it easy for readers to share, and to actually distributing your content through relevant channels.

POSTING ON YOUR SITE

You always want to make it easy for people to view, share, and embed your infographic content into their own blogs. And while you might think it's a good idea to display your content in a JavaScript lightbox that disintegrates after 10 seconds and redirects someone to your Deal of the Day, people will likely respond as Chris Farley did when told that he wasn't really drinking caffeinated Colombian coffee crystals—"angry." The best approach is to use an introductory paragraph or two to give context to the infographic in the blog post, and then to post it directly. You might also consider posting a lot of the graphic's information in text format. This will make it easy for search engines to read the information, and also to make the content accessible to people with impaired vision who use software that reads websites' content to them. Most blogs are 550 to 600 pixels wide, so if you are using an image that is wider than your blog, you should allow people to click through to the full-sized infographic view. It is very important to have the full-sized infographic on an actual .html page (Figure 5.1).

This is helpful for a few reasons. First, it helps decrease the content's bounce rate (people visiting one page on your site and then closing the browser or hitting the back button), as people who visit the blog post directly will click through to view another page—the one with the wide infographic view. Second, you will be able to track the actual engagement with the wide view of the page in your analytics dashboard, because the .html page can have your analytics script running.

A few years back, people often had an enormous amount of social bookmarking icons in their blog posts. Some even had drop-downs with 100-plus options for sharing. Now, it is more important to guide people to share in the social communities that you want to reach. It is fairly common nowadays to have Twitter, Facebook, and Pinterest as your options, and then an option to email the post. Providing social buttons for any other social platforms where you want to have a presence—such as StumbleUpon, Reddit, or Tumblr—would also be helpful, as long as you don't go overboard or clutter your blog's design. Keep in mind that these particular sites might not always be your most beneficial options for encouraging sharing—social news sites come and go, and you might need to change these options regularly, especially to target the most relevant channels.

It all depends on who your audience is. If you want to reach a more professional audience, you likely would want to make it effortless to share to LinkedIn. The bottom line is to make it easy for people to share and take full advantage of the customization options that most of these sites allow. For example, Twitter's official button allows you to populate @yourcompany in the tweet when someone clicks the button, and to suggest that people follow @yourcompany after tweeting the post.

Surprisingly, we still encounter content—multiple times every single day, on reputable blogs around the web—that has a Twitter share button that posts messages as "via @addthis" (which is the default text populated in tweets by AddThis, a commonly used social sharing plugin) or without any mention of their own company or publication Twitter handle. This approach costs your brand a lot of followers over time. You should always display the buttons as counters showing the quantity of shares of your content, which can help you reach a tipping point once you have momentum in the quantity of shares on an individual post. Utilizing such social proof to encourage new visitors to share your content, based on the visual evidence that many other people found it to be shareable, also helps those same people see your site as well regarded and established. Ultimately, it is most important to encourage sharing in the communities that are apt to be interested in your subject matter. This typically requires an ongoing process of reassessing which communities are the most important and effective for promoting your content. However,

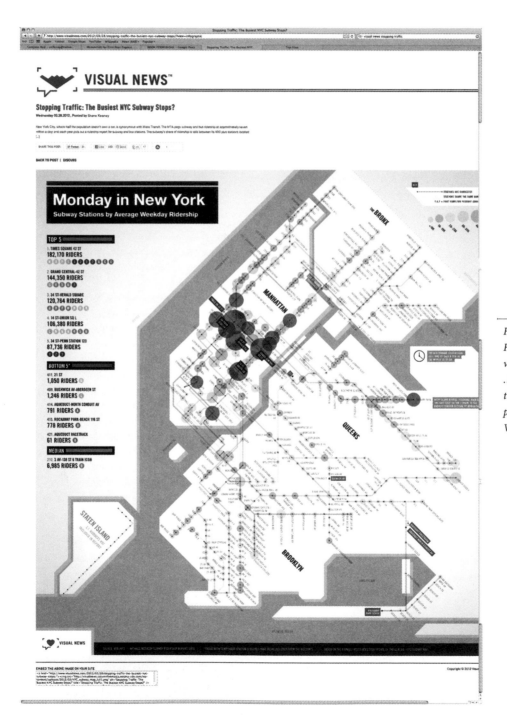

Figure 5.1
Full-sized infographic
view on a standalone
.html page after clicking
through from the image
preview in the blog post.
Visual News.

it's good in all cases to have a diverse group of people discovering, submitting, sharing, and voting on your content.

To make it easy for people to share your content, you should also be sure to give people an embed code. We have an easy-to-use embed code generator on our site, and you can see the format here:

```
<p><strong></strong><br /> <a href="LINK"_"blank">
<img src="IMAGE" width="500" height="" border=""
alt="" /></a></p>
<p>Via <a href="http://columnfivemedia.com/work-types/
infographics/"> SOURCE #1</a> for <a href="SOURCE
LINK" target="_blank">ORIGINAL SOURCE</a></p>
```

You can change any of the fields in ALL CAPS, and the image width as desired.

The code for allowing people to embed interactive data visualization will vary based on whether you create it in Flash or use JavaScript, HTML, or CSS instead. Interestingly, this is part of what makes it a bit tricky to utilize interactive content in a content marketing campaign. It typically costs two to three times as much to create basic interactive content in Flash as compared to a static infographic; however, you won't necessarily see two to three times as much sharing. In fact, you might find that fewer people actually embed the interactive, especially if the piece is particularly wide and not easily embedded by Joey Donut in a Tumblr blog. It becomes even more challenging to justify the cost of regularly creating interactive graphics when you go the mobile-friendly route; it takes more time to develop the same interactive functionality in JavaScript/HTML5/CSS3, especially if you need to support older browsers. As we mentioned in Chapter 2 (Infographic Formats), there are many good reasons to create interactive data visualizations, especially as an on-site resource for people who are already coming to your site or as part of your software product. Including these more complex pieces as part of your content marketing campaign on occasion can be a valuable showcase for your brand. Additionally, with some strategic effort you can potentially get a lot of distribution and coverage of the content. If the process of creating the content is also particularly interesting, you can get even more mileage by describing how you made the showcase piece.

Last, while it is great to get Twitter followers and Facebook likes, it can be challenging to get your message in front of those people again. Many people are too busy or don't care to read every update from every person or brand in their feed every day on every social site. While it might not seem as sexy, compiling a simple newsletter (we use and love MailChimp) can help you determine who is interested in your content. It also allows you access to the place where we engage with content the most—the email inbox. If someone likes you enough to let you into his or her sacred land of email, you can begin to transform that person from someone who is casually entertained by your brand into someone who actually buys from you. Make sure that you have a strong call to action for the e-mail subscription, and take the time to experiment with your messaging and placement in order to maximize the visibility and the number of subscribers.

DISTRIBUTING YOUR CONTENT

Once you have covered all of the fundamentals for making your own site's content shareable, one of the most powerful ways to distribute it is to identify the media outlets that are most relevant to your subject matter. Remember: journalists and bloggers are busy and inundated with manipulative, pushy, and downright boring requests every day. So take the time to think about ways that you can provide value to them, while respecting their journalistic integrity. Getting past the stigma created by spammy use of infographics—think of content as irrelevant as "10 Things You Don't Know About Giraffes" being used to promote a waterbed company in Nebraska—is one of the current challenges in distributing infographics to journalists.

It is great for everyone that journalists and readers alike are turning a more critical eye towards infographics (just like they would with video or written content as well). It helps the industry to mature and sets the bar for achieving widespread distribution higher for content creators. Ideas have to be stronger than ever, and your data and research must be sound. As we see the rise of people making infographics of questionable quality using do-it-yourself tools, it is more imperative than ever that you have a solid concept with excellent copy and interesting information in addition to quality design.

There are several ways that we help the journalists who regularly feature the content that we create and distribute for clients. We have found that calling out the highlights in text format, creating "ClickToTweet" links that they can use in their posts, and cropping sections of the image so that they can break up the infographic into sections for a long-form article are all very effective ways to ensure that we are providing value to the publisher. Keeping journalists' subject expertise in mind on an ongoing basis when initially brainstorming content ideas is a better way to provide content that is relevant to their readers—

rather than just asking for a favor every time.

Another great way to get media outlets to notice your content is to identify partners who are interested in co-branding with you. It usually doesn't make sense for a web-based publisher to commission infographics for a few hundred dollars from a freelancer, let alone a few thousand dollars from an established information design agency. This is because the content produced needs to pay for itself in advertising revenue in most cases, and this would not be profitable without a high volume of traffic or a paid sponsor of the content.

However, you can co-brand content with such a trusted and valuable publishing partner, involve them in your brainstorming and design process, and provide them with the information graphic at no charge. Again, the key here is to create material that has mutual value; a one-sided approach is doomed to fail. You will need to abide by the publisher's style guide and editorial guidelines in order to co-brand the piece with them, and of course respect their journalistic integrity.

When you commission a piece from an infographic design agency and give them design attribution, you should use a consistent style guide for co-branded attribution on infographics. In some cases two brands will put their logos on the infographic. However, a tasteful text attribution at the bottom right of the graphic (second image in Figure 5.2) can also be sufficient in certain contexts, such as this example of content that Column Five created for History.com with research provided by their team.

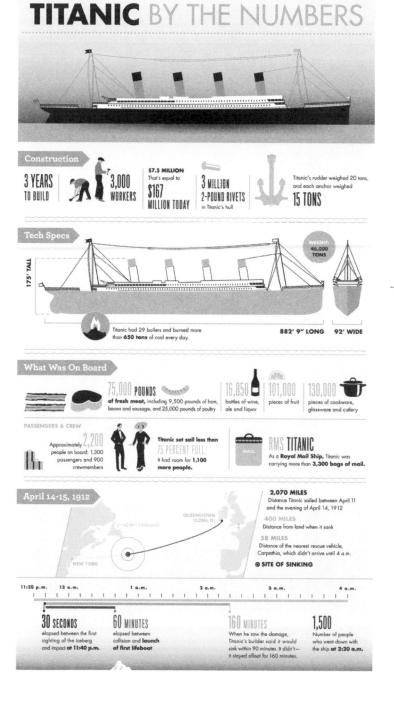

Figure 5.2
Titanic, by the Numbers.
Column Five for History.com.

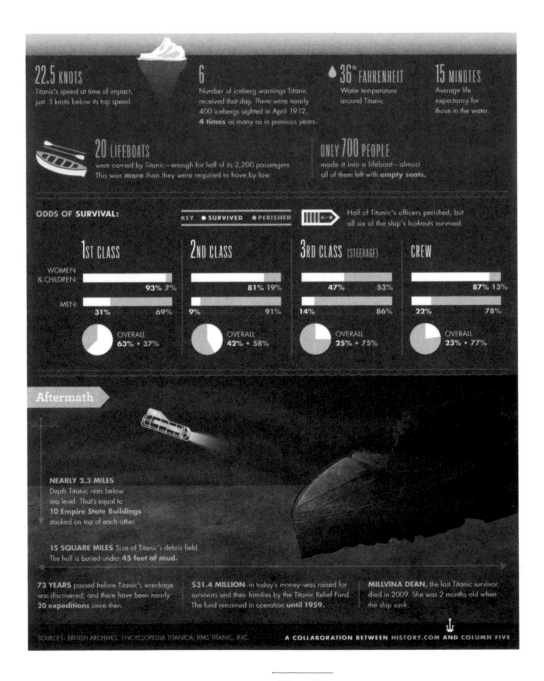

22.5 KNOTS
Titanic's speed at time of impact, just .5 knots below its top speed.

6
Number of iceberg warnings Titanic received that day. There were nearly 400 icebergs sighted in April 1912, **4 times** as many as in previous years.

36° FAHRENHEIT
Water temperature around Titanic

15 MINUTES
Average life expectancy for those in the water.

20 LIFEBOATS
were carried by Titanic—enough for half of its 2,200 passengers. This was **more** than they were required to have by law.

ONLY 700 PEOPLE
made it into a lifeboat—almost all of them left with **empty seats.**

ODDS OF SURVIVAL:

KEY ● SURVIVED ● PERISHED

Half of Titanic's officers perished, but all six of the ship's lookouts survived.

1ST CLASS

WOMEN & CHILDREN: 93% 7%
MEN: 31% 69%
OVERALL **63% • 37%**

2ND CLASS

WOMEN & CHILDREN: 81% 19%
MEN: 9% 91%
OVERALL **42% • 58%**

3RD CLASS (STEERAGE)

WOMEN & CHILDREN: 47% 53%
MEN: 14% 86%
OVERALL **25% • 75%**

CREW

WOMEN & CHILDREN: 87% 13%
MEN: 22% 78%
OVERALL **23% • 77%**

Aftermath

NEARLY 2.3 MILES
Depth Titanic rests below sea level. That's equal to **10 Empire State Buildings** stacked on top of each other.

15 SQUARE MILES Size of Titanic's debris field. The hull is buried under **45 feet of mud.**

73 YEARS passed before Titanic's wreckage was discovered, and there have been nearly **20 expeditions** since then.

$31.4 MILLION—in today's money—was raised for survivors and their families by the Titanic Relief Fund. The fund remained in operation **until 1959.**

MILLVINA DEAN, the last Titanic survivor, died in 2009. She was 2 months old when the ship sank.

SOURCES: BRITISH ARCHIVES, ENCYCLOPEDIA TITANICA, RMS TITANIC, INC.

A COLLABORATION BETWEEN HISTORY.COM AND COLUMN FIVE

Figure 5.2
Continued.

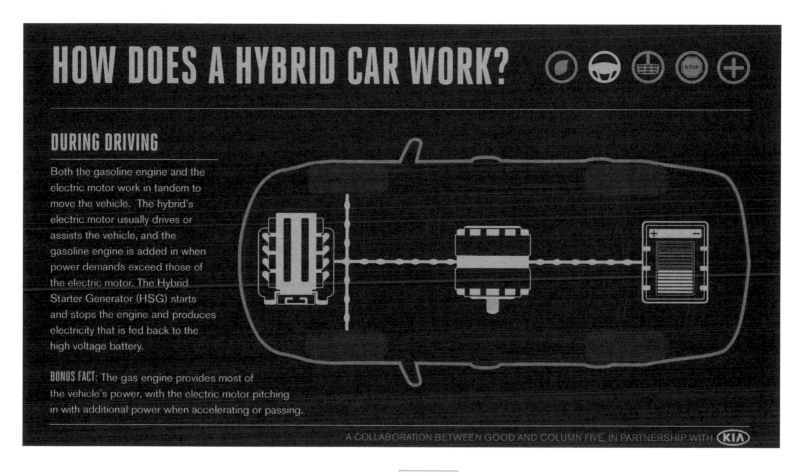

Figure 5.3
How Does a Hybrid Car Work?
Column Five for GOOD in partnership with KIA.

Keep in mind that if you try to turn it into an advertisement for your brand, you will likely have to go the "paid content" approach and work with the publication's advertising team to creative effective sponsored content. We have found the most effective way to create powerful sponsored content is for the sponsor, the publisher, and the content creator to create strong visual content that is not too brand-centric, so that the advertiser (your company in this case) can more effectively tap into the natural readership. *GOOD* does an amazing job of this as a publication, such as in this collaboration with their advertiser, Kia, in which we created an interactive graphic explaining how a hybrid engine works (Figure 5.3). The branding for Kia is tasteful, and the content is relevant to both their brand and the publication's readership.

You can also create co-branded content with another company in your industry. One of you can take the lead on the design (or work with a professional designer/agency), while the other does the research and provides the information. Web analytics company KISSmetrics has regularly done an excellent job of this, as you can see in Figure 5.4 in collaboration with Klout below.

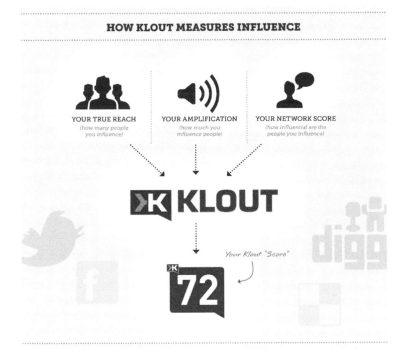

Figure 5.4
Got Klout?
Column Five for KISSmetrics.
(Continued on page 158)

VITAL STATS *(as of 11/2011)*

ESTABLISHED **2008**

TOTAL CAPITAL RAISED **$11M**

MONTHLY UNIQUE USERS **320K**
(speculative data from compete.com)

COMPANIES USING KLOUT'S DATA ... **2,500**

OF PEOPLE THAT KLOUT
REGULARLY CRAWLS DATA FOR **100M**

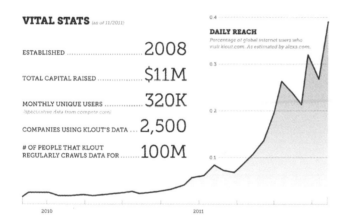

DAILY REACH
Percentage of global internet users who visit klout.com. As estimated by alexa.com.

KLOUT SCORE VS. # OF RETWEETS

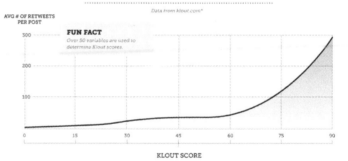

Data from klout.com*

AVG # OF RETWEETS PER POST

FUN FACT
Over 50 variables are used to determine Klout scores.

KLOUT SCORE

KLOUT SCORE VS. TWEET HALF-LIFE

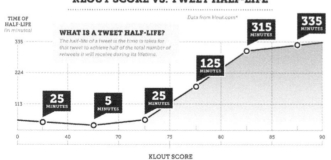

TIME OF HALF-LIFE *(in minutes)*

Data from klout.com*

WHAT IS A TWEET HALF-LIFE?
The half-life of a tweet is the time is takes for that tweet to achieve half of the total number of retweets it will receive during its lifetime.

25 MINUTES **5** MINUTES **25** MINUTES **125** MINUTES **315** MINUTES **335** MINUTES

KLOUT SCORE

THE BENEFITS OF "KLOUT"

(and the Klout business model)

Some think of Klout as a high-level screening process for industry experts. Because Klout knows which people are the most influential in a given category, it makes sense that companies are very interested in working with Klout to put products in front of those who would be most likely to use and talk about them.

COMPANIES
(companies have products that they'd like to promote)

KLOUT
(Klout allows companies access to industry experts)

INDUSTRY EXPERTS
(industry experts get products from companies and talk about them)

HOW TO INCREASE YOUR "KLOUT"

1 CREATE CONTENT WORTH SHARING
Think about the shareability of content before you post
it. Try to post content that has a high shareability factor.

2 START A DISCUSSION
One of the easiest ways to increase your Klout
score is to have more action taken on your
messages. You can do so by starting a discussion.

3 CONNECT OTHER NETWORKS
Be sure to connect your other social
networks (Facebook, Youtube) to Klout.

4 BUILD A NICHE COMMUNITY
When you have a niche community of
your own, you'll be able to get retweets
and drive conversations easily.

5 ENGAGE WITH INFLUENCERS
Engage with influential users in your niche.
Jump into their conversation, message
them and respond to their messages.

*KISSmetrics can help you determine where
your most active users are coming from!*

KISSmetrics   Let's talk: **+1 (888) 767-5477**

PEOPLE PAY YOU. NOT PAGEVIEWS.

KISSmetrics is a powerful web analytics solution that helps you make smarter
business decisions. Try KISSmetrics for FREE: **kissmetrics.com/signup**

Special thanks to **@klout** and **@askaaronlee**

* http://corp.klout.com/blog/2011/11/the-life-of-a-tweet/

Figure 5.4
Continued.

As you continue to establish the credibility of your company blog by following the best practices outlined in the Editorial Infographic Production section of Chapter 4 (Editorial Infographics) and treating it like a publication, you can also establish one-way syndication (informal or formal agreements to republish your content on someone's site) or even cross-syndication (exchanging content with or without compensation to each other's sites). This can be a great way to get additional distribution for your content, as well as free content for your own site. It also allows you to build a strong ally in your industry and helps support the content through the PR and social media engines we have outlined above. It is beautiful when you get enough momentum behind a piece of content through social media promotion that it supports your media distribution in turn—and you then get placement on a reputable site that regularly does well in social media channels. That scenario gives you social media promotion success, which leads to a huge PR win, which then leads to more social media promotion success! This is particularly powerful when you have a strong editorial story living within your proprietary data—something that we'll discuss further in Chapter 6 (Brand-Centric Infographics).

Last, you can position someone in your organization as a "guest author." One of the best ways to establish thought leadership is to become a regular guest contributor to your target publications. We have done this ourselves to establish thought leadership, and to create additional channels for distributing the content that we create for clients. It can be difficult to get in the door, so the most important thing is to start building a body of writing to demonstrate examples of your work. You can also offer specific ideas that you would like to post in order to have someone on the editorial team preapprove them.

PATIENCE PAYS DIVIDENDS

It is exciting to create infographics that go viral and attract hundreds of thousands of unique visitors. However, it is important to remember that you can't hit a home run every time—and that hitting singles and drawing walks is a good way to score runs as well. Say you create a piece for a niche audience that is exclusively targeted to a specific journalist and they post it, but it only sends 200–300 clicks back to your site. The number of visits or pageviews in your own analytics report does not tell the whole story. If you can see that thousands of people liked and shared your branded content on a publisher's site, you know that there were even more brand impressions on your content, and perhaps best of all, in the context of a reputable third party talking about you rather than talking about yourself! The new relationship with a journalist and the exposure to a new audience are far more valuable than vanity metrics such as pageviews.

Ultimately, you must be patient, and it helps to measure your branding campaign's success by asking your customers how they first heard of you, which will yield qualitative responses that wouldn't appear in your analytics dashboard. Further, when you see traffic, links, customers, and press mentions continuing to come your way through a successful piece of content with a long shelf life that was published six months ago, you will start to taste the sweet benefits of residual payoff from the time and money you invested in creating beautiful content and treating your company like a publication.

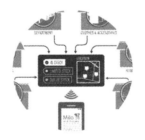

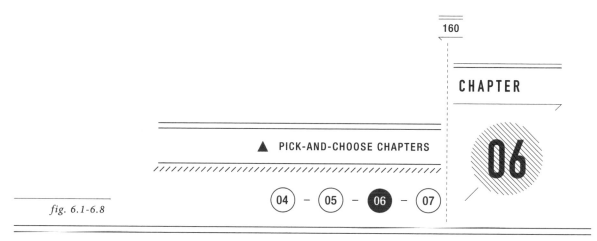

CHAPTER

▲ PICK-AND-CHOOSE CHAPTERS

(04) – (05) – **06** – (07)

06

fig. 6.1-6.8

BRAND-CENTRIC INFOGRAPHICS

181

Infographics can be an incredible tool in explaining your business, communicating its value, and holding your audience's attention while you do it. As we discussed in the previous chapter, editorial content tends to have more broad appeal, thus garnering more attention and adoration. However, you don't want to overlook the utility of information design in communicating a more branded message. We call this *brand-centric* content; that is, it is not intended merely to shed light just on any relevant, interesting topic in order to attract attention.

Instead, its goal is to communicate very specific ideas related to a company, its mission, and details about the products and services that it offers. This chapter will show how you can make traditional methods of communicating your value proposition more engaging by visualizing certain elements of them. We have identified several common areas of this communication that benefit greatly from the application of infographics.

"ABOUT US" PAGES

If you are a new or relatively unknown company, each visitor to your site should be thought of as a valuable prospective customer. It is therefore essential that you make your company's purpose instantly clear, since visitors are likely to leave as quickly as they came. You must present what you do, why you do it, and how it gets done to each visitor in a way that is both direct and appealing. This information is most often contained on a site's "About Us" page, and it typically consists of a few sparse paragraphs of formatted text describing the company's history, location, and purpose.

Unfortunately, customers will probably skim over and not really read content like this if it is standard and predictable. That's exactly why this is a great opportunity to make your purpose and unique value proposition stand out. This information should be front and center on a start-up's homepage, not relegated to a sub-page of the site. Using infographics to display this information will bring the content to life, and ensure that your visitors are getting the message quickly and clearly.

If potential customers don't commonly understand the need for your product or service, infographics can help to set the stage and explain this need. This is a good opportunity to visualize industry statistics, demographic details, or problem statements. This setup is shown in Figure 6.1, which shows an explanatory infographic Column Five designed for shopping search site Milo.com in 2010, before eBay acquired them.

The "Did you know . . ." section on the left side of the page highlights the industry landscape, and describes the current and projected need for a solution. This sets the stage for the infographic diagram that depicts Milo's service on the main part of the page. Doing this allows the brand to tell its complete story by presenting adequate background information, thus strengthening their message's value.

Figure 6.1
Example of infographic used in an "About Us" page.
Column Five for Milo.com.

The main diagram shows how Milo works in a simple way that reflects the playful brand's style. This example demonstrates a few good practices for developing an infographic for an "About Us" page.

 MAKE YOUR PURPOSE CLEAR ⟶

You must keep your statements concise in order to maximize their impact. Milo uses one sentence to explain their very simple mission, and two very short sentences to describe how they aim to achieve it. They then include two additional paragraphs at the bottom to describe the service in more detail for those who desire more information. It is important to note that these paragraphs are not necessary in order to understand the company's mission and service. Because you'll be dealing with site visitors' (very) limited attention, you'll want to keep the essential messaging short and sweet, and deliver it up front.

2 ─ CHOOSE YOUR BULLETS WISELY ──────────→

As with all infographics, it is important to decide what to include and what to omit. While it is tempting to regale the reader with the endless benefits of adoption when speaking about one's own company or product, that's not the most effective approach. Look at your analytics to determine the average amount of time users spend on each page, and you will realize that you likely don't have this luxury. For example, Milo wanted to convey a few things that were essential to understanding the value of the service:

- They work with local, not online stores
- They work with a diverse range of store types
- Their service shows location and availability of items
- Their service is available on a mobile app

This very simple diagram quickly conveys each of these points to give viewers an immediate understanding of the product. It is important to limit the points you want to highlight to maintain the visualization and the overall message's impact.

3 ─ AVOID INDUSTRY-SPEAK ──────────────→

Keep your messaging accessible to those who may not be familiar with your industry's common terminology. Using "inside baseball" terms on your site doesn't make your company sound more advanced; it makes you sound more generic and less accessible. And while you want to avoid talking down to your customers, you also want to avoid speaking to them like a robot. The "About Us" page is a great place to inject some personality into your brand messaging, and connect with your customers on a human level.

PRODUCT INSTRUCTIONS

Chances are that a product is probably not very well designed if someone needs a detailed explanation of how it works. Inevitably, however, the need will arise to give at least some basic instruction on how to use a product—whether it is a toy, tool, mobile app, or SaaS solution. But reading the instructions is roughly the last thing anybody wants to do after purchasing something they are excited about. It feels like buying a new car with tires that need to be inflated before you can drive it. It creates a mandatory barrier to entry, which immediately diminishes your product's appeal. That's why it is incredibly valuable to have the initial instruction experience be not only simple, but also as inviting as the product itself. You need to consider your customers' interaction at this stage as thoughtfully as their experience of actually using the product. Visualization can help immensely in this regard, since it enables you to keep instructional content short and stimulating, ensuring that product instructions feel more like finding a $20 bill in the glove box than filling a flat tire.

Using visual cues in place of wordy descriptions will help keep the content direct and concise—which your customers will love. But where do you start? One way to approach the form visual instructions will take is to look at the product or interface itself. It is logical and intuitive to visually represent a product's anatomy in its instructions; providing a supporting diagram will serve to familiarize the user with the product more quickly. While this is not always the best solution in the end, it is a strong way to start envisioning the format your instructions could take. If your product is a physical object, you have a unique opportunity to display a diagram of its anatomy while calling out its various features and applications.

This immediately eliminates the need for any text to describe location, proximity, or relationship of features, and instantly clarifies how customers can use it. While it's not uncommon to include such visuals in product-assembly instructions, directions for use, by comparison, are often far more daunting and typically span sheets of text. A prime example of a product in need of visual instructions is the classic board game. Nothing says "family fun night" like plowing through three pages of monochromatic 9-point type in order to understand the rules, right?

If you have a digital product such as a mobile app or SaaS solution, you also have a great opportunity to explain a potentially complex user interface by using infographics. While the user experience should be intuitive, an introduction or explanation of the various features can come in quite handy to get the user up to speed quickly. We have found from experience that motion graphics work fabulously for this purpose. Because your customer is likely already viewing the product on a computer or mobile device, video is an appropriate medium for an introduction. The main features can typically be distilled into a short (1–2 minute) clip that runs users through the interface to familiarize them with it.

A great example of this application is a project that we worked on with Myxer Social Radio. We walked users thorough the interface functionality of their new mobile app, which allows friends to listen to music at the same time. The video can be found at http://goo.gl/OpcDP. The goal of this motion graphic was to communicate quickly and clearly how to use some of the application's key features. To maintain users' attention, we kept the piece short—around 90 seconds—and fast-moving. There is not always enough time to show new users every feature and functionality; however, it is ideal for featuring the basics and encouraging users to explore more for themselves.

VISUAL PRESS RELEASES

The world of PR is undergoing a significant transformation, and these changes will continue in the coming years. Journalists and notable bloggers are inundated with emails from companies and PR agencies, all of whom are seeking a write-up of their latest tidbit of news. Traditional methods of pitching these "stories" are decreasing in potency, and companies are looking for new ways to draw attention to their news. The type of content that readers want to consume is changing as well. As we discussed in the previous chapter, the world of media is becoming increasingly editorial in nature. In other words, readers want a story. The typical press release, which likely consisted of a company bio followed by a collection of revenue stats, or a list of new features of an app's latest update, is rarely interesting to the average reader. People want more, and brands are looking for ways their press releases can make a splash—not see them drown after only a few days.

Companies and PR agencies recognize this changing landscape, and our company has fielded a lot of requests recently to find new ways to make this content interesting and appealing to journalists and readers. Using infographics to convey this messaging not only stands out to media contacts; it also provides a way to tell a story without being lengthy and boring. Our work with several brands provides good examples of how to execute a visual press release effectively.

For example, using infographics to display your company's statistics, such as revenue growth, user base expansion, or notable product performance, can quickly communicate a rise in a product's popularity or viability—something that's always appealing to journalists looking for the hottest new trends. This is especially common in the tech industry, where companies can often experience hockey stick–like growth curves or develop remarkably innovative products that disrupt a traditional industry. Visual representations of such statistics help to contextualize the data and clarify what makes these numbers so impressive.

One great example of such a graphic is a piece called "The Lifecycle of a Web Page" that Column Five created for StumbleUpon, the social discovery platform (Figure 6.2). The purpose of this graphic was to show some of the impressive numbers surrounding StumbleUpon's user engagement, and compare those to competing social networking sites such as Twitter and Facebook. StumbleUpon sought to communicate their platform's value to content creators in an effort to encourage further sharing. It also placed them in the middle of the ongoing discussion of the use and value of social media sites, and provided insight into how people interact with them.

The result was increased mentions of StumbleUpon in the press and prominent blogs as well as a useful piece of collateral for the company's business team to use, to show partners and clients the nature of their platform's traffic. The keys to the success of this infographic were that statistics included were both interesting and significant and the tone of the piece was matter-of-fact. Nothing kills the good vibes you have going with your reader like injecting a sales-sounding message to draw conclusions and make recommendations to the reader. When you have impactful facts that speak for themselves, there is no need to add, ". . . so the next time you share content, consider the platform that outperforms Facebook AND Twitter by 900 percent!" The data should tell the story itself; don't be afraid to let it talk. Another good example of utilizing company statistics is this graphic created for SlideShare: http://goo.gl/L38d9.

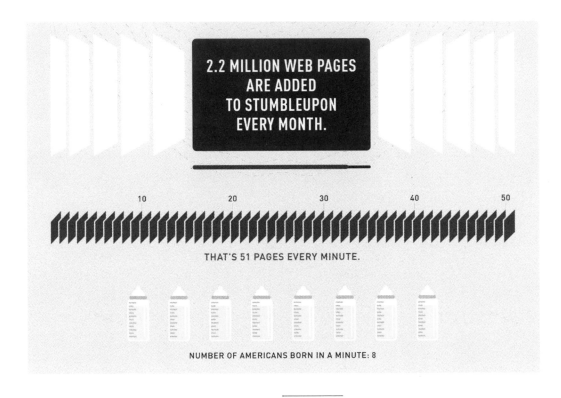

Figure 6.2
Example of a visual press release.
Column Five for StumbleUpon.

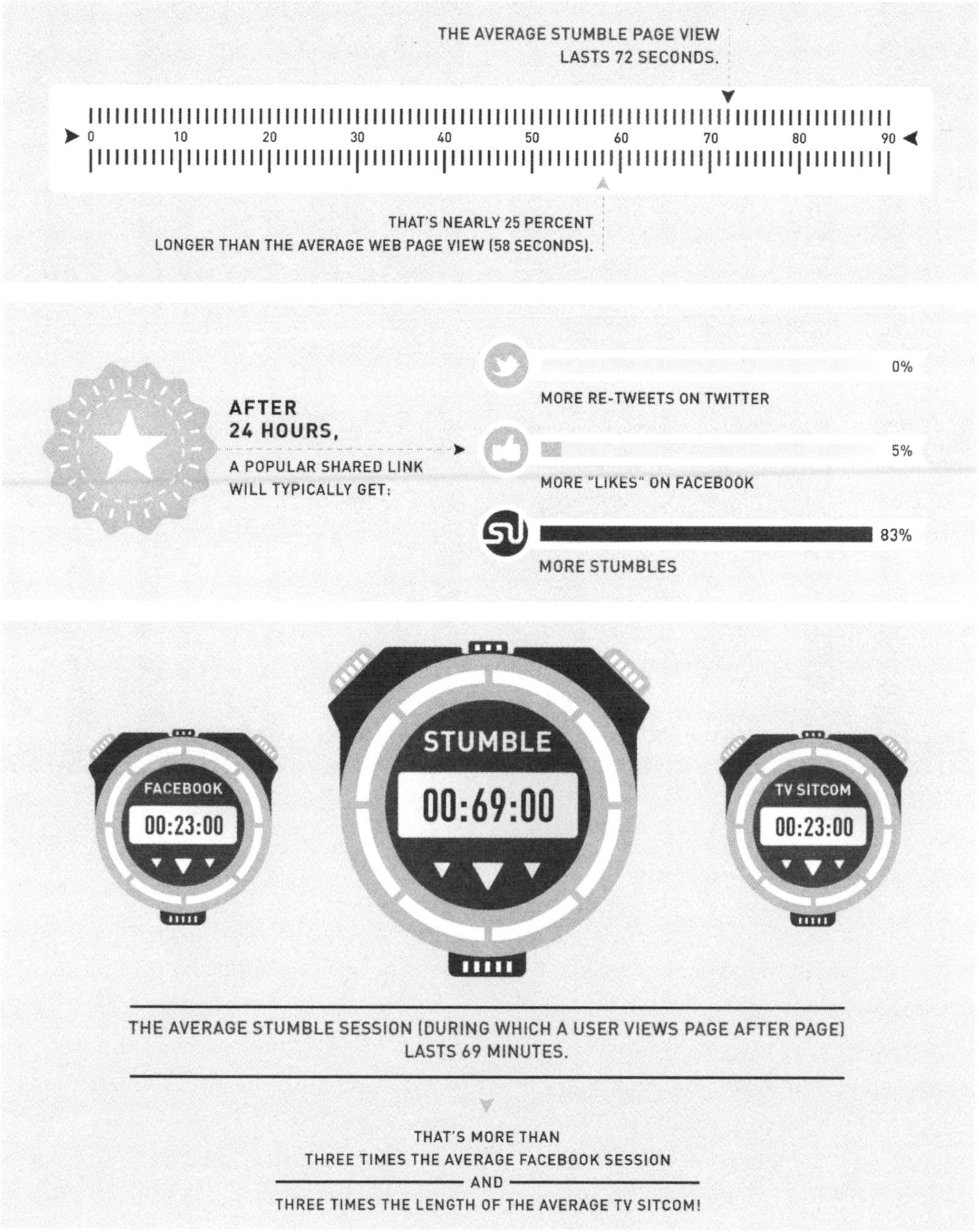

THE AVERAGE STUMBLE PAGE VIEW
LASTS 72 SECONDS.

▼

|||||||||||||||||||||||||||||||||||||||||||||||||||||||||||||||||||||||||||||||||||||||||
▶ 0   10   20   30   40   50   60   70   80   90 ◀
|||||||||||||||||||||||||||||||||||||||||||||||||||||||||||||||||||||||||||||||||||||||||

THAT'S NEARLY 25 PERCENT
LONGER THAN THE AVERAGE WEB PAGE VIEW (58 SECONDS).

**AFTER
24 HOURS,**

A POPULAR SHARED LINK
WILL TYPICALLY GET:

0%

MORE RE-TWEETS ON TWITTER

5%

MORE "LIKES" ON FACEBOOK

83%

MORE STUMBLES

FACEBOOK
00:23:00

STUMBLE
00:69:00

TV SITCOM
00:23:00

THE AVERAGE STUMBLE SESSION (DURING WHICH A USER VIEWS PAGE AFTER PAGE)
LASTS 69 MINUTES.

▼

THAT'S MORE THAN
THREE TIMES THE AVERAGE FACEBOOK SESSION
————— AND —————
THREE TIMES THE LENGTH OF THE AVERAGE TV SITCOM!

Figure 6.3
Example of a visual press release. 15 Years of Entertainment.
Column Five for PlayStation.

Another nice way to bring attention to your company's achievements is to take a nostalgic look at your history. Whether your company is only 3 years old or 30, you can use a timeline to highlight accomplishments and milestones. Of course, how much this information appeals to the average reader will depend on how familiar they are with your company—and how impressed they are with your achievements. The level of appeal will also affect the media pickup of the piece, so you'll want to be both conscious of and realistic about these facts. For instance, many people care about and can relate to the history of a company like Apple; we have owned their products and experienced their evolution through the years. But not every company will have the same broad appeal. Temper your expectations accordingly.

We have also created these types of graphics for internal purposes, to remind employees where the company has been, and where it is going. A good example of this is a graphic we created to mark PlayStation's 15th anniversary in 2011, shown

5.18.04

The PlayStation® console hits 100 million units sold worldwide, becoming the first video game console to reach the 100 million mark.

11.1.04

SCEA launches an ultra-compact PlayStation®2 computer entertainment system. Online games can now be easily accessed and enjoyed via a built-in network connector.

3.23.05

The PSP-1000 system is the very first handheld entertainment system of the PlayStation® family. It adopts UMD® optical disc as playable media and is equipped with a high-resolution LCD screen that enables the system to achieve stunning visual and sound quality.

11.17.06

The PlayStation®3 computer entertainment system launches in North America utilizing large capacity Blu-ray Disc media along with a built-in hard disk drive. The system supports downloading games and many types of digital content items via the PlayStation® Network.

9.30.09

PlayStation®2 system reaches over 140 million units sold worldwide.

10.1.09

The exclusively digital PSP®go system arrives in North America, featuring a sliding display panel and a 16BG storage system in place of the UMD® drive, ideal for consumers who want to enjoy games as well as digital content from any location.

6.9.10

The PS3™ system becomes the first home console to offer stereoscopic 3D game content via firmware update 3.30. Stereoscopic 3D movie playback for PS3™ system is announced for later in the year.

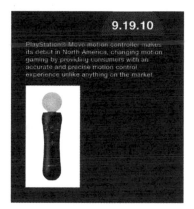

9.19.10

PlayStation® Move motion controller makes its debut in North America, changing motion gaming by providing consumers with an accurate and precise motion control experience unlike anything on the market.

in Figure 6.3. We centered the content on the various PlayStation consoles Sony has released over the years, and highlighted the evolution of technology leading up to their most recent release, PlayStation Move. This is clearly a company history that appeals to a specific (albeit large) group of people: those who own or have owned PlayStation consoles and games.

Knowing this target audience, the ideal strategy would be to seek out specific sites, blogs, and other media outlets that might want to cover the topic. A plethora of popular gamer sites, some of them specifically PlayStation oriented, likely would be interested in the news, and video game publications might want to feature the graphic. PlayStation should reach out to of these outlets individually with a unique and personal pitch. Of course, not all brands are as familiar as PlayStation, and it might not be as appealing to a mainstream publication. That is why it is important to target niche and industry-specific outlets that would be particularly interested in your company's history.

Showcasing your company's trove of proprietary data and highlighting its value to outsiders can also be the basis of very strong content. The great thing is that this approach doesn't just talk about your company's value; it displays it. One of Column Five's first clients, online personal finance and budgeting tool Mint.com, allowed us to execute this style of visual press release perfectly. Because of the services it provides, Mint possesses large amounts of anonymous financial data about users' spending, saving, and borrowing habits. No other company has access to such a well-rounded profile of Americans' monetary assets and habits. In an effort to spotlight the remarkable aggregation of this information, we produced several infographics on specific topics such as Valentine's Day flower purchases, a comparison of average spending on coffee at the major shops (Figure 6.4), or how shopping at luxury retailers around the holidays had changed over the years. In April 2010, we looked at how

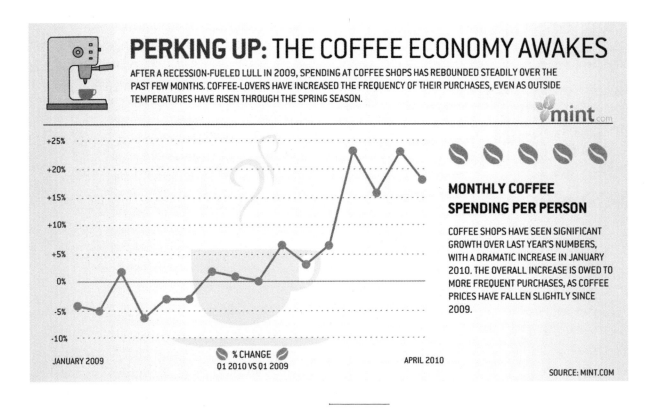

Figure 6.4
Example of a visual press release. Perking Up.
Column Five for Mint.com.

Americans had changed their saving habits during the recession (Figure 6.5). This was a great opportunity to not only bring attention to their data, but also to tell a very interesting story: that all it took was a severe economic meltdown to get Americans to start saving more and spending less! The key to great success in this realm is to find an interesting story in your data that will attract a broad audience and spread widely. If you can inform and entertain the viewer while drawing attention to your company's data, it is truly a win-win.

Visual press releases can cover many other topics; they are not limited to the three ideas mentioned. The key here is to be able to create something that stands out and entices journalists to cover the topic. Using an infographic format enables journalists to easily pair their article with your visualization, which in turn will bring attention and validity to your company's release.

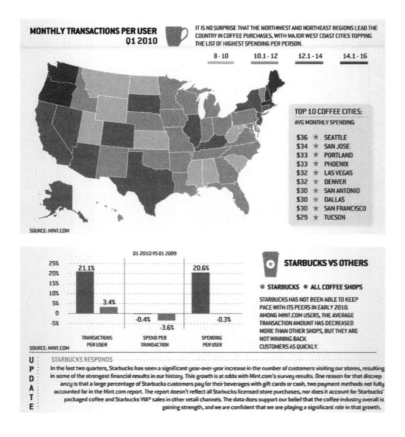

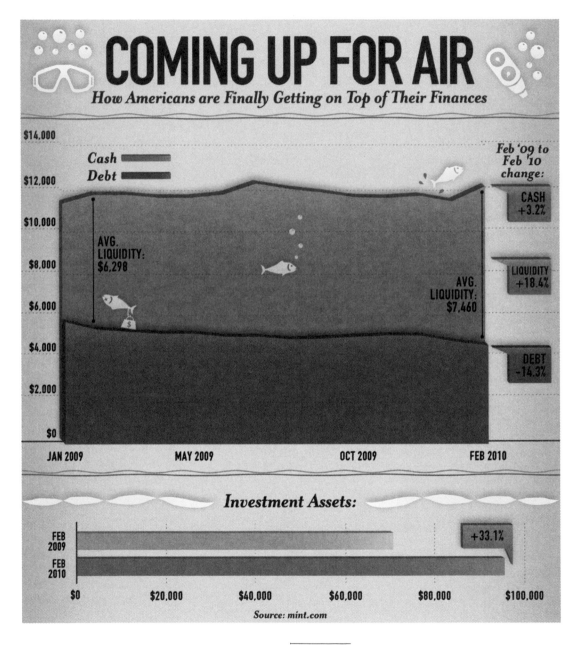

Figure 6.5
Example of visual press release. Coming Up for Air.
Column Five for Mint.com

Figure 6.6
Example of presentation design.
(Continued on pages 176-177)

PRESENTATION DESIGN

The principles of visualization and infographics are nothing new in the world of presentations. Decks have used data visualization since the first man, long ago, saved his own job by presenting a beautiful collection of graphs that trended up and to the right. Enlisting charts to show company trends and insights is now commonplace in the business world. What presentation design most typically lacks, however, is the actual element of design. While PowerPoint has undeniable utility, most people would agree that it is somewhat lacking in the aesthetics department. The software itself is only partially to blame; the onus is on the creator.

This section will discuss best practices for applying infographics to presentation design, building on the foundation of data visualization that is already common practice (Figure 6.6).

Figure 6.6: *Continued.*

1 — DIVERSIFY YOUR VISUAL REPERTOIRE

The first thing you must understand is that information design is not limited to the visualization of data, in presentation design or any other application. It can and should be used to visualize other concepts such as hierarchy (org charts), anatomy (portfolio allocation), and chronology (timeline of events). Beyond the bar graphs showing sales figures and monthly projections, there are many more opportunities to explain concepts with visuals that will engage your audience and clarify your key points.

2 — MINIMIZE SLIDE CONTENTS

You might notice a pattern here. Just like other applications, you should minimize the total content you display at any one time in order to maximize its impact. If your audience is reading paragraphs on your slide, they are not listening to what you have to say. Keep your visuals simple, and use them as talking points for your presentation. Eliminate as much text as possible, since you'll probably repeat anything that is written in sentence form during your speech.

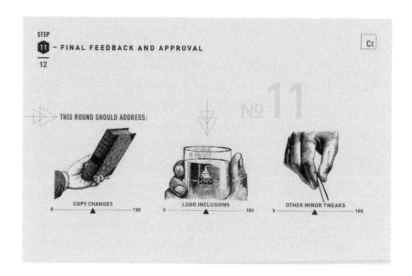

SOCIAL BUTTONS
Make sure you have the official Twitter counter, Facebook 'like' counter, Google +1 button, and StumbleUpon counter installed. We can install a custom WordPress plug-in for you if you need help with this.

PROMOTIONS
Within five days of initial publishing, we implement a tripartite approach in our Social PR promotion:

1/ Submit infographic to social news and networking sites such as Digg, StumbleUpon, Reddit, Facebook, Twitter, and Google+.

2/ Next, we target relevant media outlets and publications to republish the piece.

3/ Finally, we approach industry-specific blogs and infographic design sites for additional pickup.

RESULTS
Please allow up to 30 days for the full effects of our promotional efforts to be realized. Often we get the pickup we want right away, but sometimes it can take several weeks for a piece to reach its potential.

OUR PROMOTION PROCESS IS EVER-EVOLVING, AND WE TAILOR IT TO FIT EACH CLIENT'S INDIVIDUAL NEEDS.

STEP **11** / 12 — FINAL FEEDBACK AND APPROVAL   Ct

THIS ROUND SHOULD ADDRESS: No. 11

COPY CHANGES   0 ▲ 100

LOGO INCLUSIONS   0 ▲ 100

OTHER MINOR TWEAKS   0 ▲ 100

③ - USE COLOR SPARINGLY ⟶

Color is a unique tool that you should use with care. Bold colors imply emphasis on a notable item, and when colors are used everywhere, it is difficult for people to determine where to direct their attention. When everything is highlighted, nothing is highlighted. Use this power to highlight sparingly on each slide, to point the viewer to the main thrust of your messaging.

④ - KEEP IT COHESIVE ⟶

The most frequent flaw in the design of a deck is likely the inconsistency among its various elements. Fonts vary; charts and graphs are borrowed from different sources; and company logos exist in varied formats, colors, and resolutions. As an agency that specializes in design, we understandably find these piecemeal creations more perturbing than the average person. However, the effect of a well-designed, polished presentation is undeniable—whether it is one that you share just within your company, or at a public speaking engagement. Of course, not every presentation occasion warrants the commission of a designer to create the deck, but we believe that many do. If the situation requires you to make a strong impression, it is essential that the various elements of your presentation fit together seamlessly. You want your audience to feel as though you have chosen your visuals as expertly as you have chosen your words.

ANNUAL REPORTS

Since this is the most important document that your company will create all year, you should treat it as such. An annual report can contain storytelling, insightful commentary, heartfelt letters to shareholders, and rich data. Unfortunately, many are simply unapproachable. They are long, wordy documents that employees and stakeholders are likely to scan for highlights rather than actually read. They do, however, contain countless opportunities for visuals that can arise from storytelling and data. In-depth commentary can still exist, but infographics can help break up the text and highlight the areas and points to which readers should direct their attention.

The Michael J. Fox Foundation's (MJFF) 2010 Annual Report is a great example of how to communicate stories and messages through illustration and infographics. Column Five created a series of five individual illustrations to be included in the report, each to explain a concept behind the MJFF's unique approach toward Parkinson's disease research. Figure 6.7 is an illustrated diagram showing how the MJFF works to use drugs that the FDA has already approved, thus saving the time and money needed to approve new drugs. This type of information helps to inform MJFF donors of the important parts of their strategic approach—information that might have been lost in paragraphs of text. Note that the illustrations in this example were designed to supplement the body text of the report, not replace it entirely. They bring the highlights to the forefront by providing the reader with visuals that immediately engage them in the essential messaging.

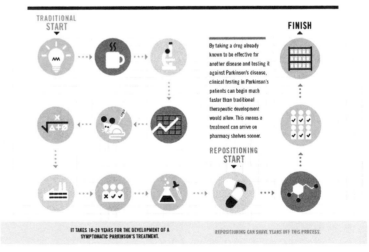

Figure 6.7
Example of an annual report.
Column Five for The Michael J. Fox Foundation.

TRADITIONAL

STREAMLINED

THE FOX EFFECT

Identification of a drug target typically unfolds in an uncoordinated way as different labs analyze it from discrete angles, often at the expense of opportunities for collaboration. MJFF is orchestrating efforts to encourage sharing data and resources early in the process so that LRRK2 can evolve toward practical drug therapy faster.

NEW TREATMENT

OVER $30 MILLION IN MJFF INVESTMENTS IN LRRK2 THERAPUTIC DEVELOPMENT TO DATE.

OVER 30 LABS IN THE LRRK2 BIOLOGY CONSORTIUM.

OVER 3,000 INDIVIDUALS IN THE COHORTS WITH MUTATIONS IN THE LRRK2 GENE.

Using infographics in an annual report is also a strong way to draw attention to your company's big wins for the year. The Human Rights Campaign (HRC) did just this in their 2011 annual report. They approached Column Five to create a completely visual report while emphasizing the progress that had been made in the fight for equal rights for the LGBT community.

The report walked the viewer through the HRC's work for equal rights, translating issues such as Congressional support and current laws across the country (Figure 6.8) into compelling visual information. Using infographics to convey this type of information allowed us to "show rather than tell" viewers the progress that had been made over the course of the year, and clearly communicate the value that the organization is providing. This annual report design went on to win an AIGA 50 award, earning it further attention and recognition. The MJFF and HRC reports are two examples of how clearly communicating your company's value in visual ways can take many forms, some of which we will discuss in the following chapter.

Figure 6.8
Example of an annual report.
Column Five for Human Rights Campaign.

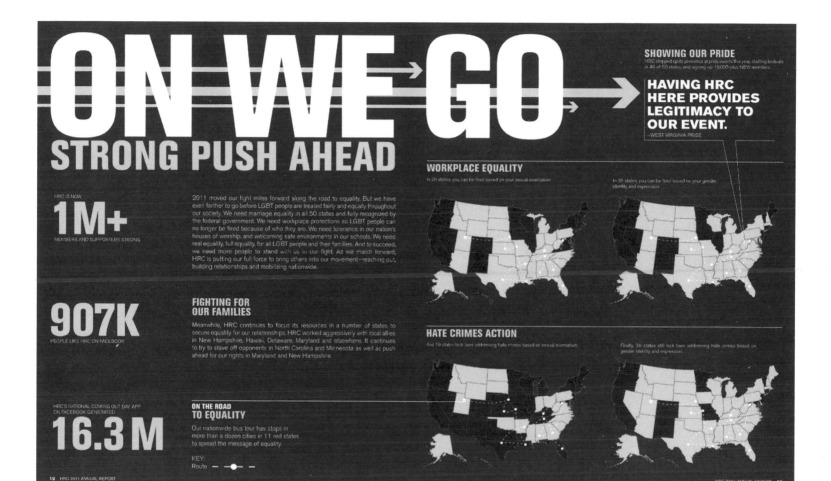

ON WE GO

STRONG PUSH AHEAD

SHOWING OUR PRIDE
HRC stepped up its presence at pride events this year, staffing festivals in 46 of 50 states, and signing up 19,000-plus NEW members.

HAVING HRC HERE PROVIDES LEGITIMACY TO OUR EVENT.
—WEST VIRGINIA PRIDE

HRC IS NOW
1M+
MEMBERS AND SUPPORTERS STRONG

2011 moved our fight miles forward along the road to equality. But we have even farther to go before LGBT people are treated fairly and equally throughout our society. We need marriage equality in all 50 states and fully recognized by the federal government. We need workplace protections so LGBT people can no longer be fired because of who they are. We need tolerance in our nation's houses of worship, and welcoming safe environments in our schools. We need real equality, full equality, for all LGBT people and their families. And to succeed, we need more people to stand with us in our fight. As we march forward, HRC is putting our full force to bring others into our movement—reaching out, building relationships and mobilizing nationwide.

907K
PEOPLE LIKE HRC ON FACEBOOK

FIGHTING FOR OUR FAMILIES
Meanwhile, HRC continues to focus its resources in a number of states to secure equality for our relationships. HRC worked aggressively with local allies in New Hampshire, Hawaii, Delaware, Maryland and elsewhere. It continues to try to stave off opponents in North Carolina and Minnesota as well as push ahead for our rights in Maryland and New Hampshire.

HRC'S NATIONAL COMING OUT DAY APP ON FACEBOOK GENERATED
16.3 M

ON THE ROAD TO EQUALITY
Our nationwide bus tour has stops in more than a dozen cities in 11 red states to spread the message of equality.

KEY:
Route — ● —

WORKPLACE EQUALITY
In 29 states, you can be fired based on your sexual orientation.

In 35 states, you can be fired based on your gender identity and expression.

HATE CRIMES ACTION
And 19 states lack laws addressing hate crimes based on sexual orientation.

Finally, 38 states still lack laws addressing hate crimes based on gender identity and expression.

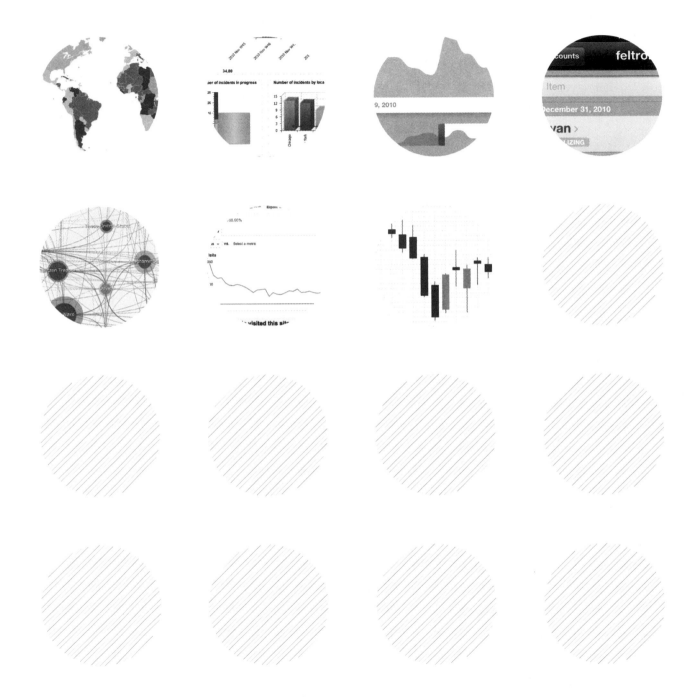

CHAPTER

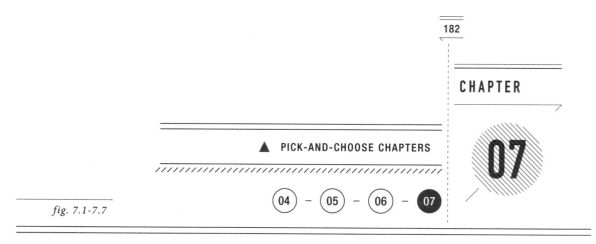

▲ PICK-AND-CHOOSE CHAPTERS

fig. 7.1-7.7

(04) – (05) – (06) – (07)

DATA VISUALIZATION INTERFACES

In previous chapters, we have discussed various applications for creating a visual story with data and information, most of which are based on a narrative approach. In this chapter, we will look at more explorative applications, specifically the use of data visualization in interactive interfaces. Companies and brands can use these types of visualizations in web applications, software, or mobile apps, and the visualizations can be executed in a variety of different ways. These interfaces display data in ways that provide the viewer with information that, with viewer analysis, can be readily transformed into insight.

Dave Campbell, a Technical Fellow at Microsoft who works on solving problems surrounding big data, presented one model of this transformation. We see the evolution from *Signal > Data > Information > Knowledge > Insight* as refinement increases, outlined in Figure 7.1. This process is similar to the DIKW Hierarchy— typically used in a more philosophical context— which presents the key components of *Data > Information > Knowledge > Wisdom.*

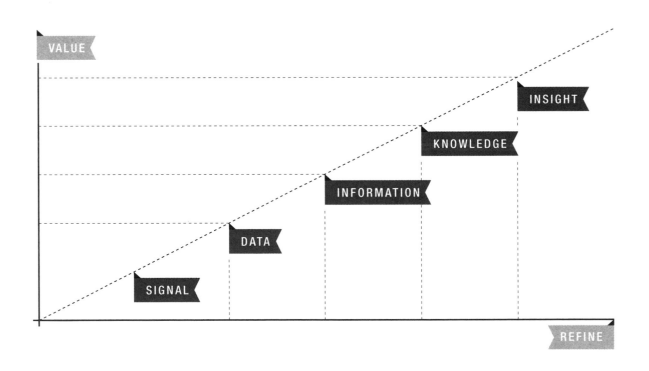

Figure 7.1
Dave Campbell's model of information refinement.

Displaying data in interactive visualizations makes it easier to transform this data into information because it's grouped in meaningful ways that allow viewers to recognize trends, patterns, and correlations, which are also referred to as *phenomena*. Once a viewer recognizes those patterns, he is able to transform that information into knowledge by understanding what it means within its given context. Viewers can then derive insight from this knowledge, which allows them to make inferences and take action.

While this content will never be editorial in nature, it can still vary slightly on the spectrum from narrative to explorative. Businesses commonly use dashboards to exhibit predetermined metrics that they have established as key performance indicators. The fact that the exhibitor will use a selection process to determine what to show the user in advance makes it a moderately narrative experience. Conversely, the experience should be much more explorative when data is displayed as a resource, whether for the sake of transparency or to encourage people to find their own stories and insights.

There are many diverse applications for infographics and data visualization in this area. In this chapter we will talk specifically about two of these: dashboards and what we call visual data hubs.

A CASE FOR VISUALIZATION IN USER INTERFACES

Though many lament the fact, it is undeniable and arguably unavoidable that our daily view of the world increasingly comes through the lens of a computer display. While our visual system is almost incomprehensibly adept at detecting, recognizing, and comprehending objects in the physical world—thanks to millions of years of evolution—our eyes don't have as much experience with the digital world. This is why we must understand the capacities of our visual system and create digital interfaces that best serve it. Developing a strong synergy between our cognitive systems and our technology's increasing computational capabilities will only lead to enhanced communication and substantial increases in productivity.

One of the major opportunities to enhance our cognition as it pertains to the human-computer relationship is in the use of images. We know from Chapter 1 (Importance and Efficacy) that the mind is able to instantly detect and recognize a visual image with which it is familiar, bringing with it a host of associated experiences. Common imagery in a user interface allows viewers to navigate through programs quickly, by prompting them to recall what the imagery represents and where it will take them (Ware, p. 228). This is a strong argument for using more iconography in interface design; it enables quicker recognition of navigation systems while simultaneously enhancing aesthetic appeal. The introduction of illustration can benefit interfaces that visualize data as well as those that don't.

DASHBOARDS

Dashboarding is an area that has been using information design to communicate key business metrics for decades. In terms of purpose, these interfaces have embodied many of the best practices surrounding visual communication. Yet their aesthetic and creative value is often lacking (Figure 7.2). This is an area of great opportunity in business communication; while well intentioned, the dashboard's traditional format and appearance could benefit from a bit of a makeover.

It's easy to see that traditional dashboard inclusions are designed to make analysis incredibly simple for the viewer. They reduce an entire organization's worth of data to a few line charts, fuel gauges, and traffic-light-style color coding. Each business is unique, and as with all design, dashboards should cater to the information they display. Since companies now track more of the data that will inform their decisions, it is appropriate that they begin to think of new ways to display them. Creative and innovative use of infographics has made it possible to display more data in less space, thus providing viewers with greater insight in the same amount of time.

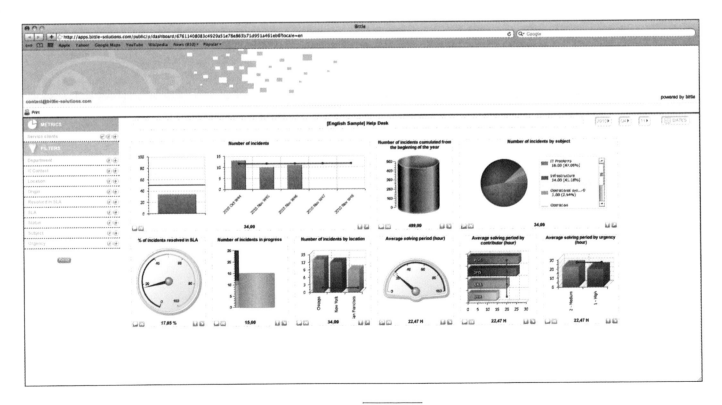

Figure 7.2
Example of traditional dashboard design.

Individuals and organizations can apply infographic thinking in a few different areas to improve the way that they report data, regardless of the audience. One example might be analytics programs or tools that service-based companies use to report their performance to clients. These applications are usually designed to give a clear picture of the information reported, enhance insights, and inform future decision making. To do this, take cues from the narrative approach we have discussed in previous chapters. The display should not only present the information, but also facilitate a deeper dive into the information to find the source of a problem. The following are key areas to consider when crafting this narrative while designing such a dashboard.

1. *Sequence*

   The order in which you present the content is essential to telling the story clearly and logically. Showing causal relationships in this way helps increase understanding and speed of comprehension.

2. *Hierarchy*

   Consider the most important information for the viewer to see, and weight it accordingly. Draw attention to important areas by allocating them more space and using color and type to distinguish their content.

3. *Context*

   In dashboards, as well as other infographic applications, words are not the enemy. Use language to help guide viewers through the experience and ensure that they are given a full understanding of what they are looking at, and how it relates to other elements on display. Even when parts may seem self-explanatory, introductions to each section are a good opportunity to explain specific metrics' nuances and implications.

Dashboards also need to adapt to the changing world of data. Organizations should consider new formats to accommodate the growth of information and how users interact with it. The average person is becoming more data literate—that is, they are more comfortable sorting through increasing amounts of information to gain the insights they need. This calls for a greater flexibility of display options. Gone are the days when a red, yellow, or green light alone should guide our insights. We need more granularity; people will understand information as long as it's displayed clearly.

A great example of this flexibility is Google Analytics' user interface (Figure 7.3). Their web-based analytics software is an intuitive platform that allows users to see a high-level summary of their traffic, with granular data that can be drilled into to highlight the sources, demographics, and geography, among others. This provides great insight into the key metrics of a website, enabling users to make important decisions about the type of content they produce, and the demographics they target. Various date ranges can be selected to give users an ability to see a great amount of detail within a simple interface. While Google Analytics is not a dashboard in the traditional sense, this functionality lends itself well to the application.

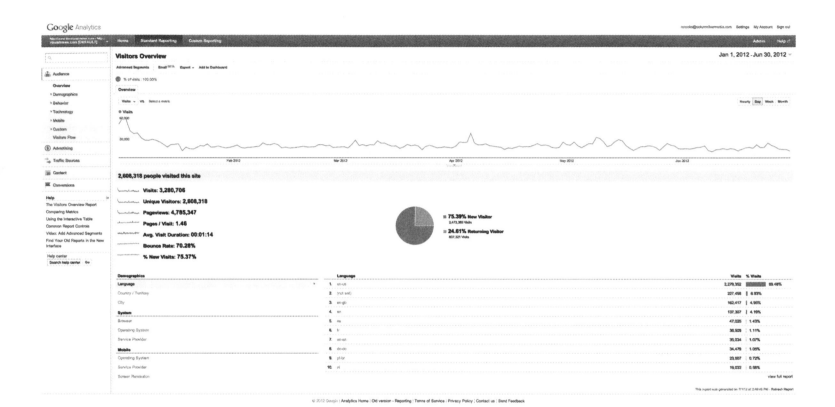

Figure 7.3

Google Analytics user interface.

VISUAL DATA HUBS

Another key application that has become more prevalent in recent years is using data visualization in interactive interfaces that allow users to explore data. This is typically most valuable for companies seeking to display their proprietary data—either for individuals or for the media—and to earn branding value from such exposure. Creating a hub with the data, and enabling user exploration and analysis, can be very beneficial to both the brand and the viewer who can use it as a resource. As it relates to the interactive formats described in Chapter 2 (Infographic Formats), these would typically be updated monthly or annually with the most recent data.

The visualization of user-selected data, which aids in identifying insight, further amplifies this benefit. These hubs should be designed to be inherently *explorative*; they should encourage users to draw their own insights from their findings, without prescription. However, this approach should not be limiting. There is also great opportunity to implement a narrative on top of the explorative data, drawing user attention to points of note. Many businesses could take cues from the *New York Times*, which does an excellent job of maintaining this balance in the publishing world. Providing a complete data set to explore in various ways, while also highlighting key factors that may have had an impact on that data can be a very strong approach.

Brands can implement this type of interface for various objectives. The first is to provide a resource for users that allows them to pull information from the hub and use it to inform their decisions relating to a specific subject. Liveplasma.com, a visual discovery engine for music, movies, and books, is one such example. Visitors simply type in the name of an artist, movie, or book title, and the site generates a network map visualization that offers related media suited to their taste (Figure 7.4). For example, a visualization for a music selection allows you to see artists with a similar musical style, whose circle size in the graphic represents their relative popularity.

Depending on the data you have, this can be a valuable resource, a fun tool, or an attention-getter for your business. Such an interactive visualization could be a central part of your product, a supplementary marketing tool to attract new customers, or some combination of both. Either way, if you have interesting data, you should provide them to users for their exploration. An interface that visually represents such data can be enticing, entertaining, and ultimately useful for your users.

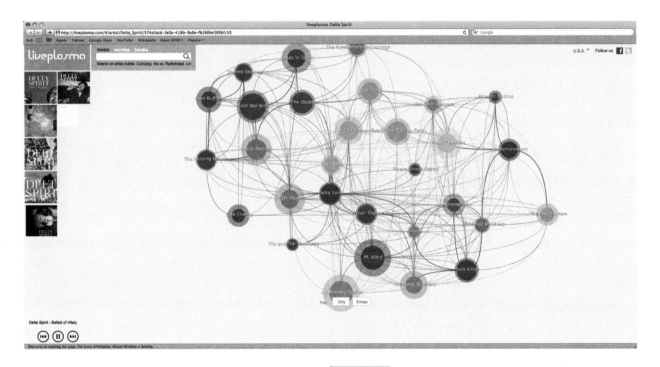

Figure 7.4
Liveplasma.com interactive interface.

These visual data hubs can also be great for getting media attention for your business. In fact, many are built just for that purpose. Providing a resource for journalists to find topics for new stories is a quick way for your company to be mentioned in articles and thought of as a key future source of news insights.

A great example of this is a project Column Five built for the Heritage Foundation, in partnership with the *Wall Street Journal*, that showcases their Index of Economic Freedom (www.heritage.org/index). This index is the organization's best-known and most important research, so they were looking to bring attention to it by allowing users to cross-analyze the data in many different ways. We wanted to provide users with a rich exploration experience that went beyond just charting the data, to enable them to compare countries' relative economic indices.

As such, one of our key additions was a heat map that enabled users to see geographical trends and isolate specific regions to get a greater level of detail (Figure 7.5). To allow wider accessibility on mobile devices and to create a responsive user experience, we used the D3 JavaScript library and SVG format, as described in Chapter 2 (Infographic Formats) for the world map, which the user could essentially zoom into when viewing specific regions. This kept users from having to load a new map image of each region each time they made a new selection. Using SVG made it faster to display an overview of information, into which anyone can drill deeper to find specific and potentially newsworthy figures.

In recent years, we have seen a marked increase in the number of sites that use interesting information design in their interfaces. We believe that this trend will grow dramatically in the future, thereby giving brands incredible opportunities to provide users with increasingly rich, interactive, data-driven experiences that will encourage greater engagement, entertainment, and ultimately insight. Dashboards and visual data hubs introduce a strong basis for thinking about these opportunities, and we will continue to see the evolution of innovative integration in these areas. Dashboards will improve as increased attention is paid to crafting the story they are telling, aided by the adoption of greater flexibility and variety of data displays. By contrast, visual data hubs are a more amorphous application, and as more companies seek to showcase their data in the coming years, and provide incredible value to both individuals and media in the process, they will manifest themselves in new and interesting ways.

However, the applications certainly don't stop there. Nicolas Felton's Daytum iPhone app brings data visualization to the quantifiable-self movement, and enables users to track and create infographics from the data recorded throughout their everyday lives (Figure 7.6). Online brokerage firm TD Ameritrade is using data visualization in their Trade Architect tool, which gives users an interactive dashboard to track stock market trends along with their own investment portfolios (Figure 7.7). These are just two examples of infographic use in user interface design. Countless more are springing up by the day as companies realize the benefits of information visualization.

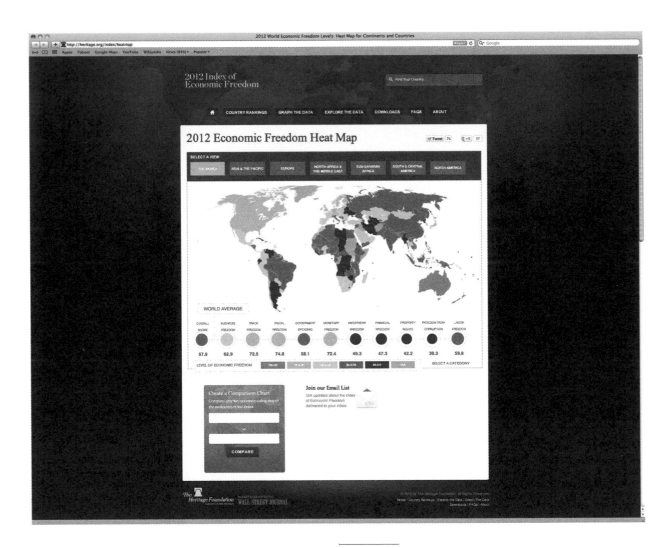

Figure 7.5
Economic Freedom Heat Map.
Column Five for The Heritage Foundation.

Figure 7.6
Daytum iPhone app.

Figure 7.7
TD Ameritrade's Trade Architect tool.

We will likely see a notable shift from prescriptive data presentation toward more explorative experiences that put the user in the driver's seat. Narrative presentation certainly has—and will continue to offer—incredible value in certain applications, specifically those that allow companies to drive a very specific message home. However, the growth and increased openness of the data landscape necessitates a more open display than has ever been imagined before. This is not to say that these approaches are mutually exclusive. We also see great opportunity in implementing a hybrid approach. That is, providing the underlying data for the viewer to explore, while calling out areas of interest.

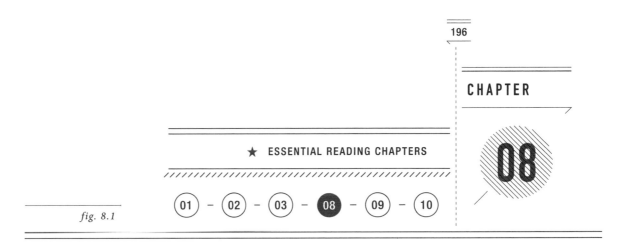

CHAPTER

★ ESSENTIAL READING CHAPTERS

fig. 8.1

(01) – (02) – (03) – **(08)** – (09) – (10)

08

WHAT MAKES A GOOD INFOGRAPHIC?

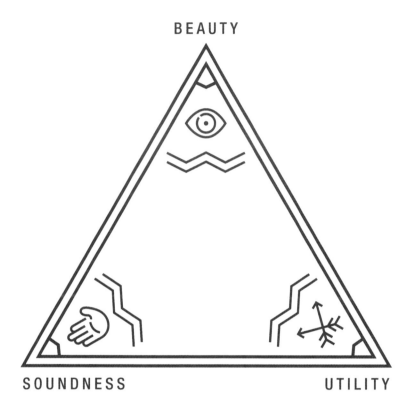

Figure 8.1
Vitruvian Principles.

In order to answer this question, we must apply a critical framework through which we can understand and measure quality. When you look at a good infographic, everything about it makes sense. A good infographic, to borrow again from Horace's thoughts on the role of a poet, leaves you feeling informed or delighted.

In Chapter 1 (Importance and Efficacy), we discussed the value of infographics as visual solutions to communication problems. Vitruvius' principles of good design serve as three components by which we attempt to measure quality of these solutions (Figure 8.1). A good infographic has all three:

- *Utility*
- *Soundness*
- *Beauty*

UTILITY

With respect to utility, infographics must employ an objectives-based approach. Essentially, the utility of an infographic is measured by how it enables a brand to reach its objectives.

We established in Chapter 1 (Importance and Efficacy) that all infographics communicate information. And, there are two approaches to communicating: explorative and narrative. Therefore, to measure the quality you must consider the approach.

To recap, explorative infographics provide information in an unbiased fashion, enabling viewers to analyze it and arrive at their own conclusions. This approach is best used for scientific and academic applications, in which comprehension of collected research or insights is a priority. Narrative infographics guide the viewers through a specific set of information that tells a predetermined story. This approach is best used when there is a need to leave readers with a specific message to take away, and should focus on audience appeal and information retention.

It is important to think about these two approaches in a non-hierarchical way. Each is unique, and their effectiveness is ultimately judged by how well they enable a brand to reach its communication objectives, regardless of how readers interact with the information.

SOUNDNESS

Good infographics also communicate something meaningful. Communicating a message worth telling provides readers with something of value. While infographics can be a powerful vehicle of communication, they are sometimes produced arbitrarily or when a cohesive and interesting story isn't present. If the information itself is incomplete, untrustworthy, or uninteresting, attempting to create a good infographic with it is more than a fool's errand; it's impossible.

We discussed the common mistakes found in infographics with Cliff Kuang. He receives hundreds of pitches each day from people wanting their infographics featured in his "Infographic of the Day" column, often from brands, agencies, and designers that are trying to generate press for themselves. Kuang said the most frequent mistake these individuals make is that their subject matter is not interesting. According to Kuang, "Infographic producers (from brands to designers) tend to confuse the amount of time they put into researching, copywriting, and designing an infographic with the level of willingness that an audience has to read the content." In short, if no one cares what the infographic is communicating, then how can it be good?

In Chapter 4 (Editorial Infographics), we briefly discussed some of the questions we ask ourselves during our ideation process, specifically relating to editorial content. While not every infographic is or should be editorial in nature, these questions are helpful in determining the types of infographic ideas that lead to good infographics. Infographic content should relate to its intended audience, whether it is a broad or targeted one. Therefore an infographic that is sound is one that has meaning and integrity.

BEAUTY

While the information is of the utmost importance when it comes to soundness, what is done with the information—essentially, how it is designed—is also important. With this in mind, there are two things to consider: format and design quality. If an inappropriate format is used, the outcome will be inferior. Similarly, if the design misrepresents or skews the information deliberately or due to user error, or if the design is inappropriate given the subject matter, it cannot be considered high quality, no matter how aesthetically appealing it appears at first glance.

An infographic's design should be prescribed, with regards to appropriateness and effectiveness, by the objectives and the information being displayed, not individual preferences. The design is the application of a visual solution to the problem; it is representative of the approach as a whole, rather than individual elements (e.g., an illustration or icon). According to Moritz Stefaner, "information visualization and information graphics work best when they take the recipient and the data seriously." This advice reflects the old adage that form should follow function.

This is why we must contextualize our perception of beauty. Some people like illustrations of monkeys or pirates alongside their charts and graphs; others consider anything other than black, left-aligned Helvetica Medium on white to be "noisy." Both of these solutions can be effective and be considered good given the proper context. Picking the right visual solution may require you to use intense illustration or data visualization, or both. It's all about finding the right visual representations of the information, based on the story.

Because an infographic's design also takes your specific objectives, the information, and the audience into account, there are endless possibilities for how beauty can be manifested. In the following chapter, we will discuss two main visual elements used in infographic design—illustration and data visualization—and explain our approach to each.

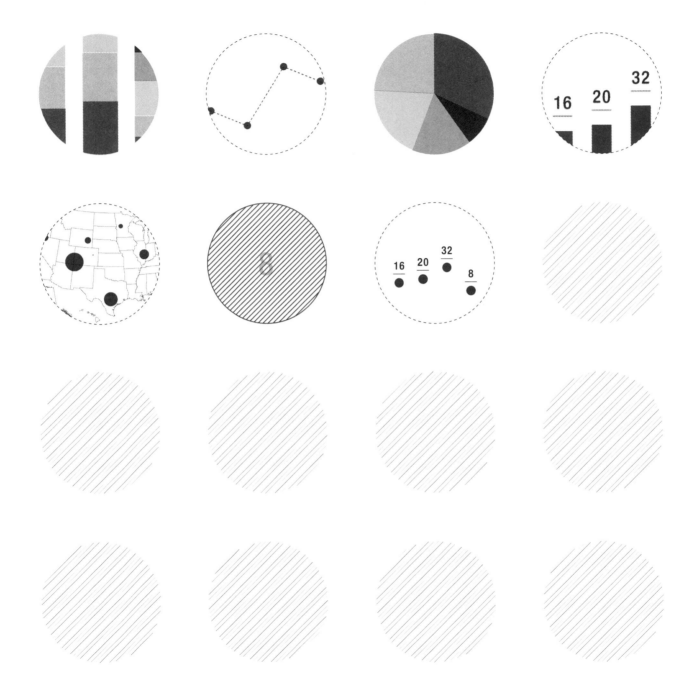

CHAPTER

★ ESSENTIAL READING CHAPTERS

fig. 9.1-9.23

(01) – (02) – (03) – (08) – ● 09 – (10)

INFORMATION DESIGN BEST PRACTICES

In the previous chapter, we discussed what makes a good info-graphic. Now we will discuss the best ways to design your information. Illustration and data visualization are the two major components of infographic design. Based on your objectives, you will use one or both to varying degrees.

Broadly speaking, narrative infographics tend to use more illustrative design, while explorative infographics need to represent an unbiased view of the data, and thus have little use for illustration. We've found that most people want to create infographics with an approach that takes a nod from both types. As with anything design related, it's all about finding a balance.

ILLUSTRATION

Chapter 1 (Importance and Efficacy) introduced the tools that we use to make infographic content visually interesting. As we know, we can only measure the quality of these visual elements—or *illustration* (iconography, framing, visual metaphor, and illustration)—when we're using them. In other words, an absence of representative iconography does not necessarily mean that we're missing the mark. We should also assume that we only use them when the message and objectives dictate or allow them to be included. And it's the designer's (or brand's) responsibility to figure this out. Effectively, the appropriateness of illustrative design elements will vary based on the information and the audience.

Using illustration in infographics is the source of much heated debate among academics, designers, and other experts. We don't have a hard-and-fast rule about illustration use—how much, what style, and the like—beyond the notion that its use, the degree to which it is used, and its style all ought to be dictated by the message and its objectives. That said, these debates typically have two aspects that tend to get mixed up:

- Is illustration *appropriate* for use in an infographic?
- Are the illustrative design elements used in a specific infographic of *good quality*?

Of course, if your objectives do not require you to use any illustrative design elements, then you needn't use them. Based on your individual project or situation, the best practice might be to avoid them altogether. And that is a perfectly acceptable approach. If your objectives call or allow for them, then the same rules or best practices that apply to our measure of quality for design in a broader sense—utility, soundness, attractiveness—should apply to the individual visual elements.

IT'S ALL ABOUT THE INFORMATION!

The information is the most important part of the infographic. You must consider the use of any illustration with this in mind. Mastering execution and finding the balance between appeal and clarity is in itself an art. This section is not about framing techniques or iconography design per se. The best way to think about the use of illustration is in what role its addition plays in the quality of the design.

We recently conducted an interview with Robin Richards, a respected designer in our industry, in which we discussed the role that illustration should play. Richards's perspective is as follows:

"[Illustration] can help showcase and bring things to life, but there's a fine line between [this and] it becoming distracting. It should be more of a supporting than a leading role. If the designer isn't careful, what he's designing can become purely an illustration, rather than an infographic. You want the illustration to support the story that the data is telling, rather than detract from it."

We should be clear: these principles that we discuss are not meant to curtail creativity, or restrict designers. We do, however, believe that infographic design should be afforded the same type of critical framework that a serious practitioner from any field would appreciate. And we're convinced that helping to establish this critical framework will lead to improvement within a field that currently tends to have one foot in academia and one in the world of online marketing in a very fragmented manner.

WHEN ILLUSTRATION CAN BE HARMFUL

If not used properly, illustration design can and will be harmful to this message. For example, illustration can distract and would not be appropriate for an explorative infographic, because people will spend time looking at the visuals while trying to determine what the message is. As we've mentioned, the sequence should always be information first, design second. However, the message in a narrative infographic has already been established. Therefore, this is a case where good illustration is capable of playing that supporting role we referenced earlier.

Illustration can also be harmful if it misleads people when used improperly, not because illustration is innately misleading. The most common mistake we encounter is the accidental distortion of the data's display. We also frequently see people who use illustration to hide the fact that their message is either incomplete or meaningless. That said, illustration can help to inform and delight. Good illustration can be very powerful, and can create value for readers, and help move the story along. According to Kuang, "Good illustrators are good at staying on the side of enticement and not trickery. Once you get into trickery, you betray someone's trust."

DON'T CONFUSE APPROPRIATENESS WITH QUALITY

At Column Five, we love good illustration. In fact, many of our designers have backgrounds as illustrators, and we do plenty of more traditional studio work that is purely graphic design and illustration. Illustration can be extremely effective when helping to tell a story. It just has to be done correctly, when the situation calls for it, and in a way that makes sense. Based on the determinants of one's objectives—audience and content—there are two things to keep in mind:

1. *Audience appropriateness*
   Who you are talking to will have an impact on your decision to use illustration or to not. We've used the example of the bullion, and the shareholders, so this should make sense at this point.
2. *Content appropriateness*
   We've also mentioned that editorial content tends to be more illustrative, and depending on the brand, many brand-centric applications can use illustration without inherent issues—including "About Us" pages and product instructions.

   We also see instances in which illustration is used in poor taste. There are no shortages of infographics online that deal with morbid or serious information but almost seem to make light of the subject matter through illustration. Subject matter such as starvation, HIV/AIDS, or extreme poverty require a certain level of sensitivity, and these are situations in which illustration can sometimes do more harm than good. And that's not to say that illustration should never be used to facilitate understanding of a serious subject magger, but rather that discretion should always be employed.

DATA

When we asked *Visualize This* author Nathan Yau what makes a great infographic—as we'd done with so many others—his response was, "Good data and a designer that understands it. You can always tell when someone doesn't really know much about what they're displaying, and if you don't understand, then how are you supposed to explain anything to your readers?" Essentially, you must always know what you are saying before you try to say it.

DEALING WITH DATA

So, before we get into designing with data, we need to discuss what data types and relationships we encode with charts and graphs. Keep in mind that we didn't write this section with the intention of creating the definitive set of best practices for designing with data. There are already a number of books that address this. Stephen Few's *Show Me the Numbers: Designing Tables and Graphs to Enlighten* and Dona Wong's *The Wall Street Journal Guide to Information Graphics* are two great books that cover this subject matter quite well. To clarify, this section is meant to be but a primer, and a chance for you to learn a thing or two about some of the most common mistakes that you probably see on a daily basis—without even realizing it. And ideally, you'll be able to implement these practices when it comes to your own design.

DATA TYPES

Most people recognize about seven types of quantitative data, but in order to keep this chapter succinct, as well as address our primary aims, we'll only discuss two of them: *discrete* and *continuous*, which we find to be among the most commonly used data types:

- Discrete
- Categorical
- Nominal
- Ordinal
- Interval
- Continuous

Discrete—A set of data is said to be *discrete* if the values within it are distinct and separate; that is, they can be counted (1, 2, 3, . . .). Examples might include the number of kittens in a litter, the number of patients in a doctor's office, the number of flaws in one meter of cloth, gender (male, female), or blood group (O, A, B, AB).

Continuous—A set of data is said to be *continuous* if the values belonging to it may take on any value within a finite or infinite interval (read: exist in any range; e.g., 1.2, 1.21, 1.21211112, etc.). You can count, order, and measure continuous data; for example, height, weight, temperature, or the time required to run a mile.

One way to determine whether your data is discrete or continuous is to ask yourself if it is possible for the data to take on values that are fractions or decimals. If so, then, my friend, you're most likely dealing with continuous data. It's important to understand these differences, because they will play a role in how you decide to graph your data.

GRAPHING RELATIONSHIPS

Next, let's look at how we encode (design with) the data through charts and graphs (which we'll collectively refer to as "graphs"). Graphs are a representation of the relationships in quantitative information. The shape the information should take—or the graph type that you should use—is thus based on the type of relationship. As such, different types of graphs can display some types of relationships better than others. Therefore, the first step in conveying any quantitative information through graphs is identifying the relationship type. This will help provide structure to your approach, as well as help rule out inappropriate graph types.

In the book *Show Me the Numbers: Designing Tables and Graphs to Enlighten*, author Stephen Few lays out seven types of relationships that that are most commonly graphed (Few, p. 66). Because this chapter is only meant to serve as a primer, we will only address what we believe are the four most common relationships that people tend to visualize in infographics, from the following:

- Nominal comparison
- Time series
- Ranking
- Part-to-whole
- Deviation
- Distribution
- Correlation

Nominal Comparisons

This is the most basic relationship to understand. Nominal comparisons represent a nominal scale; their function is to display several subcategories' quantitative values so that they can be easily compared to each other. An example of the type of message that ought to be conveyed through this type of comparison is that the value of *X* is larger than that of *Y*, or that the value of *B* is twice as large as the value of *C*.

Quantitative values in a nominal comparison graph are represented by categorical subdivisions (eg. *B* or *C*) are independent of one another. They should therefore be designed in such a way that communicates the uniqueness of each value. Bar graphs work really well for this type of relationship—especially if the scale is large and you want to highlight the differences between the values. You can also shorten the range and replace bars with simple data points, known as a dot plot.

Time Series

A time series relationship consists of a number of relationships between categorical quantitative values that are distributed across divisions of time. Time series graphs are used to show trends, or how values change over time. They take a single measure for each line and plot change (positive and negative) in its quantitative value over time. These are the most popular types of graphs used in business.

These kind of graphs should always have time measurements along the x-axis (from left to right), with quantitative values plotted along the y-axis. The most commonly used graphs to show time series relationships are lines (with continuous data) and vertical bars (with discrete data). Dot plots can also be used, as well as a dot plot with lines connecting the various points.

You'll want to avoid horizontal bar charts. We typically represent time as something that moves from left to right, rather than top-down.

Ranking

Graphic ranking relationships are all about communicating the ordering—from highest to lowest, or vice versa—of quantitative values of a set of subcategories.

If the goal is to show ranking, then you want to use a graph type that brings attention to the quantitative values of each subcategory. Bar graphs (vertical and horizontal) are extremely useful for visualizing ranking relationships; the ordering of categorical subdivisions should be selected according to the purpose of highlighting the highest values (descending order) or the lowest values (ascending order). Dot plots can also be used, if narrowing the quantitative scale aids in the display of the ranking relationship.

Part-to-Whole

The goal in graphing a parts-to-whole relationship is to show how a set of categorical subdivisions' quantitative values relate to one another as parts of a whole. By displaying a ratio, a part-to-whole graph uses percentages as the unit of measure. When graphing part-to-whole relationships, the sum of all individual quantitative values must always add up to 100 percent. A common example of when part-to-whole relationships can be used is when people want to show budget breakdowns; essentially what percentage of a budget is used for what.

Pie charts are the most common graph types used for part-to-whole relationships; however, they have their limitations. You want to avoid using a pie chart if you have more than a handful of categorical subdivisions. A stacked bar chart is also a good option; this is especially true if you would like readers to be able to compare the composition of two separate stacked bars, with the same categorical subdivisions. For example, if you wanted to show the favorite colors of students from three separate classrooms. Bar (horizontal and vertical) graphs and dot plots can be useful as well, but both are less popular than those previously mentioned for this type of relationship.

VISUALIZATION

Now, on to the fun stuff. This section will discuss the common graph types, reiterate what they're best used for, and explain how to use them effectively. Based on your newfound knowledge of data, you should be able to figure out what type of graph is right for you. When it comes to infographic design, the goal of any designer, according to Nathan Yau, is to establish "clarity from complexity." You can almost always determine the appropriate graph type based on the relationship type, but in most cases there are a number of acceptable options. Figuring out which graph makes the most sense to you is sometimes about what you think is the best (read: most effective) way to convey your message to your audience. And sometimes it's only after graphing the data in several different ways does the best option become obvious.

In this section we will discuss the proper use and best practices for what we see as the most commonly used and misused graph types:

- Dot plot
- Line chart
- Vertical bar graph
- Horizontal bar graph
- Stacked bar graph
- Pie chart
- Bubble chart

Dot Plot

As discussed, you can use dot plots to show nominal comparisons (Figure 9.1), time series (Figure 9.2), ranking (Figure 9.3), and part-to-whole relationships (Figure 9.4). Dot plots can be used with either discrete or continuous data. They essentially consist of a set of dots plotted along an x-axis according to qualitative values (e.g., subcategories), and vertically on the y-axis according to quantitative value. Dot plots are most commonly used to show time series relationships, with the various points along the x axis representing sequential points in time. In this case, the y-axis could be thought of as the "value axis" and the x-axis could be referred to as the "time axis." Trends can be identified based on a change in height of dot placement along the x-axis.

When using dot plots to show a time series relationship, the scale does not have to start at a zero baseline. For the other relationships they do, however. For a time series relationship, the scale can be truncated if there is a story worth telling in the data that would otherwise be obscured by using a very large scale. However, you should use discretion when attempting to do this; a good rule of thumb is to use a scale in which the range of the dot plots consists of two-thirds of the graph's total height, in order to display data trends more clearly. Additionally, if your goal is to show a time series relationship with continual data, you can throw a line on it, connecting the points (Figure 9.5). Essentially, you can use a series of straight lines between the points, which will help guide the reader's eyes from left to right.

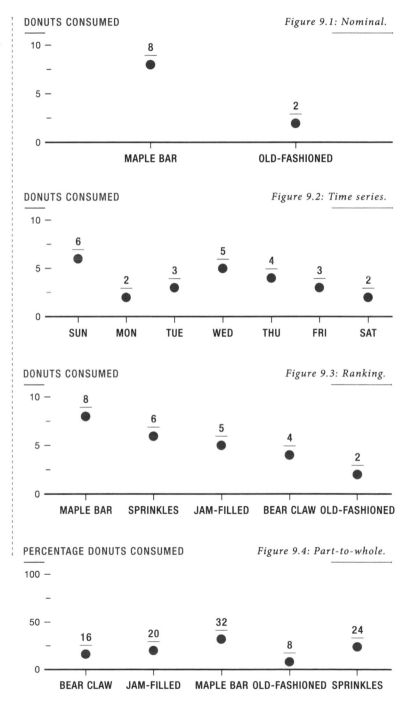

Figure 9.1: Nominal.

Figure 9.2: Time series.

Figure 9.3: Ranking.

Figure 9.4: Part-to-whole.

Line Chart

We use line charts to show time series relationships with continuous data (Figure 9.6). As could probably be imagined, your line
chart could have the dots at specified intervals (days, months,
years, etc.) or it can omit them. With line graphs, the *x*-axis
should always represent time, while the *y*-axis should represent
a quantitative value that changes over time. Line charts are very
handy because they allow users to identify specific values at
various points in time, as well as to identify trends, such as when
and how much a value is changing. Charting multiple values on
the same graph allows readers to further identify the relationship between categories; for instance, an increase in one variable
and a decrease in another, or even an increase or decrease across
all variables.

As with dot plots, the scale on line charts has a lot to do
with how the message is conveyed. For example, using too large
a scale runs the risk that viewers may gloss over a very important story in the data. However, using too small a scale might
lead you to overemphasize minor fluctuations. As with dot plots,
designers should plot all of the data points so that the line chart
takes up two-thirds of the *y*-axis's total scale.

Most people would argue that line charts are very easy to
understand, and should be kept that way. Showing too many
lines on one chart can tend to look too busy; therefore, it is best
to keep the chart to four or fewer clearly labeled lines. If you
need to show more than four categories, you can use the practice
of paneling (Figure 9.7) and a constant scale for consistency.

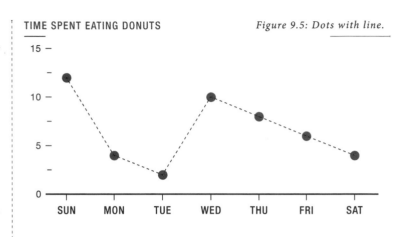

TIME SPENT EATING DONUTS   *Figure 9.5: Dots with line.*

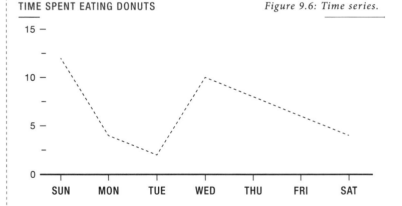

TIME SPENT EATING DONUTS   *Figure 9.6: Time series.*

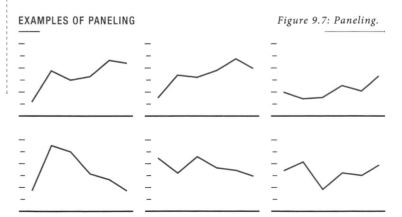

EXAMPLES OF PANELING   *Figure 9.7: Paneling.*

Bar Graph (Vertical)

Bar graphs are the most straightforward and versatile of all graph types. You can use them to display nominal comparison (Figure 9.8), time series (Figure 9.9), ranking (Figure 9.10), and part-to-whole relationships (Figure 9.11). Bar graphs can use discrete or continuous data, and there's really not a lot that you can't do with them. Similar to line charts, vertical bars have qualitative values listed on the *x*-axis and quantitative values on the *y*-axis. They can also be rotated 90 degrees for horizontal placement (more below), upon which the axes' value types would be swapped.

The value of a bar graph is that it makes it easy for the reader to understand what is going on. You should resist all urges to overcomplicate things. The first rule about bar graphs is that they must always have a zero baseline. This is because we use the length of the bars to compare them against each other, and if we truncate the scale, the story becomes distorted.

According to Dona Wong, the perfect distance between two bars in a graph is half the width of one of the bars (Wong, p. 63). Typically each bar within a graph should be the same color, and you should avoid any intense patterns if it distracts from understanding the visualization.

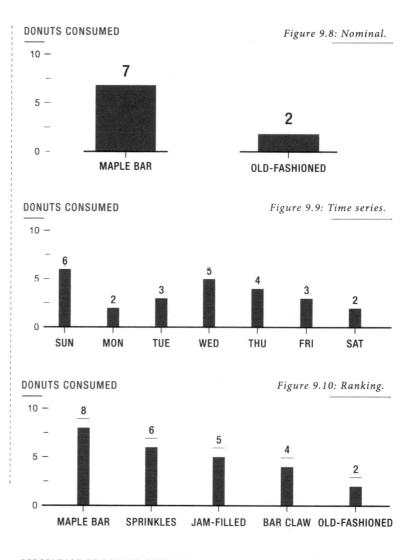

Figure 9.8: Nominal.

Figure 9.9: Time series.

Figure 9.10: Ranking.

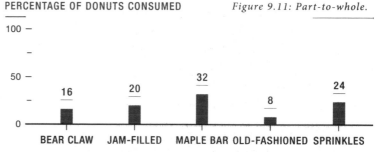

Figure 9.11: Part-to-whole.

Bar Graph (Horizontal)

All of the rules that apply to vertical bar graphs essentially apply to horizontal bars (Figure 9.12). One limitation of horizontal bars, however, is that they are not good for showing time series relationships. While they could theoretically be used for this, it's not recommended because we are accustomed to reading about time from left to right (at least in the West).

As with vertical bars, ordering is often important, especially if you are showing a ranking relationship (Figure 9.13). It is very helpful to the reader to create a hierarchy that highlights either the lowest- or highest-value subcategories at the top. Alphabetical ordering is the other acceptable method (Figure 9.14). One urge that designers should resist is to place grid lines along the *x*-axis, because it can overcomplicate the visual. But the biggest horizontal bar chart *faux pas* of all is to use leftward horizontal bars when the values are actually positive. The *x*-axis starts at zero in horizontal bar charts; thus any bar to the left of that baseline might be viewed as having a negative value. This mistake is very common among web-based infographics, and it tells the opposite story than what is actually found in the data.

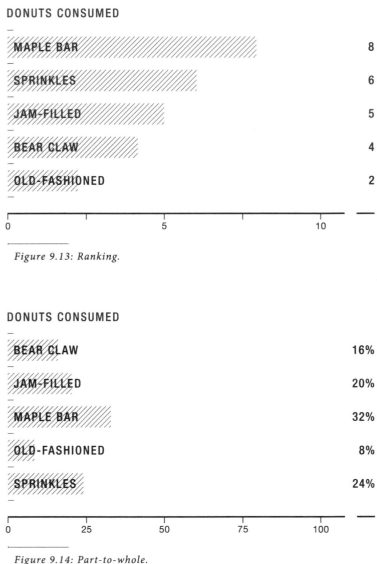

Figure 9.13: Ranking.

Figure 9.14: Part-to-whole.

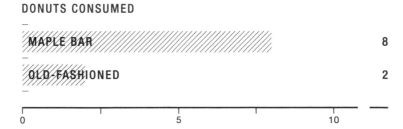

Figure 9.12: Nominal.

Stacked Bar Graph

Stacked bars are most often used when there is a need to display multiple part-to-whole relationships. Stacked bars use discrete or continuous data, and can be oriented either vertically or horizontally. While the aggregate of each bar can be used to make nominal or ranking comparisons, this graph type is used when the composition of each bar tells an interesting story that provides the viewer with greater insight (Figure 9.15).

One variation of the stacked bar is known as the 100 percent stacked bar, of which all of the subcategories add up to 100 percent (as is the case with the pie chart), therefore removing this nominal comparison between bars. Instead, this allows the viewer to focus on the comparative composition of each bar without the distraction of relative scale. With 100 percent stacked bars, the size of each segment represents a percentage of the total bar and is typically labeled accordingly. One hundred percent stacked bars are typically used when there is a need to show a time series relationship as well, (e.g., how one's donut consumption compares to that of his friends) (Figure 9.16). Most would argue that this type of visualization is easier to understand than multiple pie charts as it enables the viewer to directly compare segments on the same axis with relative ease.

Both types of stacked bars can be used with only a single bar, similar to how a single pie chart can be used (Figure 9.17). They are most useful when (as was mentioned before) there are more than a handful of subcategories that make up the part-to-whole relationship, and using a pie chart won't simply won't cut it. From a design perspective, they are much easier to label, as their orientation is linear, not circular. Since the area of each segment represents a percentage of the whole, it is acceptable to label each segment as a percentage, a quantitative value, or both. In determining what is best, you should consider which label is more interesting and provides greater context to the viewer.

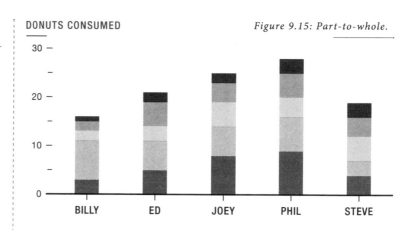

Figure 9.15: Part-to-whole.

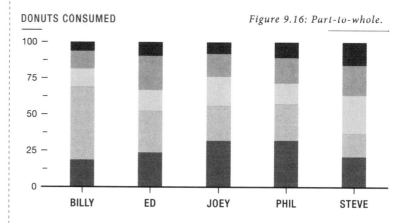

Figure 9.16: Part-to-whole.

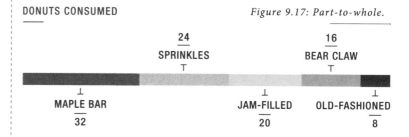

Figure 9.17: Part-to-whole.

Pie Charts

As previously discussed, we use pie charts for making part-to-whole comparisons with discrete or continuous data (Figure 9.18). While many people ardently oppose the use of pie charts in general, we believe they can serve a purpose. And since they are so widely used—and convey relationships between data so intuitively—we decided that we'd better explain how to use them properly.

The real value of pie charts is their usefulness in communicating big ideas quickly. However, they're not very useful in comparing the values of the subcategories between pies (as stacked bars can be), or showing the changing makeup of a part-to-whole relationship over time. This is because it's hard to compare the sizes of multiple pie "slices" (essentially the angles of their points next to each other) in the same pie or across multiple pies.

There are several rules to consider when using pie charts, the most important of which is that the sum of all the subcategories' quantitative values must always equal 100 percent—no exceptions. And as we've previously stated, you should really only use pie charts when you have a handful of subcategories (the jury is still out on whether or not seven is acceptable). Allowing any more than five slices can make it troublesome for readers to fully grasp what is going on with the data. If you have about 10 or more subcategories, simply use another graph, such as bars or stacked bars, to avoid confusing the reader.

When arranging the parts of the pie chart, the largest section should always start at the top, and go clockwise from 12 o'clock. Similarly, the second largest section should always start at the top and go counterclockwise from 12 o'clock. Any additional sections should be placed down below. The logic behind this is that readers read top down, and will therefore read the most important subcategories (arguably the largest) first.

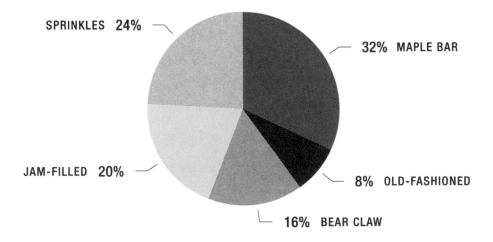

Figure 9.18: Part-to-whole.

Bubble Charts

Bubble charts are a type of area chart that use discrete or continuous data and can be used to display nominal (Figure 9.19) and ranking (Figure 9.20) relationships. You would seldom use them to show only a time series or part-to-whole relationship. Bubble charts can be used to compare subcategories' values, in either side-by-side comparisons, or in more elaborate graph types such as bubble plots (when showing ranking and time series) and bubble maps (if geography was germane to the story being told) (Figure 9.21 and 9.22). They are most valuable when the range of data set is large, and there is a good amount of variance between the smallest and the largest subcategories. They can also be useful when using bar charts simply looks awkward.

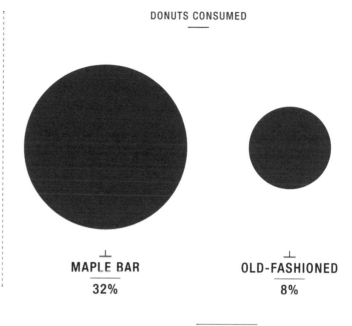

Figure 9.19
Nominal.

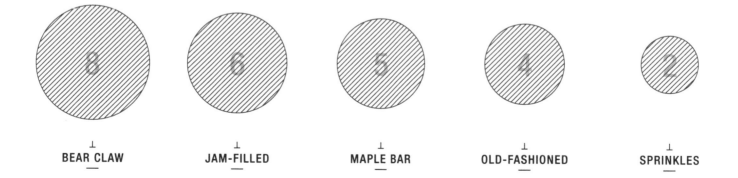

Figure 9.20
Ranking.

Bubble charts are botched quite frequently. It's important to note that the total area (not the radius) of each bubble chart represents a subcategory's quantitative value. How bad can bubble charts look if you use radius to scale instead of total area? If a designer is trying to use bubble charts to show the difference between two quantitative values—say 2 and 4—the area of the latter should be twice as large as the former. But if they are basing scale on radius, the graph will be designed in a way that distorts the data. The differences become more pronounced with more difference between the values (Figure 9.23).

Because bubble charts have their limitations in conveying information clearly, you shouldn't overcomplicate them by adding too much detail, manipulating the shapes to make them into money bags, or the like. You also want to avoid using shapes that are not entirely circular (e.g., a money bag or ring with a big ol' diamond on it). This'll just end up looking strange. While they are good for conveying high-level differences between subcategories' values, people also want to understand the information as well—which works best if the differences between the bubble sizes are not very great.

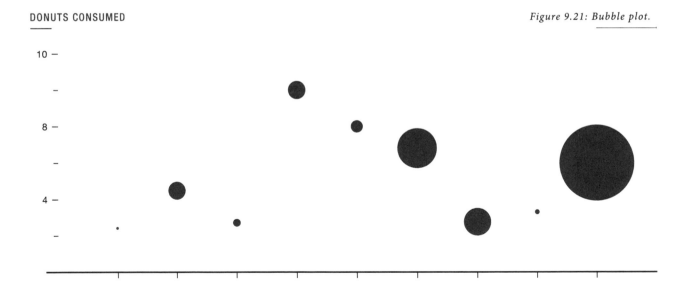

DONUTS CONSUMED

Figure 9.21: Bubble plot.

Figure 9.22: Bubble map.

Each graph type has its own rules governing what to do—and sometimes even more importantly, what not to do—based on the ultimate goal of communicating the message clearly and effectively. It is the designer's responsibility to select the best option, as there are often several for the type of chart you could use based on your data. Sometimes the best option is obvious; other times, it takes trying a few options to determine which graph best conveys the story you're trying to tell.

This chapter covered the importance of applying our critical framework to any qualitative design, regarding both the appropriateness of use and quality. We also made a brief introduction to designing with data. As we've mentioned, a number of authors have contributed more extensively to these topics, beyond what we could cover in this chapter. We encourage you to read more about design and data and how you can use both to become a better communicator.

Figure 9.23
Correctly vs. incorrectly sized bubble charts.

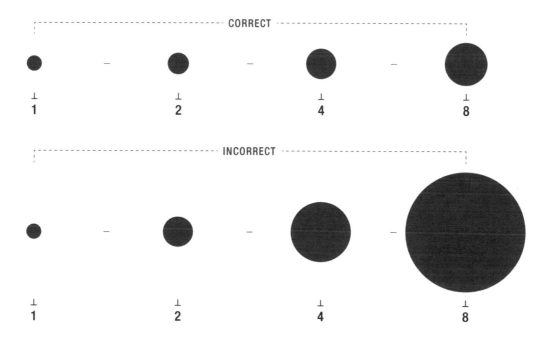

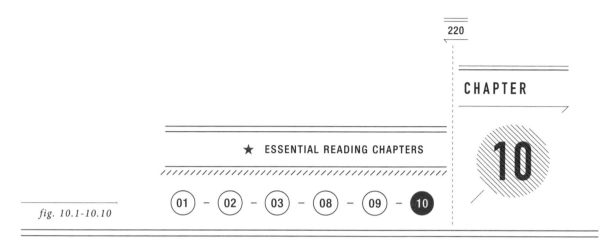

CHAPTER

10

★ ESSENTIAL READING CHAPTERS

fig. 10.1-10.10

01 – 02 – 03 – 08 – 09 – 10

THE FUTURE OF INFOGRAPHICS

The future of infographics is marked by the increased automation of data visualization, powered by software that will make these capabilities more accessible to everyone. This is coupled with the recognition that human creativity will still play an essential role in crafting a strong story and customizing a visualization.

Infographic thinking is everywhere you look. It has officially hit the mainstream, and the message is clear: people want to be informed and entertained. Individuals are also becoming more fluent in understanding data. For example, with mobile apps empowering the quantified-self movement, people engage with visualizations of data gathered from their daily activities in order to make (in some cases) a lifestyle change.

As we have shown, there are many applications in which enticing visuals serve to burn a beautiful analogy into the viewers' brains to help them retain the information and take action accordingly. You can see a wide range of data-driven imagery in many of today's wired cities: an attractive visualization of citywide network activity displayed over a train station entrance, augmented reality–style overlays for viewing information at an airport (Figure 10.1), and a car that displays its own vital health statistics. Today, we also have data exhibited as art (Figures 10.2, 10.3, and 10.4) at museums around the world, visualizations in live sports broadcasts, and of course, their increased prevalence in movies (Figure 10.5) and TV commercials (Figure 10.6).

Figure 10.1
Infographically enhanced Observation Deck B at Zurich Airport.
ART+COM.

Figure 10.2
Statistics Strip for "Work. Meaning and Worry" exhibition, Deutches Hygiene-Museum Dresden.
ART+COM.

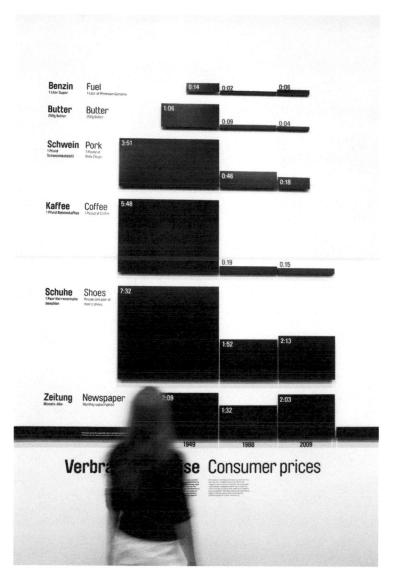

Figure 10.3
The Concept of Sustainability. ART+COM.

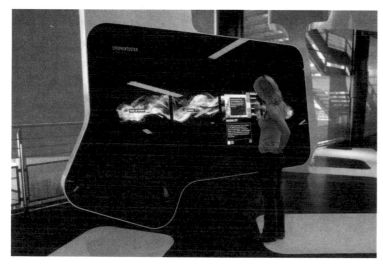

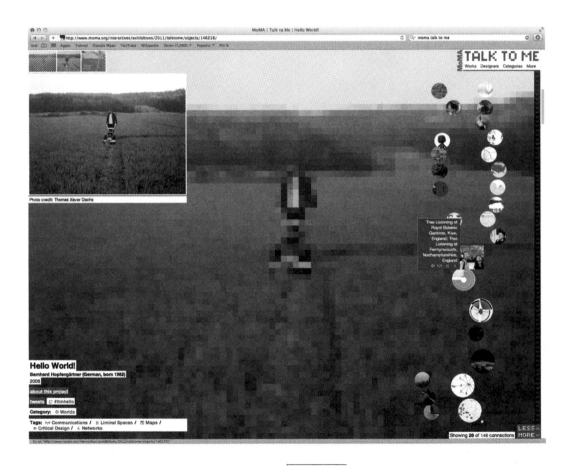

Figure 10.4
"Talk to Me" exhibit at Museum of Modern Art in New York City.
Stamen.

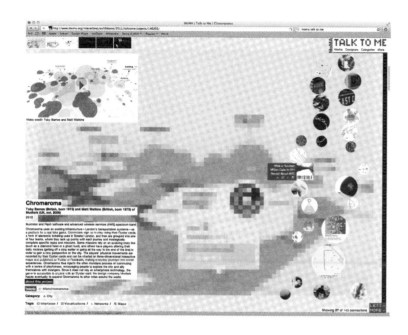

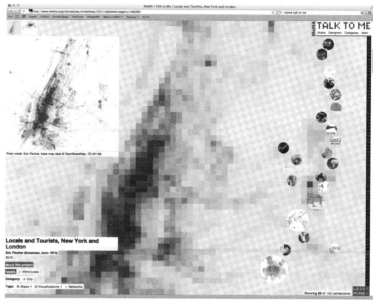

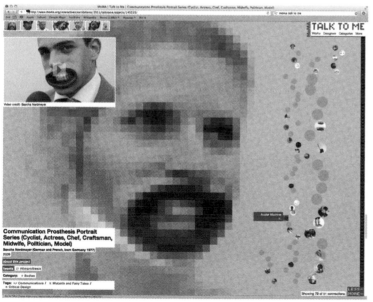

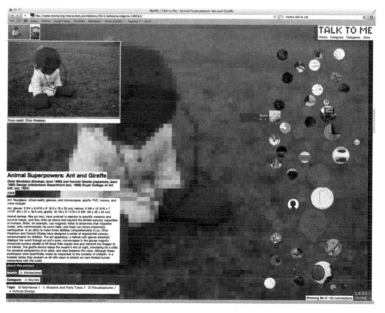

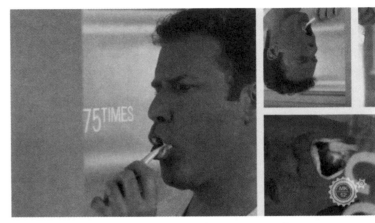

Figure 10.5
Infographic overlays from the movie Stranger Than Fiction.
Sony Pictures.

Figure 10.6
Commercial: Big Things Are Happening.
Cisco.
(Continued on pages 234-235)

Figure 10.6: Continued.

"THE REAL **IMPACT** OF THE INFORMATION **REVOLUTION**

ISN'T ABOUT **INFORMATION MANAGEMENT**

SOCIAL BUSINESS SOFTWARE WILL BECOME A **$5 BILLION** BUSINESS BY 2013

USER | GROWTH
FACEBOOK | TWITTER
620ᴍ | 157ᴍ

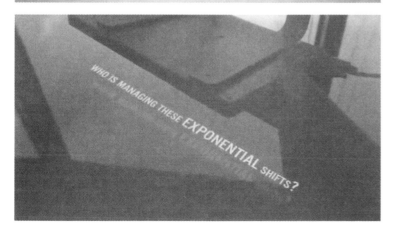

WHO IS MANAGING THESE **EXPONENTIAL** SHIFTS?

together we are the human network. **CISCO**

We can't help but think about artificial intelligence when imagining data visualization's limitless future. We envision the days when machines will try to entertain one another by telling stories around the fire that draw from an aggregation of the entirety of human knowledge, as eventually consolidated by the Google hive mind. You can imagine that visualizing data and putting together entertaining visual stories would be an elementary task for these robots. Perhaps not surprisingly though, these omniscient AI beings will instead end up spending entire days arguing about what the monolith represented in *2001: A Space Odyssey*.

However, you probably aren't lucky enough to be thinking about how to build such machines in the near future. Chances are, you're much more concerned about finding a competitive edge in your business communication—whether you are doing so externally or internally, for marketing purposes or to gain deeper insights into your business. To that end, here are three trends that will be shaping the future of infographics:

1. *Democratized Access to Creation Tools*
2. *Socially Generative Visualization*
3. *Problem Solving*

In all of these areas, we see the importance of original thinking and creativity combined with the efficiencies of using better technology to power visualizations.

DEMOCRATIZED ACCESS TO CREATION TOOLS

What will be the fate of the medium if the web becomes increasingly flooded with infographics? Some say people will become disillusioned based on the prevalence of low-quality designs, brought about by the automation of their creation. On the other hand, the time spent creating and consuming infographic content will lead to better understanding of data, and the best practitioners will also continue to innovate and compete, which will help raise the bar for quality and increase demand for stronger conceptual work, especially for brands that want to stand out from the pack.

To frame this properly, it is helpful to think of the widespread use of video on the web. With ready access to the tools to create and upload videos, we see a huge variation in quality, with more noise and less signal. It does not make sense to say "I hate videos" after seeing a lot of bad ones, as video is still an established and viable medium of communication. When asked how he felt about industry concerns over the democratization of visualization tools, data visualization expert Ben Fry said,

"The same argument has been made with any technological leap since the beginning of time. Books printed en masse had a similar reaction. The Internet came along and everybody could post things on [it], and wouldn't that be the end of the world? The important thing is to focus on the literacy aspect of [whatever the medium is]. The more that people do the work, [the more it] goes to improve the conversation of what's good, bad, useful and what's not."

Essentially, an entire medium of communication does not become ineffective simply because some people are using it poorly.

In fact, it is great that people are creating more and more infographics; it forces the industry to mature whether people are using them for research, journalism, content marketing, or business insights. The popularization of infographics will also lead to more innovative solutions to increase the efficiency of the medium and further refine our critical framework for assessing their quality.

As it applies to the future of visual journalism through data (which can be extended to include corporate blogs that function as online publications rather than merely as a platform for company announcements), automation tools can help maintain an accurate representation of data by helping reduce human error while increasing the speed of implementation. It can be challenging to break time-sensitive news with accurate and engaging visuals, so we utilize a suite of software that we have developed internally to visualize the data in the most appropriate chart, graph, or map, and to include relevant custom illustration to add to the graphic's appeal. This particular application—which we think of as one key component of *Visual News*—is a great example of how automation and tools can be tremendously helpful in creating editorial content. There is also growing demand within organizations for customized software that allows employees to create template-based, infographic-style reports that they can customize, to some extent, in order to allow nondesigners to generate on-brand visual materials in a very intuitive way.

It's important to maintain a consistent style that adheres to your brand guidelines, and you can also look for opportunities to use illustration—especially in your external-facing, marketing-driven content, which needs to be more enticing. We have the tools today to create custom interfaces that combine the capacity to quickly visualize quantitative data with the ability to customize the editorial angle and qualitative analysis. Multiple stakeholders in a project can use such software to explore the data and to provide observations and insights, so that we can then add the qualitative perspective. Thus, data visualization software is increasingly used in the process of exploring data to find stories. As this trend continues to grow and evolve, the tools will keep improving to empower beautiful visualizations to tell a meaningful story.

SOCIALLY GENERATIVE VISUALIZATIONS

We also see a significant opportunity in the creation of living, breathing infographics. Much of the data visualization that you see on the web is difficult for Joey Donut to embed in blogs. That is not a problem in some cases; for example, when companies employ explorative, interactive visualizations as an on-site resource. You can create landing pages to showcase these data hubs, and produce deep links within the content to allow viewers to drill down further into topics that are interesting or relevant to them. However, if it is essential to have media outlets republish your content more readily, then you want to make it more easily embeddable and shareable, or at least provide journalists with high-resolution images of project highlights that they can use in the coverage.

One way to do this is through an application of dynamic interactive infographics that we call *socially generative visualizations*. This novel approach combines the best aspects of traditional static infographics and classic interactive interfaces with a new purpose: to allow the viewer to interact with the content in a more meaningful way by contributing to and actually being a part of the measured data that is displayed. The data and visuals are updated with each subsequent user interaction with the product, thereby providing each new consumer with a potentially different experience than those who came before. This allows the content to have perpetual relevance, as it is always updated within the original context. In order to make the material more engaging from the outset, you can start with a large sample size of data, such as the Hunch piece below shown in Figure 10.7.

Beyond the distribution potential of such content, your brand can help drive user acquisition by making it into an advanced form of interactive polling that ties to your registration process and/or product. Further, you can potentially drive more users by creating calls to action within the content after allowing people to answer the questions for themselves and see the results updated in real time.

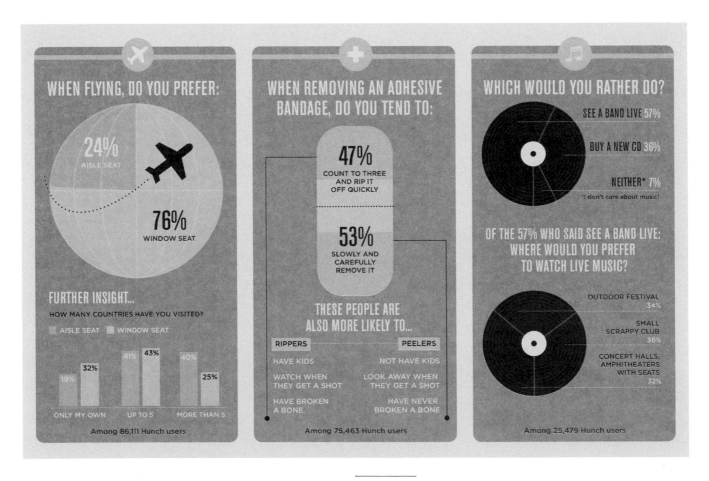

Figure 10.7
That's What THAY Say.
Column Five for Hunch.
(Continued on pages 240-241)

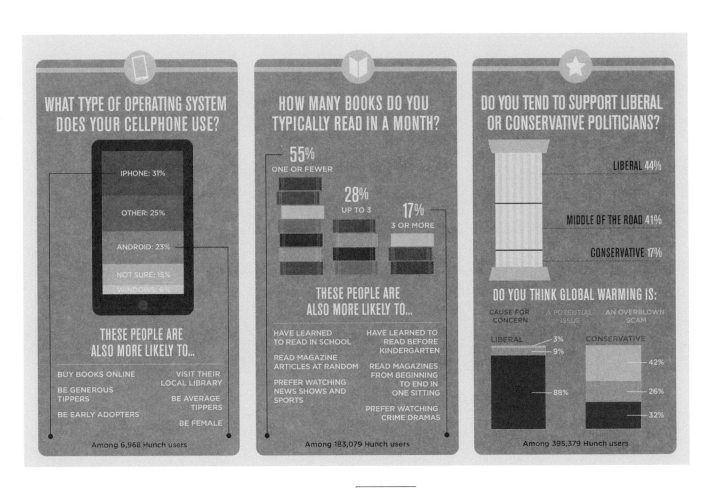

WHAT TYPE OF OPERATING SYSTEM DOES YOUR CELLPHONE USE?

IPHONE: 31%

OTHER: 25%

ANDROID: 23%

NOT SURE: 15%

WINDOWS: 6%

THESE PEOPLE ARE ALSO MORE LIKELY TO...

BUY BOOKS ONLINE   VISIT THEIR LOCAL LIBRARY

BE GENEROUS TIPPERS

BE AVERAGE TIPPERS

BE EARLY ADOPTERS

BE FEMALE

Among 6,968 Hunch users

HOW MANY BOOKS DO YOU TYPICALLY READ IN A MONTH?

55% ONE OR FEWER

28% UP TO 3

17% 3 OR MORE

THESE PEOPLE ARE ALSO MORE LIKELY TO...

HAVE LEARNED TO READ IN SCHOOL

HAVE LEARNED TO READ BEFORE KINDERGARTEN

READ MAGAZINE ARTICLES AT RANDOM

READ MAGAZINES FROM BEGINNING TO END IN ONE SITTING

PREFER WATCHING NEWS SHOWS AND SPORTS

PREFER WATCHING CRIME DRAMAS

Among 183,079 Hunch users

DO YOU TEND TO SUPPORT LIBERAL OR CONSERVATIVE POLITICIANS?

LIBERAL 44%

MIDDLE OF THE ROAD 41%

CONSERVATIVE 17%

DO YOU THINK GLOBAL WARMING IS:

CAUSE FOR CONCERN   A POTENTIAL ISSUE   AN OVERBLOWN SCAM

LIBERAL   3%   CONSERVATIVE

9%

42%

88%   26%

32%

Among 395,379 Hunch users

Figure 10.7
Continued.

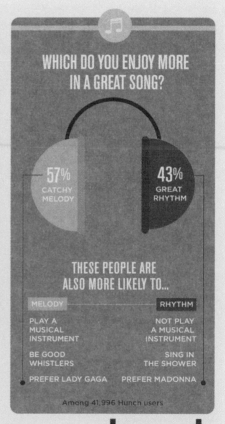

WHEN YOU GO TO THE MOVIES DO YOU TEND TO BUY:

13%	12%	42%	33%
POPCORN OR CANDY	DRINKS	BOTH	NEITHER

DO YOU TEND TO ENJOY MOVIES WITH AMBIGUOUS, OPEN-ENDED ENDINGS?

YES   NO   SOMETIMES

POPCORN OR CANDY
- 12%
- 28%
- 60%

DRINKS
- 15%
- 23%
- 62%

Among 25,627 Hunch users

WOULD YOU CONSIDER YOURSELF MORE OF A DOG PERSON OR A CAT PERSON?

61% DOG PERSON

31% CAT PERSON

8% NEITHER

SOME FAVORITE TV SHOWS FOR EACH GROUP:

DOG	CAT
SEINFELD	X-FILES
SATURDAY NIGHT LIVE	BIG LOVE
HOUSE	XENA: WARRIOR PRINCESS

Among 69,393 Hunch users

WHICH DO YOU ENJOY MORE IN A GREAT SONG?

57% CATCHY MELODY

43% GREAT RHYTHM

THESE PEOPLE ARE ALSO MORE LIKELY TO...

MELODY	RHYTHM
PLAY A MUSICAL INSTRUMENT	NOT PLAY A MUSICAL INSTRUMENT
BE GOOD WHISTLERS	SING IN THE SHOWER
PREFER LADY GAGA	PREFER MADONNA

Among 41,996 Hunch users

hunch

© 2011 Hunch Inc.

As we discussed in Chapter 2 (Infographic Formats), the need for manual updates is an inherent challenge in many static infographics, and even some interactive infographics. By spending the time upfront to create an interactive experience that dynamically updates the data visualization, your content will always be fresh and viewers can engage with the content and see the impact of their information on the infographic.

One example is this piece for GigaOM from 2010 (Figure 10.8), in which we analyzed first-year sales predictions for the iPad. Today, we could build on that same piece to aggregate and display user responses and predictions, and also use other interactive functionality that we could update to show how current sales compare to the original predictions. If you would like to contribute to one of these socially generated visualizations, check out www.visualnews.com/money (Figure 10.9), where we analyze and collect new data to take a fun look at financial behavior across different demographics.

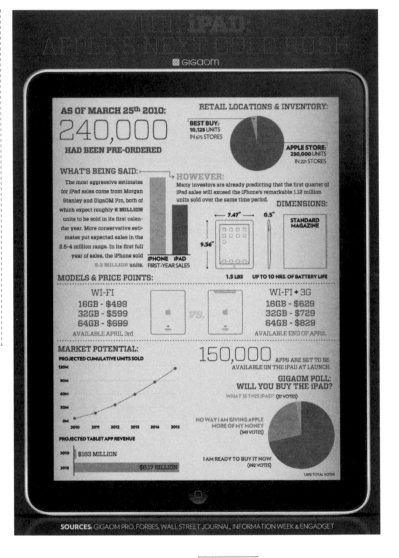

Figure 10.8
The iPad: Apple's Next Gold Rush.
Column Five for GigaOM.

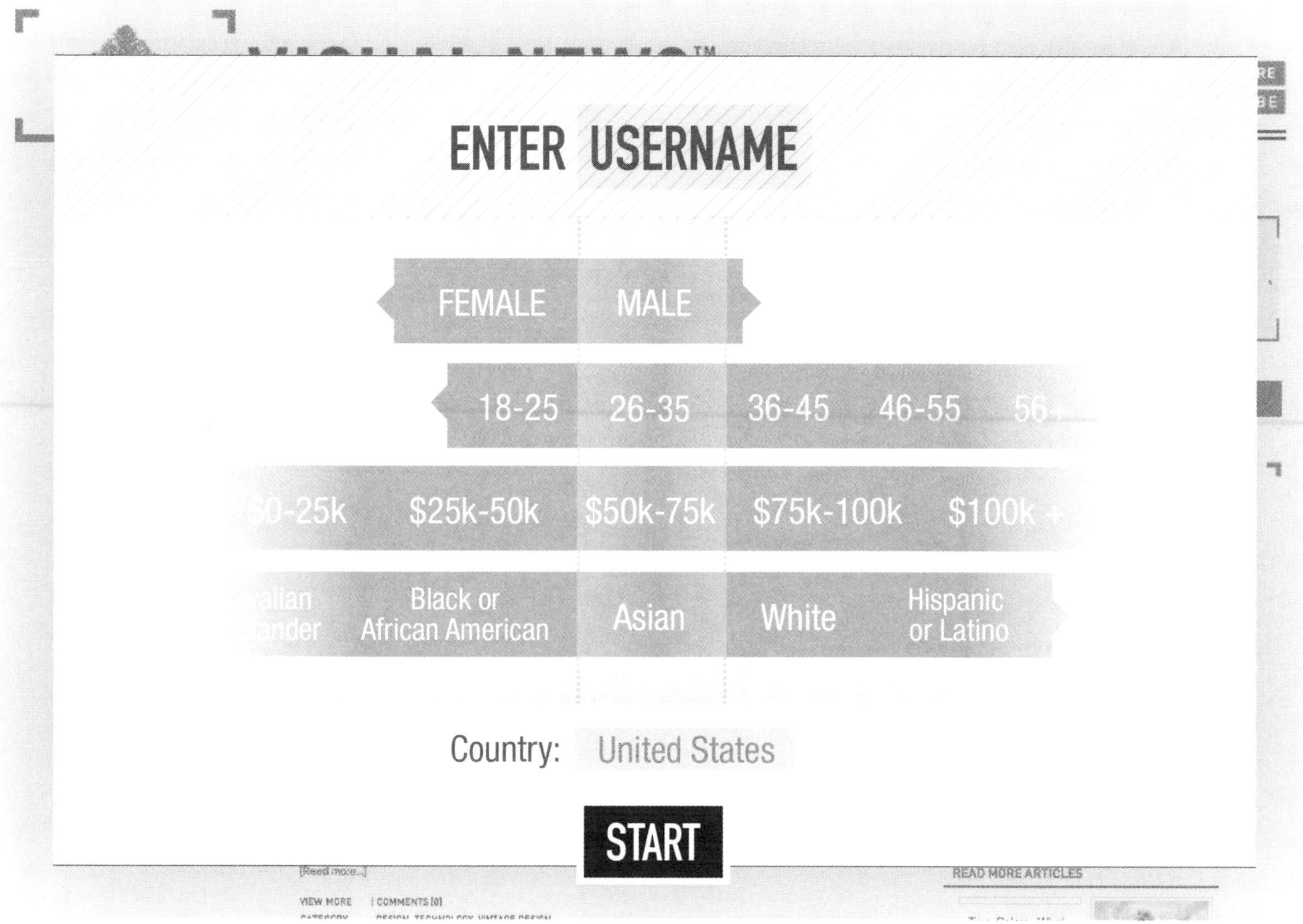

ENTER USERNAME

FEMALE MALE

18-25 26-35 36-45 46-55 56+

$0-25k $25k-50k $50k-75k $75k-100k $100k +

Hawaiian Islander Black or African American Asian White Hispanic or Latino

Country: United States

START

Figure 10.9
Socially Generated Visualization at www.visualnews.com/money.
Visual News.
(Continued on pages 244-246)

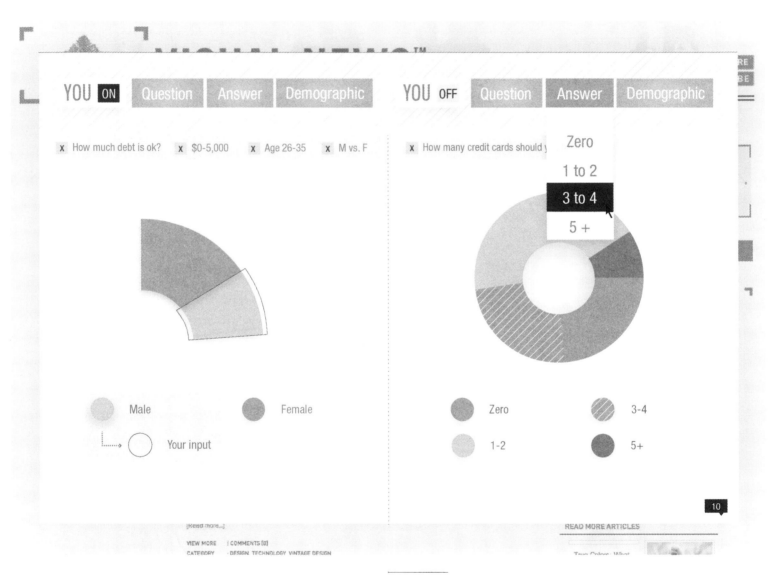

Figure 10.9
Continued.
(continued on page 246)

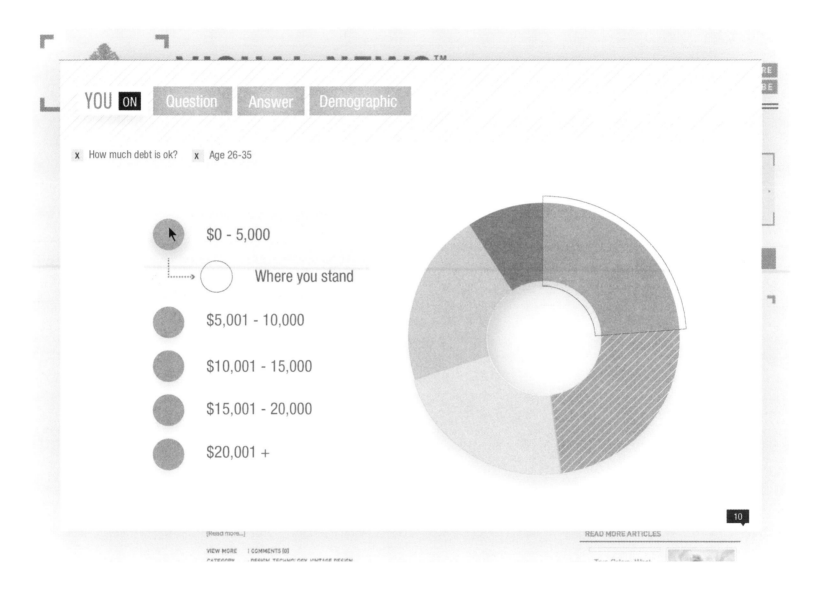

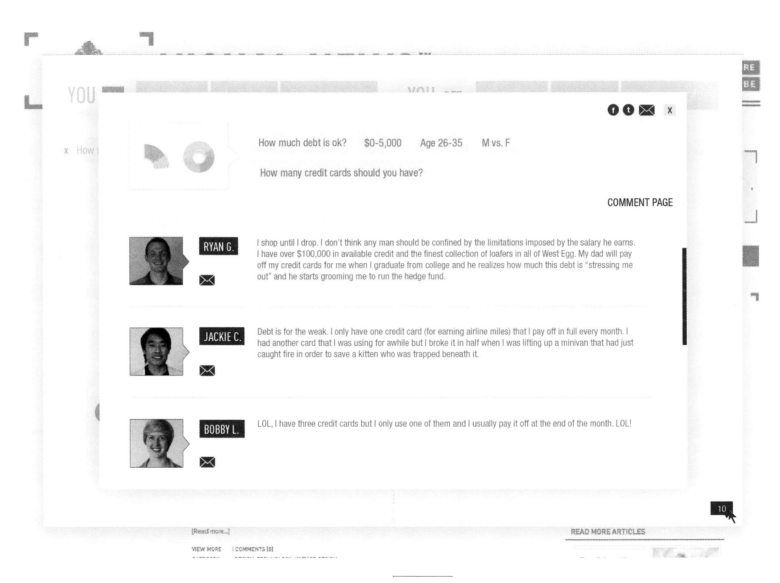

How much debt is ok? $0-5,000   Age 26-35   M vs. F

How many credit cards should you have?

COMMENT PAGE

RYAN G.

I shop until I drop. I don't think any man should be confined by the limitations imposed by the salary he earns. I have over $100,000 in available credit and the finest collection of loafers in all of West Egg. My dad will pay off my credit cards for me when I graduate from college and he realizes how much this debt is "stressing me out" and he starts grooming me to run the hedge fund.

JACKIE C.

Debt is for the weak. I only have one credit card (for earning airline miles) that I pay off in full every month. I had another card that I was using for awhile but I broke it in half when I was lifting up a minivan that had just caught fire in order to save a kitten who was trapped beneath it.

BOBBY L.

LOL, I have three credit cards but I only use one of them and I usually pay it off at the end of the month. LOL!

Figure 10.9
Continued.

Socially generative visualizations are a significant innovation in creating evergreen editorial content and will be used more frequently, reflecting the demand for more interactive experiences online. According to Nathan Yau,

"In the short-term, infographics will grow more interactive, like what we've seen already with work from the *New York Times*. People will continue to demand more as they consume more and grow more data savvy. That said, the Internet is still a place to find quick entertainment or a distraction, so there will still be a place for the more design-heavy infographics, but those with more thought put into the actual content will grab (and deserve) the most attention."

It will become increasingly crucial to involve your audience in this approach to visual storytelling by producing socially generative visualizations.

Beyond interactive content within the editorial context, there are further developments with far-reaching implications. As Moritz Stefaner writes,

"We have seen first prototypes of tools for collaborative visualization, where users can work on, analyze, discuss and annotate data sets together, be it in real-time or asynchronously. Another exciting prospect is the combination of simulations with interactive visualization—what if you could not only see the federal budget outcomes or worldwide CO_2 emissions, but investigate cause and effect of changes to the underlying data in an interactive simulation?"

Indeed, this approach has the power to revolutionize industries far beyond content marketing and business communication.

PROBLEM SOLVING

Bill Gates once attributed the initial spark that led to his charitable organization, the Bill and Melinda Gates Foundation, to an infographic (Figure 10.10) that he had seen in an article in the *New York Times*. As told by Nick Kristof:

"In September, I traveled with Bill Gates to Africa to look at his work fighting AIDS there. While setting the trip up, it emerged that his initial interest in giving pots of money to fight disease had arisen after he and Melinda read a two-part series of articles I did on third world disease in January 1997. Until then, their plan had been to give money mainly to get countries wired and full of computers. Bill and Melinda recently reread those pieces, and said that it was the second piece in the series, about bad water and diarrhea killing millions of kids a year, that really got them thinking of public health. I was really proud of this impact that my worldwide reporting and 3,500-word article had had. But then Bill confessed that actually it wasn't the article itself that had grabbed him so much—it was the graphic. It was just a two column, inside graphic, very simple, listing third world health problems and how many people they kill. But he remembered it after all those years and said that it was the single thing that got him redirected toward public health."

No graphic in human history has saved so many lives in Africa and Asia.

We have also recently encountered more ways to use such innovation for the good of society, as a growing number of nonprofit organizations seek deeper insights in their qualitative and quantitative data. Matthew Summer, CEO of iCoalesce, which uses data visualization in educational program evaluations, is working to make all field survey data accessible through a mobile-friendly web application for an organization working closely with homeless populations in Orange County, California.

This allows individuals working in the field to view housing availability for homeless individuals in real-time, and place people in need of homes in places that are appropriate for them based on important characteristics such as medical needs. Working with the homeless population poses some particularly baffling real-world challenges, and the unstructured data that is collected can make it very difficult to derive updated, accurate information about important things such as bed availability in homeless housing units. As Summer tells us of the challenge of helping solve this type of problem with visualization:

> "We have seen time and again . . . large data sets dropped in our laps that had some sort of schema, but lacked real design, in terms of the ability to communicate meaning or knowledge. We see this as a problem, and certainly an undesirable situation for a knowledge worker, because it eats up time and money reverse engineering meaning out of the data. This happens most with proprietary data systems designed for a niche service [such as] Homeless Management Information Systems."

This clearly emphasizes the need for clean research design and consistent data collection methods. However, data that have already been collected—say, regarding individual homeless persons—still have qualitative value, and can still be measured and analyzed even if they are in various formats with incomplete records in some cases. This means that a system that is flexible enough to handle such inconsistencies is necessary. Summer continues:

> "I think we can all agree [that] data without meaningful analysis and interpretation is generally useless. It is important

to ensure that the back-end of your system is not only helpful in organizing messy, unstructured data, but that you also systematize the way that data is collected in a more organized manner in the same system from today forward."

On the backbone of such a flexible system, we can design front-end interfaces that allow people in the field to access real-time data. This helps reduce the inherent problems of relying upon a printed report of bed availability—even if it was created that very morning. This demonstrates one way that we can use data visualization to make a lasting, meaningful impact on society by providing valuable real-time insights. With the rise of social entrepreneurship, we expect that there will be an explosion of innovative uses of data visualization to empower a new breed of businesses and organizations that care about helping people.

BECOMING A VISUAL COMPANY

Whether you have already tested the waters and implemented infographic thinking in your organization, or this is all new to you, it is important to solidify the goals and metrics you will use to assess how effective your information design efforts are. Keep in mind that it's also important to experiment; it can help you realize unique opportunities for producing engaging, original content. As Nathan Yau suggests,

> "When you think of visualization as a medium rather than a monolithic tool, it's something much more flexible that can be used for a lot of things. It's also more exciting. You can tell stories with data through analysis, journalism, or art." "Visualization can be fun or serious; it can be beautiful and emotional or barebones and to the point. In the end, it's still all about the data, and visualization lets you see what you might not find in a table. There are stories in the numbers,

and visualization can help you find or tell them."

As we have discussed, there is room at the table for the data analysts and the storytellers, and there are valid situations for applying both perspectives.

So, what is the key to transforming our communication through visualization that has the ability to provide meaningful insights and engage viewers? Our ability to further develop and utilize tools that will aid in the processing and display of vast amounts of information, coupled with the human creativity essential to making the message both relevant and appealing. We must encourage increased accessibility to these tools, enabling a greater number of people to create and share infographics. While this will decrease the average quality in the short-run, it will also be central to the development and progress of the medium. This will also help further establish the critical framework by which we judge quality, as we collectively develop a deeper understanding of the many applications for their use. Finally, we must uphold the value of human creativity in shaping the world of visualization, and continue to empower people to create visual stories that will inform, entertain, and inspire.

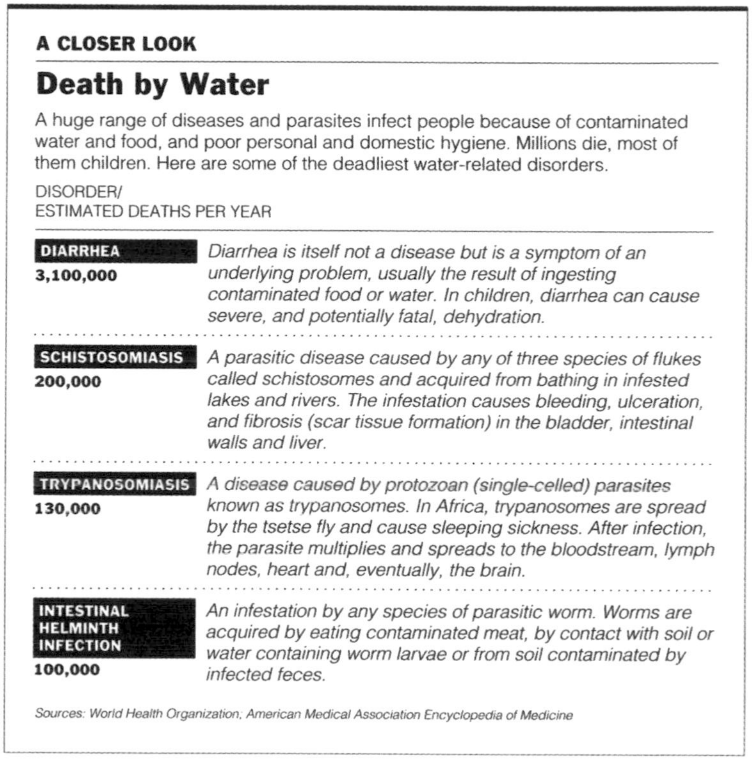

A CLOSER LOOK

Death by Water

A huge range of diseases and parasites infect people because of contaminated water and food, and poor personal and domestic hygiene. Millions die, most of them children. Here are some of the deadliest water-related disorders.

DISORDER/
ESTIMATED DEATHS PER YEAR

DIARRHEA 3,100,000	Diarrhea is itself not a disease but is a symptom of an underlying problem, usually the result of ingesting contaminated food or water. In children, diarrhea can cause severe, and potentially fatal, dehydration.
SCHISTOSOMIASIS 200,000	A parasitic disease caused by any of three species of flukes called schistosomes and acquired from bathing in infested lakes and rivers. The infestation causes bleeding, ulceration, and fibrosis (scar tissue formation) in the bladder, intestinal walls and liver.
TRYPANOSOMIASIS 130,000	A disease caused by protozoan (single-celled) parasites known as trypanosomes. In Africa, trypanosomes are spread by the tsetse fly and cause sleeping sickness. After infection, the parasite multiplies and spreads to the bloodstream, lymph nodes, heart and, eventually, the brain.
INTESTINAL HELMINTH INFECTION 100,000	An infestation by any species of parasitic worm. Worms are acquired by eating contaminated meat, by contact with soil or water containing worm larvae or from soil contaminated by infected feces.

Sources: World Health Organization, American Medical Association Encyclopedia of Medicine

Figure 10.10
Death By Water, the graphic that saved millions of lives.
New York Times.

FURTHER INFOGRAPHIC GOODNESS

Access all of these links and more infographic inspiration at
www.columnfivemedia.com/book/links

Blprnt - Jer Thorp
www.blprnt.com

Chart Porn
www.chartporn.org

Column Five
www.columnfivemedia.com

Cool Infographics
www.coolinfographics.com

Data Blog - The Guardian
www.guardian.co.uk/news/datablog

Data Desk - Los Angeles Times
www.datadesk.latimes.com

Datavisualization.ch
www.datavisualization.ch

Eager Eyes
www.eagereyes.org

Fast Company's Co.Design
www.fastcodesign.com/section/infographic-of-the-day

Feltron - Nicholas Felton
www.feltron.com

Five Thirty Eight: Nate Silver's Political Calculus
fivethirtyeight.blogs.nytimes.com

FlowingData
www.flowingdata.com

Francesco Franchi
www.francescofranchi.com

Graficos
graficos.lainformacion.com

I Love Charts
ilovecharts.tumblr.com

Information Aesthetics
www.infosthetics.com

Information Is Beautiful
www.informationisbeautiful.net

Interactive Things
www.interactivethings.com

Junk Charts
junkcharts.typepad.com

Malofiej
www.malofiej20.com

The New York Times - By the Numbers
blow.blogs.nytimes.com

The New York Times - Unofficial
chartsnthings.tumblr.com

Stamen Design
www.stamen.com

Substratum Series
www.substratumseries.com

Edward Tufte and Graphics Press
www.edwardtufte.com/tufte

Visualising Data
www.visualisingdata.com

Visual Loop
visualoop.tumblr.com

Visual.ly
www.visual.ly

Visual News, a Column Five Publication
www.visualnews.com

Well-Formed Data
www.well-formed-data.net

THANK YOU

Jason's Thanks

Thank you to my wife Nicole, for putting up with me and believing in me. I deeply appreciate your love and support these past 12 years. You are such a great mom to our sweet little Lucy. I also want to thank my parents and family for teaching me to take time to pay attention to matters of the heart and soul.

Thank you, Ross and Josh, for your loyal friendship, and for always working on ways to communicate more clearly with each other and pushing me to grow on so many levels.

Josh's Thanks

Thank you to my incredibly supportive and loving parents and family, who have always encouraged me, and have been there for me. Thank you also to Kelly who has always been very patient and understanding with me in general, but especially while we were writing this book.

Thank you also to the best business partners a man could ask for. Jason and Ross, I truly value our friendships, and it's been an amazing experience building a business together and coauthoring a book with you both.

Ross' Thanks

Thank you to my lovely wife, Jessica, who graciously and gracefully endured my writing on our honeymoon—and has consistently supported my pursuits regardless of which way they tip the oft-lopsided scales of my work-life balance.

Thank you to Jason and Josh for your hard work, insight, and candid feedback throughout the writing process. I am incredibly grateful for an enjoyable and fruitful partnership, and lasting friendships over the years.

Thank you to our clients who entrust us with their communication and pay us to do what we love. We are greatly appreciative of the business relationships and friendships we have built with each of you.

We'd also like to thank our much-respected friends and colleagues who were kind enough to contribute to this book, in the form of interviews, discussion, research, and providing graphics for our use. This includes Dr. Craig Rusch, Dr. Joel Schwarzbart, Nathan Yau, Nigel Holmes, Cliff Kuang, Moritz Stefaner, Robin Richards, Matthew Summers, and Dr. Andrew Vande Moere. A special thanks to Brian Dashew and the entire team who helped us create the Visualization of Information course at Columbia University.

Finally, we owe a special thank you to the Column Five team for their commitment, creativity, and humor, which have helped build an environment where we can make great things and love coming to work everyday. They are an amazing group of people and we are very fortunate to work closely with each of them daily. They are:

Colin Dobrin, Brian Wolford, Jarred Romley, Andrew Effendy, Madeleine Nguyen, Luis Liwag, Marshall Meier, Andrea Bravo, Jake Burkett, Shane Keaney, Vince Largoza, Nick Miede, Brad Woodard, Vannarong 'Rev' Run, Ian Klein, Kaede Holland, Katie Rogers, Alina Makhnovetsky, Katy French, Adrian Walsh, Chase Ogden, Travis Keith, Taylor Fallon, Arturo Wibawa, Kelsey Cox, Stuart Inskip, Melody MacKeand, Chris Carlino, Walter Olivares, Sean Parent, Neil Spencer, Jay Cross, Jake Kilroy, Jeremy Fetters, Brian Almeida, Charles Lam, Alicia Adamerovich, Danny Miede, Trevor Rogers, Sara Bacon, Scott Raney, Jane Youn, Nicole Rincon, Huilin Dai, Adam Grason, Kirk Wells, Andrew Janik, Evan Cole, Paul Sanchez, Ben Starr, Steven Shoppman, Jessica Czeck, Shawn Saleme, Skye Jordan, and Brian the Brain.

INDEX